Front Line Warfare

A Handbook For Christians
in the Trenches

by Chip Hill

 Unless otherwise identified, Scripture quotations are from The New International Version of the Bible.

For correspondence write:
Malcolm W. (Chip) Hill
HC-1 Box 202
Monterey, VA 24465

Destiny Image Publishers
P.O. Box 351
Shippensburg, PA 17257

"Speaking to the Purposes of God for this Generation"

ISBN 1-56043-008-7

For Worldwide Distribution
Printed in the U.S.A.

TABLE OF CONTENTS

ACKNOWLEDGEMENT

I want to express my sincere thanks to all my brothers and sisters at Word of Faith Church in Monterey, VA and Faith Covenant Family Church in Hot Springs, VA. Your steadfast love and support, and your priceless friendship are blessings I could not do without.

To my precious wife, Darlene, the most outstanding woman of God I've ever known. Thank you for everything you are to me. Words cannot express my gratitude. Your support, your honesty, and your love are some of my most valuable gifts from God.

And finally, I dedicate this book to one of my most precious spiritual mentors, Helen Wallace, my mother in the things of God. Helen departed this life to be with her Lord while I was completing the manuscript for this book. The void her passing leaves in my life cannot be filled by another. Helen was one of a kind; I wish you all could have known her in this life. Look her up in heaven.

PREFACE

As the human race rapidly advances toward the end of this age, spiritual battles will grow increasingly violent. The glamour that has accompanied so much of the "front line warfare" of the Church against the powers of darkness will no longer exist. Only those men and women who answer a genuine call from God, and those who have experienced a thorough baptism of His power to enable them to engage the enemy, will survive the front line warfare that is to come. A firing-line faith, one that is born in fervent, consistent prayer and abundant times in the Word of God, will be the only brand of faith that will emerge victorious from the end-time fields of battle.

Paul, the great apostle, rightly prophesied: "But mark this: There will be terrible times in the last days" (2 Tim. 3:1). Grievous, hard-to-bear days are at hand, and it will be with much fear and trembling that God's men of war will have to work to carry out their orders. This is not to say they will fear the devil and his hordes, but they will possess a healthy understanding that their sufficiency is to be found in God alone, and that their enemy is indeed the most cunning and capable foe that has ever existed.

Concerning these last days, Jesus said, "For then there will be great distress, unequaled from the beginning of the world until now — and never to be equaled again" (Matt. 24:21).

This is a time for alarm, Church! The trumpet call that comes forth in this book is clear, because if the trumpet does not sound a clear call, who will get ready for battle?

The Scriptures promise, "Thy people will volunteer freely in the day of Thy power" (Ps. 110:3, NAS). This is the day for which the army of Almighty God has been preparing! When life-and-death causes are involved, patriotic people step forward, and today they are stepping forward by the tens of thousands to give heart, soul, mind and strength to serve the King of kings.

You are one of the soldiers called to volunteer in this hour. I pray that this book will inspire you to rise up and be counted!

FOREWORD

The conference is over, the big PA systems carefully packed up and loaded into the vans. The main speakers gather their notes and their briefcases and go on to yet another conference. The local pastors, rejuvenated, inspired, and strengthened, pack their suitcases and go home. These men go back to the day-to-day routine of caring for God's people. They go back to facing the daily problems and fears of those they shepherd. They go back to the financial pressures, the social pressures, and the political pressures that surround every day. These gallant men, pastors that are truly born of God's heart, go back into the trenches, the front line of God's activity where the real warfare is, where the norm is day-to-day battles with the enemy and where victories come slowly, but just as sweetly.

It is interesting to note that even the largest of the electronic ministries still find their validity in the local pastors who take up the slack, providing the personal contact needed to minister to the people who have been reached over radio or television. These men are the trench men who go into the homes, into the bars, into the streets to truly bring the people out one by one. No matter how big the ministry, how big the publishing company, how big the radio program, the bottom line is and always will be the personal one-to-one contact that a front-line pastor has with his people. Genuine Christianity has always been a grassroots movement and it will continue to be that way.

More careful attention must be given to these pastors who work so diligently and tirelessly under the anointing of the Holy Spirit to do the work of the Lord in establishing His Kingdom in the earth. Only those who are in the trenches or who have experienced trench warfare can understand and appreciate the intensity of the battle. Only they can understand the enormity of God's grace, the wonders of His anointing, and the necessity of the gifts of the Holy Spirit in the heat of these battles.

Chip Hill is a unique blend of church planter and trench man. In fact, Chip gives new definition to the term "church planter," for he is one who rolls up his sleeves, takes up the armor and goes into battle in planting the church as well as establishing it. He comes to us with first-hand experience and knowlege of what it means to bring down the powers of the enemy, destroying speculations and every lofty thing that raises itself against the knowledge of God.

He is a man who understands both the anointing and the power of God, as well as the wiles of the enemy.

In the pages of this book you will find practical, day-by-day guidelines and support for the trench work of the ministry to which God has called you. You will learn of other pastors just like you who are in the heat of the battle every day, changing lives one at a time for His purposes in the earth.

You are not alone, but you are part of a vast army, an uncountable multitude of men and women who have responded to the Word of the Lord to go to the front lines and battle where the enemy has dug in and claimed for himself that which truly belongs to the Lord. You are part of a vast army of ministries that will declare to the Lord, "The kingdoms of this world have become the kingdoms of our Lord and of His Christ." Then your job will be done; then His Kingdom will come.

Don Nori
Publisher

1

THE BATTLES INTENSIFY

December 1986. My family and I breezed down the four-lane highway toward a small city tucked in the heart of the Appalachian Mountains. A fledgling group of Christians there was in the process of establishing a church. My wife, Darlene, and I had been asked to provide some teaching that would help to ground the believers there in the faith. As we traveled, we both anticipated an enjoyable weekend of ministry and a time of making new friends. Neither of us expected the intense spiritual warfare that awaited us. Had we been headed for Africa, Haiti, or some other third-world environment, we would have taken things much more seriously. But we were only going to a small Appalachian city that was no more than three hours from our home.

Ministry in that particular part of the Appalachians took us into the spiritual jurisdiction of satanic spirits that we had never before encountered or dealt with. These entities have ruled unchecked over that part of America for centuries. Satan's hold there was rock-solid.

The first day in town, Darlene and our two boys were violently attacked with severe symptoms of the flu. She was across town teaching a group of ladies, and the boys were with me at the home of the young man who led the church. All three became very ill with high fevers, vomiting, dizziness and bone-blasting chills. The attacks were clearly demonic, sent as a loud and clear message from the ruling spirits in the area: "We've been in control around here for years! Don't think you're going to come in here now and change things!"

That evening I ministered the Word to the men of the young church. While teaching, I took note of a deeply deceived man who was present. Although he considered himself to be very spiritual and godly, he was flowing in a spirit of witchcraft and bondage.

As I ministered the Word, the man made repeated trips to the restroom, where he could be heard chanting, seemingly some type of prayer. I grew concerned, but continued preaching. His prayers that seemingly were *for me* were really *against me.* Such prayers are often directed at their objects as curses. Here is an example: "Lord, straighten him out and do whatever You have to do in order to get him straight. Send him sickness, calamity, poverty, frustration and failure so he will see how wrong he is. Take Your anointing from him." My brother or sister, demons act on such ungodly prayers, not God! Many such cursers are in the Church in this hour, and they think they are doing God a service. We must all be careful that we don't curse what God has blessed. The prophet, Balaam, learned this lesson in Numbers 22-24 when he considered cursing those whom God was not willing to curse. How often have you wished, or even prayed, evil down on the heads of those people you don't agree with or have fallen out with? Be very careful, or you may be judged as an advocate of satan!

We must learn to protect ourselves and our families from the evil curses of deceived, angry people. By periodically exercising our God-given authority over what has been prayed or spoken against us, we can paralyze the effects of a curse. A simple, yet forceful decree, such as this one, is often all that is necessary to stay free from the curser's damaging effects:

> In the name of Jesus Christ, I break the power and influence of any and every curse that has been spoken or prayed against me and my family. By the blood of the Lamb of God, I render all such curses ineffectual, and declare us to be free! God's Word declares that we are redeemed from the curse, and that we are blessed with every spiritual blessing in heavenly places in Christ. I agree with that!

At the end of the men's meeting, as I was praying for the different needs present, the troubled man approached me, indicating that he wanted prayer. I was suspicious. I laid my hands on his chest and began praying that God would set him free from anything that might keep him from being useful to the Kingdom of God. At this point I opened my eyes, hoping to see the man with his eyes shut, his face toward heaven, and his heart receptive to the blessings I was praying for. However, I was not prepared for what I saw. He stood there, with his head cocked slightly to one side, staring deeply at me. Our eyes met, and our gaze locked into a stare down. His eyes were wide, almost perplexed looking, and yet there was something devilishly active reflecting from them. It was evident that he was trying to place a curse on me. Had it not been for the fact that God's grace had anointed me for the occasion, I might have backed down. But I stood my ground until I was confident that the Lord was finished having me pray for him. When I finished, I asked him, "Amen?" Rather startled, he replied, "Amen." That means, SO BE IT! The Lord had won that encounter — but only temporarily. In a matter of hours the man was back to his ways, and shortly thereafter he left the church. His problems were many, and he didn't really want help. If there was more I could have done for him, I didn't know it.

The following morning my family was feeling much better. The morning's service went extremely well, concluding with much personal ministry to the needs of individuals. Little had I known during the week before our visit to that city that my theme, "Triumph Over Opposition" from Isaiah 54, would be so pertinent to the situation there.

After the service, we packed our things and headed home to the mountains of Virginia. The ride home was peaceful and uneventful. That evening we retired to our beds for a restful night's sleep.

At four in the morning I was jolted out of my sleep by a tremendous pain in my stomach. The discomfort was so intense that I had to leave my warm bed and make my way downstairs to the living room in order to engage in vocal battle against the evil demonic entity that was attacking me. I walked the floor, thanking God for healing me and praising Him for deliverance. A little later that morning, the attack and its symptoms left me. Whew! I had not been attacked quite likc that for years.

Early that morning as the battle was raging, God reprimanded me for being so naive as to remove my armor and lay aside my faith after having engaged the enemy in battle as I had done in the days prior. Satan will retaliate if you hurt him, bringing you injury if you're not ready for him. He is a master at counter-offensive tactics.

God has clearly spoken that in the last days terrible times will come upon inhabitants of the earth (2 Tim. 3:1). I am becoming more convinced that forms of ministry that have been relatively easy in times past will grow increasingly more difficult in the days ahead. This will happen, not because the Church is becoming weak, but because the opposition is growing stronger. Satan has but a few years left, so he is pulling out his deadliest war plans and sending forth his choice warriors. They are rising to a much greater degree of aggressiveness than we have ever known.

Every church will have to be related to other churches that are embracing the same basic vision it has. They will flow together in unity, power and singleness of purpose. Variety will remain, short-term purposes will abound, but overall, the network of churches will be moving gingerly toward the full realization of the Kingdom of God on earth. It will become increasingly wonderful to know that there are "some more of us" over in the next county, state and nation. The comfort that comes from knowing that your flanks are covered by dependable men and women will prove invaluable as we near the consummation of this age.

Pastor, if your church is presently independent and unrelated to other churches, simply pray and ask God to unite the heart of your church to the hearts of other churches in your region of the country who share the same basic vision that you have. It doesn't mean that you have to "come under" them in some kind of binding way, it simply means you want the added strength you know comes from being a part of something larger. The sense of "belonging" that you'll gain may be one of the things that holds you steady in the tumultuous days that may soon arise.

A plurality of elders under the anointed headship of a senior elder will provide primary spiritual direction for the local assembly of believers, but in a region, a local presbytery comprised of leading men from various churches in that region will be available to provide support, counsel and general oversight for the churches of that region. Together, they will work to implement the long-term plan of God. This is often done by holding joint conventions, seminars and prayer vigils for members of all the churches of the region. Also, they can work together with evangelistic thrusts into the various communities of the region. They can also work together to protect the various flocks of God from dangerous ministry that infiltrates or moves in to unsettle works that are already established.

The apostolic teams (and there may be several with influence in a region) flowing in and through the region where their authority and anointing are received and appreciated will be available to give vital input to the presbyteries and their churches, but their main thrust will be to extend the borders of God's Kingdom into new areas.

Remember, however, that as exciting as all of this is, the most vicious of spiritual battles will coincide with God's moving. It will not be a time to take "a leave of absence," for your adversary doesn't know the meaning of such a phrase and certainly has no respect for it.

The ministries of wolves and false brethren will abound over the coming years. Paul warned the elders of Ephesus: "For I know this, that after my departing shall grievous wolves enter in among you, not sparing the flock" (Acts 20:29, KJV). The words, *not sparing*, literally mean: "not treating the flock leniently." This speaks of people who will make demands on the flock that they have no right to make. Such people demand conformity to their beliefs, will and purposes. These wolfish people don't really love and cherish the flock, rather they love and cherish themselves. Paul continued: "Also of your own selves shall men arise, speaking perverse things, to draw away disciples after them" (Acts 20:30, KJV). The perverse things to which Paul refers are not cuss words and filthy language. They are, however, the little statements wolfish people make concerning the pastor or the way he runs the church. These little statements and underminings, though they come forth guised as genuine concern, will foster confusion, a lack of faith in God's ability, disloyalty and, eventually, all-out deception in those who listen to them. Wolfish people can't build anything lasting on their own, so they seek to undermine and then take over the ministries of those who have been successful. Paul continued: "Therefore watch, and remember, that by the space of three years I ceased not to warn every one night and day with tears" (Acts 20:31, KJV). Did Paul's warnings pay off? In Jesus' message to the church of Ephesus many years later, it is written, "I know thy works, and thy labour, and thy patience, and how thou canst not bear them which are evil: and thou hast tried them which say they are apostles, and are not, and hast found them liars" (Rev. 2:2, KJV). So you see, they can be recognized, resisted and rendered ineffectual.

The apostles and elders at Jerusalem sent letters to the Christians in Asia, warning them of those who come to subvert the souls of men (Acts 15:24). To subvert means to dismantle, to plunder. Isn't it awful that these kinds of false brethren are among us today?

In his letter to Titus, Paul spoke of those "who subvert whole households" (1:11). Their motive is greed: A thirst for power, recognition, money, etc. Paul said their mouths must be stopped. Church member, please beware. There are many people moving about the body of Christ, looking for a flock into which they can sink their fangs. Stand by your pastor. Exercise faith toward God for him, so that God will protect him from the wolves in Zion. Because he is human, he will occasionally miss God's way. Allow him that, and trust God to get him back on the path. Until you've walked in his shoes, don't judge him. Leading a Spirit-filled assembly is a life and death call. Go easy on the man and protect him with your prayers. Many are out to pull him down and take over his place in ministry. If he yields to them, he is done for. Help him, don't fight him.

We are in a time of viciousness. The front line warfare ahead will leave the spiritual battlefields strewn with corpses. We must all be prepared for what is coming.

2

Planting New Churches

Anyone who is responsible for the planting of new churches is often asked the questions: "Why start new churches? Don't we have enough churches already?" The folks who ask these questions are usually sincere, well-meaning people who feel that establishing another church in their area will only pose a threat to the unity of the Spirit among the Christians there. They often reason that those involved in church planting should energetically involve themselves in one of the existing churches and work to see it brought to a place of maturity and completeness, rather than starting a new church. Many of these established churches are struggling to keep their doors open, they point out, and a new church certainly will not help matters.

I once heard Mahesh Chavda say: "There are more than enough unbelievers to go around. Therefore, churches shouldn't be fighting with one another over who has the right to exist."

We need more churches, more capable ministers of the gospel, more apostolic teams and networks of churches. In the days facing us there may be a dire shortage of authentic, New Testament churches to accurately handle the vast harvest that may be gathered in. In China, for instance, the harvest is so great that they lack an ample supply of mature ministers who are prepared to assimilate new Christians sufficiently. In Africa, the church is growing so rapidly that, in many cases, the converts must be nurtured by novice pastors and evangelists. Where mature, capable ministers are in supply, the demand sometimes placed on them is overwhelming. I believe that one day in America, Canada and Europe, the Church will be faced with the same situation, because if Jesus tarries, the explosive effect of the glorious gospel will ignite massive revival in these countries as well.

Overseas, in less-developed countries, it is imperative that new churches be planted. If they are not, the harvest of these days will be lost. Even in America and Europe the need exists, and we play the fool if we think it does not.

I once started a church in a small rural village and immediately brought down the wrath of many of the existing church leaders. By starting another church, in their thinking, I was making a statement against them. They perceived my message to be: "All of you guys failed, so I'm here to do it right." But that *was not* what I was trying to say. I was simply following a different vision than the one they had. It was no worse, and perhaps, no better than theirs, but it was the one God had birthed in my heart and had commissioned me to pursue.

That was my primary reason for beginning a brand new work. However, the Lord sometimes has His very own reasons for beginning new churches. Let us examine one of them.

Christianity in America and Europe

Why start new churches? Let us go to the Word of God to establish a case.

> *I went past the field of the sluggard, past the vineyard of the man who lacks judgment; thorns had come up everywhere, the ground was covered with weeds, the stone wall was in ruins* (Prov. 24:30-31).

To begin with, the field in this passage *could* relate directly to what we know today as the Church. In 1 Corinthians 3:9, Paul teaches that the Church is "God's field." God places redeemed human beings in charge of the cultivation and protection of His field. In our verse from Proverbs, the writer passes the field of a sluggard, that is, one who is very lazy or idle.

Secondly, the vineyard in this passage *could* also relate to the Church. In the gospel of John, chapter 15, verses 1-5, Jesus refers to the Church as the vine, or at least, as the branches of the vine. In our verse from Proverbs, the writer passes the vineyard of a man who lacks judgment.

Thirdly, we find that thorns are everywhere, and the ground of the vineyard is covered with weeds ("nettles," KJV).

Fourthly, the protective stone wall surrounding the vineyard is in ruins. The King James Version says it is "broken down."

Metaphorically, the writer of Proverbs may be writing about the Church whenever it has been under the oversight of discretionless sluggards who have allowed its stone walls to be broken down.

In America, Canada and Europe today, many denominational *and* nondenominational churches are comparable to the field and vineyard of Proverbs. Because so many of the men and women at the head of these vineyards are spiritual sluggards and lack spiritual judgment, the walls that separate the Church from the world are entirely broken down. Anti-Christian beliefs and morals have invaded many segments of the Church and have reduced those segments to an irrelevant force in shaping today's world. Blind guides and blind fools have allowed the Church to become worldly — a deplorable, pathetic mess, to say the least. Through breaches in the wall, a flood of corruption, alien seed and wild beasts have stormed into the Church to lay it waste. There will be no good fruit, no lasting fruit, coming from a vineyard such as this.

Thorns

Jesus taught that thorns "choke the Word" out of one's life (Mark 4:18-19). Thorns are the cares of this world, the deceitfulness of riches, and the lusts for other things — anything that draws your attention away from the Kingdom of God. Thorns can actually cause the pure and powerful Word of God to become unfruitful. In churches where there are these "thorns," people will merely hold to a form of godliness, but will have nothing to do with it as a force that can change them from glory to glory. The man-made traditions of religious men and women — those life-sapping rules and regulations that find no to basis in the Word of God — soon spring upbring many into bondage. Such traditions actually nullify the Word of God (Matt. 15:6).

I saw this happen many years ago when I was assigned a teaching position in one of the Sunday school classes of the church I was attending. Approximately ten teenagers were part of my class. From the first day I took the class, things began to happen. Although I was supposed to teach from a Sunday school quarterly, I felt liberty in the Holy Spirit to lay the book aside at times and discuss other spiritual issues that were more in step with where those kids were. As a result, some of the kids were brought to God. Others were brought much closer to making a decision for Christ than ever before. God was clearly working in their hearts.

One Sunday not very long after I had taken control of the class, the Sunday school superintendent sat in to evaluate the job I was doing. When she saw that I wasn't following the quarterly as closely as I was supposed to, she became very upset. Although she didn't say anything, I could see the disapproval in her eyes. Within a week I was confronted and told that it was time to "rotate" a new teacher into the class (one that would tow the quarterly line), and that my services would no longer be required. Sadly, I handed over the position to the new teacher and lost the vital contact with the kids that I had been gaining. Because I live in a small community, I have been able to follow the spiritual progress of most of those precious kids. Although they are all adults now, I remain aware of their spiritual state. Unfortunately, I have to report that not one of them is leading the abundant life of an on-fire Christian — not even the ones who came to know the Lord while I had the class. How sad. What happened to them?

A church tradition that says all Sunday school teachers must teach consistently from the denomination's Sunday school material robbed the Spirit of God of the leverage He was getting in the lives of those teenagers. Don't get me wrong, I'm not against Sunday school quarterlies; but if they are not producing the Life of God in the students, they should be scrapped! But tradition rarely allows such unorthodox decisions to be made and carried out. As a result, teachers "beat dead horses" for years on end and wonder why their classes are so dull, dead and boring.

Another pathetic, death-inducing tradition was that church's practice of rotating Sunday school teachers in and out of classes every six months or so, regardless of what the Spirit of God was accomplishing through the teaching of the current teacher. Often, unanointed teachers replaced anointed ones, and the class "died the death." Tradition said, "Give everybody who'd like to teach a chance," but the Spirit of God said, "Let only those I've called and anointed teach!" (1 Cor. 12:28)

"People" Thorns

According to some Scriptures, people are classified as thorns. If such people are allowed to remain, unchanged among God's holy seed, they will contaminate it, vex it and bring it to apostasy. (See Numbers 33:55, Joshua 23:1-13 and Judges 2:3.)

When the ungodly are allowed to infiltrate the people of God, never being challenged to accept the Lord Jesus and lead lives honoring to Him, their filth of spirit and life-style will spread like leaven through a loaf, negatively affecting the flock of God. (See 1 Corinthians 5:6.)

Sadly, many churches are filled to capacity with human "thorns" that bring vexation and demonic problems upon the people of God.

Thorns Entangle and Lacerate

Thorns, according to the Bible, have the power to entangle and lacerate (Prov. 15:19, TAB). I have known of many men and women of God who were hopelessly entangled and ripped to shreds by the hideous thorns of the evil one.

One such man went to his pastor for deliverance not long ago. He had been saved a number of years before and had grown quite strong in his walk with the Lord. Even though he was strong in many areas of his life, he failed to deal properly with one particular "thorn" that had caused him much trouble in his past life, alcohol.

As a young Christian, the novelty of life in Christ had kept him occupied with many of the facets of the Christian life that initially excite young Christians. Various fellowship meetings, Christian concerts, teaching cassettes, etc., had busied him to the point that he was rarely confronted by the power and sway of alcohol. However, after several years, the thrill of attending all of the Spirit-filled meetings in a one-hundred-mile radius began to wear off. The excitement of attending Christian concerts waned. The myriads of fine Bible-teaching tapes lost their attraction. He began staying home to watch the television, rather than traveling across town on rainy nights to hear the traveling Bible teacher expound the Word on how to remain strong in the Lord during the evil day. After all, he felt he knew all of that. Subtly and very slowly a patient devil began to convince him that he could begin enjoying a glass of wine or an occasional beer with dinner, or while watching a weekend television sporting event. No longer excited about the things God was doing in the earth (because he was no longer hearing about them), he began to settle for the little "buzz" he experienced from the glass of wine or bottle of beer. It wasn't that bad; it didn't make him cuss or act badly. As a matter of fact, it made him feel a little closer to God, a little more sensitive, or so he thought. Slowly, the enemy was pulling the wool over his eyes, all the while convincing him that things were all right between him and God.

Before long he felt a freedom to drop by the local beer joint to play a game of pool and drink a beer with the boys — all in the name of being evangelistic, mind you. He began enjoying the vulgar jokes the other men would tell, even the ones about the fallen television evangelists. Little did he realize what was actually taking place. Two thorns, the lust of other things (Mark 4:19) and bad company (1 Cor. 15:33), began to corrupt his morals and choke the Word of God out of him. They literally entangled him and cut him to pieces. He quit attending church regularly, and when he did stir himself to go, he attended those churches with preachers who compromised the Word of God, preaching a social gospel. In time, he quit attending church altogether and fell into an adulterous affair with a married woman. Alcohol and a promiscuous sexual life-style enslaved him and brought him to the brink of total disaster, suicide! By the time he realized how far he had fallen, it was almost too much for him to deal with. But the grace and mercy of God led him to his pastor, and today he is on his way out of the pit of destruction. Glory to God!

The sad thing is this: He will never be able to regain all of the precious spiritual ground he had once claimed. God forgives and loves him, and will do many fine things for him, but the lacerations he received to spirit, soul and body while entangled by the world will leave scars for the remainder of his life. The thorns of the evil one are not to be taken lightly. No matter what form they take or in what setting they're found, they remain deadly. Beware.

Weeds

Weeds, or nettles, as some translations read, always reveal the absence of God's presence and the presence of someone or something else. See Isaiah 34:13-14:

> *Thorns will overrun her citadels, nettles and brambles her strongholds. She will become a haunt for jackals, a home for owls. Desert creatures will meet with hyenas, and wild goats will bleat to each other; there the night creatures will also repose and find for themselves places of rest.*

What a picture of judgment. When God has been pushed out by the persistent rebellion of the people, other things will always fill the vacuum He leaves.

It is interesting to note that Jesus said a demon cast out seeks rest (Luke 11:24). In a vineyard full of nettles and thorns he'll find it. When nettles, brambles and thorns are fruitful, so are demons! Didn't Jesus go from synagogue to synagogue casting demons out of religious people? (Mark 1:39) I dare say it would be no different today in "Christian America," if many existing churches were to open their hearts to the full-orbed ministry of Jesus through the Holy Spirit.

I have a video cassette that contains rare footage of a mass crusade conducted in Argentina by one of that country's well known evangelists. Tens of thousands attend his crusades and are miraculously liberated from demonic torment by the manifest power of God. After the evangelist has led scores of people to the Lord with a heart-stirring salvation message, he boldly begins to renounce the power of demons over their lives. Immediately, all over the vast crusade grounds, people begin falling to the ground under the influence of demon spirits, demons that have often lain dormant or inactive for many months or years.

Under the strong, anointed decree of the evangelist, the demons begin to cry out from their captives, often causing the people to experience severe convulsions and vomiting. An army of workers, hand-picked and specifically trained for these crusades, goes to work carrying the demon-oppressed people backstage where the evil spirits are soundly evicted in Jesus' name. As I watch the video tape, I am made painfully aware of the fact that the demon-oppressed people are ordinary-looking, everyday-type people just like one sees in the stores and shops of "Christian" America and Europe. There is very little difference between them. They attend churches, drink alcohol, smoke cigarettes, read the world's newspapers, gaze at pornography, and think the same self-serving thoughts as anyone else. I maintain that if we could gather ten thousand American citizens from all fifty states and put them in the presence of that kind of anointing, we would see the same results — probably even more dramatic!

I believe that scores of our neighbors, friends and co-workers are in dire need of deliverance, as are people in every country of this fallen world. The sad thing is that myriads of them faithfully attend sweet, powerless churches every Sunday morning, churches that are infested with demon spirits! The Isaiah passage describes a haunt for jackals and a home for owls. It is a place of desert creatures; hyenas and goats and night creatures repose there and find for themselves places of rest. These are all symbols of a horde of demon spirits, ruling and reigning unhindered in the midst of the people of God.

Goats

In Matthew 25:31-46, Jesus makes it clear that there are goats as well as true sheep in Christendom. On Judgment Day the goats will be forever banished from the presence of the Lord and His true flock, being consigned to everlasting fire.

In today's world there are many cults that masquerade as Christian. However, when one compares the basic beliefs they espouse with those of the Bible, it is clear that the cults are not Christian at all. On Judgment Day they will be sorted out, not only the organizations, but also the individuals within them.

Alas, there is also a vast supply of goats in those organizations that do adhere to the basic doctrines of the Bible. They say they are Christians and even carry the Bible, but many are total strangers to the God they profess to serve. Their lives are devoid of the fruit that is in keeping with the Christian life. They are perpetual liars, adulterers and idol worshippers. Many are pornography-gazers, wife-beaters, child-molesters, drunkards and thieves. They put up a pretty good front on Sunday mornings, but live like hell the remainder of the week. The world spots them many times before their fellow church-goers become aware of the lie they live. It calls them hypocrites and uses their poor example as an excuse to stay away from genuine Christianity. They are allowed, even encouraged, to sit each Sunday in the churches of our land, and receive the same respect and consideration that a true Christian should receive. They are never confronted for their hypocrisy and are often allowed to hold important offices in the government of the church.

I used to raise beef cattle. Every October would find me trucking several loads of calves to the local livestock market to be sold.

One day as I was in my big truck waiting for my turn to back up to the dock to unload, I witnessed an elder from one of the local congregations "guzzling" down a couple of beers beside his truck. When he was finished with the cans, he threw them into the weeds nearby. I clearly remember how before he opened each can, he would crane his neck in every direction to be sure no one was watching. This old drunk wasn't fooling anyone but himself, and yet the terrible thing about it was that his pastor and fellow elders were content to leave him in a position of eldership. How utterly deplorable! Is it any wonder that most churches are in such a spiritual shambles, unable to impact their surrounding communities with the glorious gospel of Christ?

Not too long ago I was talking to a young man about his need of the baptism in the Holy Spirit. During our conversation he told how only recently he had been approached by the pastor of a particular church, one he had attended for less than a month, and had been almost begged to accept the responsibility of leading the youth of the church. The pastor was obviously thrilled by the terrific personality of the young man and was not willing to let such a prospect get away. The minister attempted to strap him with responsibility; that way he couldn't leave. However, there was no way the pastor could have known the background of the man he was trying to maneuver into such a responsible position. For all he knew, the young man could have been a child-molester, wanted by the law in five states! Sufficient time had not passed to enable the pastor to test the man's character; and yet he was willing to place the destiny of eternal souls into his young hands.

The gross lack of discernment and spiritual wisdom in many spiritual leaders never ceases to amaze me. What sobers me is that I have been guilty of this as well.

Until essential biblical criteria are known to be established in the life of a potential church member, and such issues as the new birth, repentance from dead works, water baptism and the veracity of the Word of God are dealt with, the candidate should not be received into the membership of the local church, let alone be allowed to assume a leadership position.

Everyone should be heartily welcomed to attend our general meetings, but we should never automatically assume they are members of "the general assembly and church of the firstborn who are enrolled in heaven" (Heb. 12:23, NAS). It is not until after local leadership has talked with them, observed them and become convinced before God, that they should even be considered as a growing part of the local church.

Potential members should be given time for prayerful and intelligent communication with God before deciding whether or not to become a part of a church. Membership speaks of covenant, and covenant speaks of marriage to a particular church body. It should never be entered into lightly.

Taking the necessary time when including new members in

our covenant assemblies will help to ensure that our churches do not become diluted with a mixture of saints and unregenerate sinners.

In the early days of Christianity, the presence of the Holy Spirit and the anointed, uncompromised preaching of God's Word were apt to bring such conviction on sinners who did attend church meetings that they were either drawn to their knees in repentance or were soon to flee from the presence of God's holy people in order to avoid the Spirit's convicting power. Today, however, such people are allowed to remain unchallenged and unchanged. This is anathema to God! The apostles consistently stressed the questions: "What fellowship can light have with darkness? What communion can a believer have with an unbeliever?" (2 Cor. 6:14, author's paraphrase) The Word of God instructs us not to be unequally yoked together with unbelievers, and yet we choose to ignore His command. Amos 3:3 (KJV) asks, "Can two walk together, except they be agreed?" Yet all over our land, Christian leaders are attempting to build the Kingdom of God with unregenerate sinners who have "neither part nor lot in this matter" (Acts 8:21, KJV).

When Ezra and Zerubbabel set out to build the Temple in Jerusalem in 500 B.C., their adversaries endeavored to hinder their work by infiltrating their ranks under the guise of wanting to help. Their involvement in the building process would surely have contaminated the pure work Ezra, Zerubbabel and the other fathers of Israel were commissioned to do. Zerubbabel's response to their crafty offer is noteworthy. He replied, "You have no part with us in building a temple to our God. We alone will build it for the Lord" (Ezra 4:3). Zerubbabel and the men with him had God's heart on the matter. I maintain that His heart has not changed in all the centuries since. He declares, "I am the Lord, I change not!" (Mal. 3:6, KJV). We will all do well to remember this. Too many churches today are failing to deal with the travesty of mixed congregations. They are allowing those who merely profess religion to share membership with those who do have the life of God. Churches like these will not endure the hard times to come, but will fall apart in the face of tribulation, just as a sand castle by the sea is demolished by the rising tide.

Stone Walls

Our text from Proverbs 24 mentions the fact that the stone walls are in ruins. Stone walls, applied spiritually to the Church, typify those eternal standards by which Christians of every century are to live and order their lives. When adhered to in devoted obedience, they will serve to keep the wild beasts, the night creatures and other destructive agents from entering to destroy the Church. As wild beasts enter the Church through holes in its walls, worldly attitudes and morals, the doctrines of demons gain entrance. This process may begin slowly, but soon a floodtide of corruption and death follows, and the effectiveness of the Church is diluted. The old bedfellows of compromise and tolerance gain the upper hand, and the leaven of impurity and weakness soon spreads through the whole lump of church membership. The spirit of antichrist enters in subtle ways and is soon able to lead even the most spiritual members into doctrinal error and sin.

A genuine striving for purity and power is to characterize the membership of the Church of Jesus Christ in these days, and only those believers who are responding to God without compromise can be involved in such an assembly. Only those people who are totally committed to serving and honoring Jesus can be involved in the process of building a glorious Church that will impact the world. The glory of the house God is building in the earth today, according to the prophet Haggai, will exceed the glory of all former temples of worship. We are that house, that temple of the living God. As members of it, and as living stones being built into it, we must make no arrangements with the world and its selfish attitudes and ambitions. The effect of this temple will be earth-shattering, but this effect will be nullified if we build on anything less than purity, integrity, honesty and above all — God's Word!

It greatly saddens me to have to admit that major "Christian" organizations continue to deliberate on whether or not to ordain homosexuals. Some denominations have already consented to such unscriptural ordinations! It maddens me that other groups have adopted plans to remove all male-gender references to God from their Bibles, songbooks and church school literature. Through the centuries, the Jezebel spirit has delighted in emasculating man who was made in the image and likeness of Almighty God. Now, through deceived religious men, it seeks to emasculate the Father of lights, who does not change like shifting shadows (James 1:17). However, He is still who Jesus revealed Him to be — Father! Abba! Man of war! Prince of peace! King of glory!

Halloween in Church?!?

One day a few years ago I was reading a weekly periodical published by a major Christian denomination. I was appalled as I read how one of its churches had just celebrated its annual Halloween party, complete with an "in church" haunted house for the kids. The periodical praised the church for its innovative ideas.

We must never forget that the world beholds such dens of compromise and believes they represent the Jesus of the Bible. I tell you boldly: The King of glory has nothing to do with such houses of wickedness! Because their walls are broken down and in ruins, thorns and nettles have sprung up within them, choking the very life out of the people these churches claim to be serving. Wild beasts are devouring the vulnerable flock of God!

From the midst of the rubble God is energizing a new thing, and "now it shall spring forth!" (Isa. 43:19) The Lord is calling forth, sanctioning and empowering men and women who are committed to the authentic brand of Christianity, and who are not afraid to say "No!" to the death-inducing traditions of religious dead men and the works of hell! New churches must be started and established on *proper* foundations. Existing churches that are open to change and are eager for radical reformation must be set in order. Life under the cross means relentless reformation! We dare not run from that truth. Radical, transforming action must be embraced if we are ever to realize the hopes that we may now dare for a glorious Church that will impact the world.

Be Fearless

Those of us who are committed to the vision of a glorious Church might well ponder the exhortation of God through the prophet Ezekiel:

> *And you, son of man, do not be afraid of them or their words. Do not be afraid, though briars and thorns are all around you and you live among scorpions. Do not be afraid of what they say or terrified by them, though they are a rebellious house* (Ezek. 2:6).

Mere Religion — A Rebellious House

It is certain that as the end-time army of God goes forth into the fray their most vicious opponents will be religious leaders who failed to do their job. The Pharisees, embroiled in bitter envy and jealousy, bemoaned the fact that "the whole world has gone after him [Jesus]" (John 12:19). The great apostles were continuously hounded by the "religious elite" of their day. They threw away the key of knowledge, did not enter themselves, and refused to allow anyone else to enter into the blessings of God's Kingdom. They were clearly the members of a rebellious house.

In the revelation of the end times given to John on the Isle of Patmos, a one-world religious system called Babylon the Great is unveiled. The Revelation reveals that this whore system will be drunk with the blood of the saints and with the blood of the martyrs of Jesus (Rev. 17:6). This great whore is destined to arise in the latter times, and will be comprised of the religions of the world that do not adhere to sound Bible doctrine. By strong satanic deception and delusion, they will unite in an effort to birth world unity by religious means. True Christians will reject their foolish plot and thus will be hated for being narrow-minded. But remember, it was Jesus our Lord who said, "*...strait* is the gate, and *narrow* is the way, which leadeth unto life, and few there be that find it" (Matt. 7:14, KJV, author's emphasis).

Christianity makes no room for other religions and this often gets false religious orders seething in blinding hatred toward the gospel. Nonetheless, Paul wrote, "For there is *...one mediator* between God and men, the man Christ Jesus" (1 Tim. 2:5).

Mankind will not get around the fact that "God has appointed a day in which He will judge the world in righteousness *by that man* whom He ordained, and whom He raised from the dead" (Acts 17:31, paraphrased). The fact that God raised Jesus from the dead guarantees the coming Judgment Day. "The world thinks it is done with Jesus, but it hasn't even begun with Him yet. He is at the end of the road for every man and woman" (Ravenhill).

The tomb of Mohammed is full of dust and corruption. The tombs of the Caesars are full of death. Buddha was a robber and a thief (John 10:8), and while his body has returned to dust, his soul burns in hell. Baha'u'llah's body has turned to dust and decomposing bone in the Middle East. The bodies of all the mighty kings, of the greatest military leaders, and of the most intellectually brilliant men that ever lived, lie as dust and mud in the earth. *But* the tomb of Jesus Christ is empty! On the third day, He arose and walked out of that tomb; and because He lives, we live also!

The names of the seemingly endless array of imposters and frauds will pass. The false ways of the thousands of cults and religions will eventually cease to deceive fallen men. But the way of Jesus of Nazareth will endure forever. I like the way W. Phillip Keller put it in his fine book, *A Layman Looks at the Lamb of God.* He writes:

> *If Jesus were not the Christ of God, He would long ago have been lost in the hazy mists of man's memory. Like false pretenders and crafty imposters across the ages, His record would have blown away in the winds of time. But that did not happen. Despite the most concerted efforts of human society, philosophy, governments, and ignorance to obliterate His presence and power, He has become the dearest person in all of life to a hundred million hearts from centuries past to the present.*

Time itself will prove that Jesus was and still is the Christ of God!

Why Start New Churches?

The writer of Proverbs went on to say, "I applied my heart to what I observed and learned a lesson from what I saw" (Prov. 24:32). He came to know that "a little sleep, a little slumber, a little folding of the hands to rest — and poverty will come on you like a bandit and scarcity like an armed man" (Prov. 24:33-34). Many churches in "civilized" America, Canada and Europe are impoverished for lack of spiritual diligence. There is a scarcity of purity and piety, and an absolute absence of the anointing of God. Hosea 9:6 reports that "Egypt [the world] will gather them, and Memphis [the world's seat of authority] will bury them [God's disobedient people]. Their treasures of silver [redemption] will be taken over by briers, and thorns will overrun their tents [sanctuaries of worship]." No produce, protection or life! Children going into captivity (Deut. 28:41). Sickness and disease running rampant through the assembly of God's people. Poverty overtaking them as a storm trooper. Oh the price of compromise in the Church of Jesus Christ!

The Culprits

As I read the Bible, comparing our problems today with those of Israel so long ago, I see that inadequate, sometimes bad, leaders are the hindrance to all that God wants to do. The pastors, elders, deacons, etc., in so many churches are failing to be the proper watchmen that God would have them be.

> *His watchmen are blind: they are all ignorant, they are all dumb dogs, they cannot bark; sleeping, lying down, loving to slumber* (Isa. 56:10, KJV).

The watchmen of today's Church are pastors, seminary professors and other church leaders who are supposed to be looking out for worldly trends that are attempting to come into the midst of God's people. They are compared to watchdogs whose job is to protect the sheep from the wolf, barking when they see one approaching. When they see worldliness, tolerance and compromise threatening the Church, they are to "blow the trumpet, and warn the people" (Ezek. 33:3, KJV); but today few of them can offer even a feeble bark. Why? Of course the reasons are sometimes varied, but one major reason is because they are controlled by a demonically influenced hierarchy of religious dead men. Church leaders must break free from the kind of control placed on them that causes them to compromise truth.

One praiseworthy minister, who is one of the most humble, sincere men of God I know, refused to bow his knees to such religious spirits of compromise and worldliness. I observed him for several years as he labored faithfully in an area of Virginia that desperately needed what he had to offer. Again and again his good name was assaulted by the godless spirits of antichrist that carried social influence through certain members of his parish. Following years of struggle for truth, his religious enemies sought support from the denominations's headquarters. Leaders in his denomination warned him to stop preaching and teaching subjects that offended these important members of his parish. When he chose to obey God rather than men, he was removed from his charge. Since then they have gotten what they wanted: compromise and death! The glory that was in their midst when that faithful pastor was there has long since departed, and spiritual poverty has come upon them like an armed man.

Who Are the Real Deceivers and Antichrists?

A brother just left my office. He related to me that the pastor of his in-laws' church went to a seminar on reincarnation and eastern mysticism, conducted by one of the world's leading witches. The pastor then began teaching her abominable material to his own congregation. We were appalled! Not only are watchmen failing to intercept the deadly poison an approaching wolf will bring, but now many are going out in search of the wolves themselves and bringing their horrendous teachings home to the flock!

The Church of Jesus Christ is facing perilous times. Truth is under attack and the lie is raising its ugly head and calling all men unto itself. Supposedly educated men and women are flocking to the multitude of deceivers and antichrists who offer "doors into eternal bliss" rather than Jesus Christ. We must not stand idly by and allow this to happen without a fight. It is a fight for the hearts and lives of people for whom Jesus gave His life! We must step up our efforts in evangelism.

In these last days it is going to be a battle between our Book and their books, our power and their power, our God and their gods. Prepare for the fray! The anti-Christian cults will not go away. They are committed to world "evangelism" just like we are. We must go forth in this hour for what may well be the final showdown.

Many cultists think they have seen true Christianity. They've not seen anything yet. One cult follower told me that he was once a member of a church, and that he knew what Christianity was all about. He went on to say he found much more in his new religion. I say "Baloney!" The Word of God tells us, "If they had truly been one of us, they would no doubt have continued with us" (1 John 2:18, paraphrase mine). Had he really known Jesus, he would never have turned to a false way. So what was his problem?

By and large, what has been doled out to modern society as "Christian" has been a lousy substitute. In many churches there has been an absolute famine of the Word of God. That cultist was a product of spiritual famine.

Dry Breasts and a Miscarrying Womb

So many seminary professors and pastors are offering "dry breasts" to the flocks of God.

> *Give them, O Lord: what wilt thou give? Give them a miscarrying womb and dry breasts* (Hos. 9:14, KJV).

Israel was guilty of rejecting God's Word. So God said: "Because you have rejected knowledge, I also reject you as my priests" (Hos. 4:6). He was highly dissatisfied over their improper response to the Word He had given. Not only were the people guilty, but the priests also were guilty of aborting His Word.

You have heard it said: "Like father, like son." Well, the

prophet Hosea aptly put it: "And it will be: Like people, like priests. I will punish both of them for their ways and repay them for their deeds" (Hos. 4:9).

If your way is to reject the Word of the Lord, your deeds will then be in opposition to God's deeds. You'll not live as you should live and you'll never experience the blessings God intended for you to have. As a matter of fact, you will one day find yourself fighting against God. Don't be one who aborts the Word of the Lord.

In the natural, if a woman has several abortions, she greatly increases her risk of never being able to carry a child again. What a tragedy. The womb becomes prone to reject the "seed," or in later stages of development, the growing fetus. No matter how much she wants to have the baby, because she aborted too many previous ones, she'll be unable to carry the current one to full-term and will miscarry.

In like manner, shepherds overseeing many of today's congregations have become guilty of aborting God's incorruptible seed from their hearts, just like the foolish priests of Hosea's day. The womb of the spirit is designed by God to hold and generate the life of the Word of God, but alas, so many of today's ministers have aborted the good Word. Sadly, many of them have now developed hearts that are incapable of conceiving and carrying the Word and anointing of God full-term. When such a man or woman stands in the pulpit to feed the flock of God, all they are able to offer the people are dry breasts. Because unless something is happening in the shepherd's heart, he will have little or no milk in the breast to offer the hungry. The flock may "desire the sincere milk of the word, that [they] may grow thereby" (I Pet. 2:2, KJV), but they are left to die from malnutrition of the spirit because their foolish leaders have habitually rejected the Word of God.

God deliver us from the foolish shepherds who will not give us the Truth. Away with the compromisers who have "daubed" the Church with untempered mortar! They have whitewashed the Truth, and the house will not stand in the face of the stormy wind. (See Ezekiel 13:10-15, KJV.) When hard rains come and strong winds blow, walls that are put up with untempered mortar will fall.

The Lord laments, "Many pastors have destroyed my vineyard, they have trodden my portion under foot, they have made my pleasant portion a desolate wilderness [a haunt of demons]. They have made it desolate, and being desolate it mourneth unto me" (Jer. 12:10-11a, KJV).

He continues, "The diseased have ye not strengthened, neither have ye healed that which was sick [When was the last time your pastor laid hands on a sick person?], neither have ye bound up that which was broken, neither have ye brought again that which was driven away, neither have ye sought that which was lost ..." (Ezek. 34:4, KJV).

And so God declares, "I will require my flock at their hand, and cause them to cease from feeding the flock; neither shall the shepherds feed themselves anymore; for I will deliver my flock from their mouth, that they may not be meat for them" (Ezek. 34:10, KJV).

He promises, "I will give you pastors according to mine heart, which shall feed you with knowledge and understanding" (Jer. 3:15, KJV).

Today, multitudes are pouring out of churches that compromise and are seeking those churches that have men of God who will give them what they need in order to grow and prosper in God.

The "dumb-dog" pastors have reduced the Church to irrelevancy. But a new breed of minister is coming forth nowadays that will sound a clarion call, urging the Church and nation to repent. They are anointed leaders, men after God's own heart who feed the flocks of God pure manna from heaven, even the unadulterated Word!

Apostolic men are also coming front and center in our day, men who have the call and undeniable anointing to extend God's Kingdom to the uttermost. God's sheep will be led in a way that exalts and honors the Lord in their lives, and the gates of hell will be overcome by a powerful Church with Jesus at its head. What a day to be alive! What opportunities await us! This anthem describes the heart of this rising, mighty remnant.

Moving out in the mighty power of Jesus;
Moving out in the glory of His name;
Moving out to wrestle 'way from Satan
all the captives his old kingdom claims.

Thrusting forth with weapons that are mighty;
Thrusting forth in the glory of that name;
Thrusting forth with Jesus as our Leader,
setting free the blind, sick, deaf and lame.

Holding forth the Word of Life from Father;
Holding forth a message from His throne;
Holding forth the power that redeemed us;
now to men reality's made known.

— *Chip Hill*

Outposts

Why start new churches? Because God's Kingdom will only know increase (Isa. 9:7). Jesus Christ has an "expansion mentality." With the population of the world exploding the way it is, He is determined to see His eternal Kingdom explode in numbers as well. It is destined to expand! It is exciting that you and I get to be in on what He's presently doing on the earth.

Each new church that is established on genuine biblical foundations becomes an outpost for the Kingdom of God in its area. An outpost is comprised of a small group of troops stationed at a distance from the main force. They possess a fort for protection, and their purpose is two-fold: To provide protection from attacks by the enemy, and to establish a new settlements for their kingdom's government. Each outpost resident is not merely settling the area near the fort for his government, but is also pioneering new territory for future claim.

I presently live in an area of the Appalachian Mountains that once boasted a line of pioneer forts that stretched from Pennsylvania, in the north, down through the Potomac River Valley of West Virginia (then Virginia), and on through the Jackson River Valley of west central Virginia. These forts or outposts, established by the colonial military, served as basic footholds for further frontier exploration and settlement as well as places of safety for the settlements that were built up around them. Supplies from the eastern ports were hauled to these forts by horse and wagon, and it was there at the fort that the settlers in the area found a sense of security. When the Indians were on the warpath, the settlers would often flee to the safety of the nearest fort, where they would find ample gunpowder, ammunition, food and medical supplies. When threat of Indian attacks subsided, they would leave the fort, returning to their cabins.

I think this analogy gives us an exciting idea of what Kingdom-expansion and church-planting can be like. Let us dare to see ourselves as an army of spiritual pioneers who are determined to see the kingdom we represent push into new frontiers — areas where there has yet to be a full and powerful expression of the Kingdom of God. Each new church becomes an outpost, established for the safety and preservation of those precious people who will link themselves to the vision God has given. Also, it becomes a place from which pioneers can reach out into new spiritual frontiers and seek to see the Kingdom of God extended.

In Old Testament days, captured territory always called for the establishment of outposts. Two verses describing David's military exploits reveal that, after striking down the enemy in his own territory, David and his army established garrisons (outposts) in order to enforce his victories (2 Sam. 8:6,14). Through the ministries of these many outposts, David was able to see to it that his victories were secured and established, and that peace would reign over his kingdom. The Scriptures say further, "And David reigned over all Israel; and David executed judgment and justice unto all his people" (II Sam. 8:15, KJV). As King Jesus' Word and Spirit prevail, getting the upper hand in many regions of the earth before the end comes, He too will reign, executing His judgment and His justice to His people.

The outposts become a vital arm of His kingly ministry in the regions where they are found. His judgments and His justice are legally executed by the ministers in His command (political, military and religious) who are stationed in the various outposts. And do not be ignorant of the fact that there are political and military aspects, as well as religious, to the full-orbed ministry of the Church of Jesus Christ. We are to be a highly-governed military organization on the earth, spiritually speaking, that walks in piety and great power — with God and man. The Church is not to be a weak, irrelevant, cowering little sect of people that keeps their opinions to themselves; we are to be "as awesome as an army with banners" (Song 6:10, NAS). When we speak, everyone ought to listen!

Archbishop Benson Idahosa, the founder and leader of an enormous church in Nigeria, West Africa, one day approached a woman who was the program director for the government-owned and operated television station in that nation. He asked her to be so kind as to allow him to put Christian broadcasting on the air. The programing that was already there was going from bad to worse, as even a few lewd programs were beginning to be aired. She was not even ready to consider his proposal and responded to him with a staunch, "No!" That night as he was before the Lord God in prayer, Benson asked Him what he was to do next — in order to convince the woman that she should allow God some airtime. God reminded Reverend Idahosa that he had authority in this situation, and that whatever he deemed necessary in order to gain airtime would be fine with Him. The next day Idahosa returned to the program director, very politely and diplomatically asking her to reconsider her decision. Again she was adamantly opposed to putting anything related to Jesus on the air. Idahosa's reply was awesome: "Okay, but it's going to cost you your job!"

"Who said so?" she responded.

Idahosa answered, "I said so!" He then wheeled around and departed. In just two weeks' time the woman lost her job! Her replacement was a born-again man who, after hearing from Idahosa the reason his forerunner was removed from her position, gladly gave God the time He desired. Now millions of people in Nigeria are hearing the uncompromised Word of God over government television. Benson Idahosa never complained to one man about the woman's stubbornness — he didn't even complain to God about it. He simply operated in the God-sanctioned authority that Jesus Christ has given to the Church on earth. (There will be more said about this authority in a later chapter.)

The Church as an outpost, in any given locality, is to be

inspiring awe and profound respect in the people who live there. From these bastions of strength we should be sending out "raiding parties" to wreak havoc in the strongholds of satan (1 Sam. 13:17).

From our churches we should be sending small "raiding parties" into prisons, hospitals and nursing homes. In such places, thousands of hostages sit hopelessly enslaved to the forces of satan. We should be seeing numbers of them who are "incarcerated" in these places gloriously born again.

I have seen door-to-door witnessing teams used effectively in the neighborhoods surrounding the outposts of God. Two or three evangelistically motivated believers with a strategy from God are often able to present the love of God effectively to whole households.

Let me share a few valuable tips with you on how to witness in someone's home more effectively.

Door-to-Door Witnessing Tips

1. Prior to approaching someone's home, spend at least a few moments interceding for the people you'll be reaching out to. Beseech the Lord for wisdom and anointing.

2. Bind the strong man over the household. Usually there has been one assigned by the kingdom of darkness to keep the home's inhabitants in spiritual darkness.

3. Before approaching the home, decide who on the team is going to be the main spokesman. Of course this can change once the team enters the home, but as a rule it is best to stick with the one who is predetermined to carry on a conversation with the potential converts.

4. When the team enters the home, team members designated to support the spokesman should occupy seats farthest from the potential convert, allowing the spokesman to have the seat nearest them. It is much easier to have eye contact and keep someone's attention if you are seated near them.

5. Supporting team members should keep small children or pets occupied while the spokesman shares the gospel with the targeted person(s). They should seek to eliminate as many potential distractions as possible. If the television is a distraction, they should politely seek permission to turn it off.

6. Supporting team members should not interrupt the spokesman when he is in the midst of serious sharing. This can interrupt the flow of the Spirit and squelch the flow of the anointing. Only after the spokesman offers his or her team members an opportunity to share should they feel free to add to the conversation.

7. If the person with whom you are trying to share seems hardened and closed to the idea that he needs Jesus, then try this strategy:

> "Before I leave could I at least pray for you and your family? It won't hurt anything if I pray for God to bless your home, your life and your family, will it?"

At this point most people will agree that such a prayer won't hurt anything, even if they believe it won't help either. But there is a strategy behind this move. When prayer is offered under the unction of the Holy Spirit, it brings the sweet presence of God into the scene in a way He hasn't been felt in all that has transpired in the earlier conversation. At this time it is important to pray the heart of the Father for the individual; much love and feeling must go into the prayer for it to accomplish the intended results. After a heart-felt prayer, the individual for whom you prayed may be so touched by the sweet presence of the Lord that he or she becomes ready to discuss his or her personal need of the Savior. I have seen hardened men "tenderized" by such heart-felt prayers, and with tears streaming down their cheeks, they have become receptive to the gospel that only moments before they were rejecting.

We believe it to be imperative that a church, or outpost, send out assault teams like these. A church that is not advancing on the enemy's strongholds is a church that is failing to impact the world for the Kingdom of God.

Siege Works Against the Enemy

In 1978, Darlene and I laid siege on a massage parlor in Oldtown, Alexandria, Virginia. It was in full operation not far from the home of Darlene's parents. I was appalled that such an establishment was so near their home. Often we would see pimps drive up to the place in Cadillacs with leopardskin seat covers. They would let out the young girls who worked at the parlor. It angered us to see such young girls being exploited by devil-controlled people. One night, just before we retired, God put it in our hearts to curse the massage parlor. Jesus cursed a fig tree once, and it dried up at the roots (Mark 11). He went on to exhort His followers to "Have the faith of God" (verse 22, lit.), and say to the mountain, "Be thou removed!" (verse 23, KJV). My wife and I stood up, side by side, faced the massage parlor where we could easily behold the world galloping to the pit, and cursed it. We voiced something like this:

> We curse that establishment in the name of Jesus Christ of Nazareth! By the authority delegated to us as believers, and by the faith of God that resides within us, we decree that Bunny's Massage Parlor will no more prosper, but will in fact, cease to serve as a stronghold of satan in this city. We curse it and call its ruling spirits down from their positions of authority. And Lord God, we ask you to save the girls who work there, save its management, and save every poor fool who has spent money there. In the mighty name of Jesus we pray. Amen.

It was done. We had set up a siege work against the enemy's fortress. In the weeks and months to come we simply rejoiced in God that Bunny's Massage Parlor was finished. Within a year the FBI raided it, closing not only that massage parlor, but the entire ring of massage parlors within the city of Alexandria.

I am convinced that today's Christians must regain the aggressive attitude of the early believers when dealing with the fortresses of the enemy. It has been said that all that is necessary for evil to abound is for good men to do nothing. The strongholds of prostitution, pornography, abortion and drug abuse must be besieged by the faith and resolve of sold out Christians.

If Darlene and I were effective enough to close down a ring of massage parlors in one city, just imagine what an entire nation of Christians can do if they put their hearts to it! There should be no stopping them.

Whether you sense a call to march on abortion clinics or X-rated bookstores, or maybe you feel led to enter into seasons of violent spiritual warfare and prayer concerning these deplorable social injustices, be encouraged to continue with all of your heart. Maintain your spiritual pressure, because you have God's promise that if you do not faint, you will reap in due time (Gal. 6:9).

Apostolic Flagships and Their Fleets

Each apostolic ministry, no matter how large or small, acts in a way very similar to a fleet of ships. One of the churches, usually the first one founded by the apostle, serves as the "flagship" for all the new ones that are established in the years to come.

In the navy when a fleet of warships sails to war, one ship (usually an aircraft carrier found at the center of the flotilla) carries the admiral of the fleet and also displays its flag. The fleet surrounds the flagship, providing it with an escort and a buffer zone between it and hostile forces. All ships within the fleet have constant and direct radio contact with the flagship, the admiral and his immediate team of men.

Within the expanding Kingdom of God, each new church planted by an apostolic ministry becomes a part of the fleet which is seeking to bring the peace of God to rule in the hearts of men. Thank God, there are many "apostolic fleets" being raised up by God today, and they are going forth to still the troubled waters of humanity with the good news of Jesus Christ.

Plenty of Room in the Ocean

I am sure that in World War II our government could have used many more naval fleets than those it had to send into battle. With war in both the Atlantic and Pacific Oceans, I don't think one American fleet would have argued with another American fleet, saying, "Get out of here, these are my waters!" Had we more to send forth at that time, the war may have ended much sooner and many more lives might have been saved.

In the days at hand, the Church of Jesus Christ must lay aside the spirit of competition, because no one ministry can do everything that needs to be done. All of the bona fide Christian churches in an area should be compassionately concerned with the lost and dying, how to reach them and raise them up in God; we should not be concerned over what other churches are doing. We should bless the others, allowing them the liberty they need to pursue the vision God has given them, while we also are faithful to the vision He has given us. Remember, there are more than enough unbelievers to go around.

3

THE ARTILLERY CHRISTIANS

When a fleet of warships reaches a targeted destination, perhaps the waters not far from the shores of an island occupied by the enemy, the work of the artillery crews begins. Before the smaller troop-carrying boats (ducks) can motor ashore with the men who will establish the beachheads, the big guns (artillery) on the destroyers must bombard the shores of the island in order to destroy as much of the enemy's front line as possible. The artillery "softens things up" a bit. After sufficient bombardment, the ducks are launched from the troopships to make their way through the unsettled waters toward the island. Upon arriving at the island's shore, the ducks unload their cargo; out storm the enemy's front line warriors into the fray. All the while, the artillery crew continues to bombard the island; only now, the shells are hitting a little farther inland. If the artillery bombardment is successful, only a small force of enemy soldiers will be left to oppose the men coming ashore. Beachheads will be formed at strategic spots up and down the shoreline, and from these initial bases of operation, the army will advance toward the enemy's stronghold. But had it not been for the "first-strike" efforts of the artillery crews back on board ship, the men on the beach would have had tough going.

The artillery Christians in the Kingdom of God are the mighty prayer warriors who send forth their volleys day and night for the purposes of God. All believers are called to pray, and all believers are exhorted to commune with God incessantly. But there are those committed men and women of God whose calling to pray is in the form of a special burden of intercession. They are gifted in a special way to be intercessors for the Body of Christ and the advancement of His gospel. They are often the unsung heroes of the Church who labor in prayer, unceasingly, for the plan of God to be accomplished on the earth. They are the mighty artillery Christians who pound the shores of satan's kingdom until the invasion force can establish a plantation of strength inside his borders. As apostolic ministry ventures into new territory, evangelizing the masses, planting new churches, and hastening the return of the Lord, the artillery Christians will be called, more than ever before, to "venture into the breaches [of prayer and spiritual warfare], fortifying the House of Israel and the Church, and holding fast in battle on the day of Yahweh" (Ezek. 13:5, Jerusalem Bible coupled with the author's paraphrase). The Church desperately needs men and women of war who are content to stay behind the lines of aggressive church-planting, but who are not content to leave the devil and his hordes alone. They will, in fact, enter into the warfare by staunch intercession and spiritual battle, softening up the territory into which the church-planting teams will go. The "big guns" of effectual, fervent prayer and authoritative binding of the godless, spiritual powers that be, will be the major thrust of their ministry for the work abroad. They man the spiritual cannons, throwing barrage after barrage at the enemy spirits that would seek to resist the aggressive advancements of their comrades on the front. Are these people important? Hear what Leonard Ravenhill says:

> Prayer is the most conquering outreach in the Christian life.
> Prayer is the most opposed warfare in the Christian life.
> Prayer is the most far-reaching ministry in the Christian life.

(Leonard Ravenhill, *Revival God's Way*, Bethany House Publishers, 1983.)

It is a *conquering outreach* because the Scripture says, "In *everything* by prayer" (KJV), and experience proves nothing without it. Prayer has toppled kingdoms.

It is the *most opposed warfare* because it is the bedrock of all we do for God, and without its solid foundation, we build on sinking sand. Satan knows this.

It is the most far-reaching warfare because it knows no boundaries. Prayers uttered in centuries past are finding fulfillment today. Prayers uttered from the mouths of those in chains, sitting at the bottoms of dungeons, are making an impact on the world today. And the great thing about prayer is that it knows nothing about pedigrees, only sincerity. Any sincere Christian is welcomed into the presence of God, at any time, to make entreaty for those in need. God actually welcomes the least of saints into His holy presence for this high and noble calling. When in His presence praying out of a pure heart, a believer does not remain the least of the saints of God, but actually becomes one of the most important people in God's command. In the prayer closet, lambs become lions — midgets are transformed into giants, mice into men! The place of prayer is where the foundations are laid upon which the exploits of God's people will rise.

I am more hindered in prayer than in any other Christian activity in which I engage myself. Perhaps satan has more to lose by my prayers than by any other thing I can do, so he seeks to seduce me with the pleasures and relaxations of this world. Our problem, brothers and sisters, is that we are full and satisfied with the delicacies of this life and therefore have no appetite for the better things of God. Television, current sporting events or the damning pursuit of self-satisfying hobbies has dulled our hunger for the Word and prayer, and dimmed our vision for the work at hand. Demons laugh at such Christians, giving very little consideration to us at all. Could it be that we are "wretched, and miserable, and poor, and blind, and naked" (Rev. 3:17, KJV)? Paul the apostle, that "Great Lion of God" (Augustine), had a reputation among satan's ranks, for they said, "Jesus [we] know, and Paul [we] know;" but they ask the lazy and unfounded among us, "But who are [you]?" (Acts 19:15, KJV). We have had no vision for what effectual prayer is meant to avail, we have no strong purpose in our mission for God. If one has a vision for something, he will pray until he sees it come to pass. R.A. Torrey aptly stated: "Prayer often avails where everything else fails," but alas, I don't think very many of us believe that. If you really believed that, wouldn't you be on your knees more often?

My brother and sister, the captive's cries are mounting up to heaven, and God "seeks for men and women among us, who will make up the hedge, and stand in the gap before Him" (Ezek. 22:30, author's paraphrase). The walls and hedges that are to be surrounding the lives of people, giving them protection and security from the works of darkness, are full of gaps and breaches. The enemy has pushed through and laid waste the lives of many. They lie there in defeat and intimidation, not knowing what can possibly be done to liberate them from their woes. They are languished, beaten and bruised — unable, often, even to lift a feeble cry to God. The mighty prayer warriors of God, the artillery Christians, are ever ready to rise to the challenge. They are scaling the walls, filling in the breaches, and standing fast in prayer and awesome spiritual warfare for the captives. As they fill up a gap in the hedge, they find their ministry is two-fold: they offer up prayers to God for the people they are rescuing, and at the same time, they ward off the merciless onslaughts of the enemy who seeks to enter in through the gap and deliver death to the prisoner. The prayer warrior holds his or her strategic position until victory is secured and the captive is liberated. Their victory song echoes words spoken by Job, so many centuries ago: "I broke the fangs of the wicked and snatched the victims from their teeth" (Job 29:17). Intercessors must take the hammer of truth and smash the jaws of satan, bringing deliverance to the ones who are being devoured.

I know a Christian couple who witnessed all three of their teenage children stray into the deadly ways of the world. Drugs, alcohol and sex became their life-style, much to the dismay of their parents. But they did not give up on their children.

Every morning at five o'clock, the parents arose from their night's sleep to intercede fervently for their wayward kids. After more than three years, the middle child, a son, called from another state to say that he had been truly born again and was in a halfway house getting over drug dependency. He was attending a Spirit-filled church faithfully every Sunday morning and was a part of its young people's group.

The only daughter, after a fling with the ways of the world, also gave her life back to the Lord and is today displaying a sincerity no one had seen in her before.

The third child, their oldest, has also made contact with his parents, saying he needs to get his life together, and he knows Jesus is the only way to do it.

These glowing victories did not happen on their own. A mom and dad who knew their authority and privilege in prayer were committed to stand in the gap for their kids until the battle was won.

Fasting: Adding an Extra Dimension to Our Praying

In my part of the country we have all sorts of little varmints that can be very destructive. If it weren't for varmint hunters, they would easily take over the countryside, running many people out of their homes and means of livelihood. Woodchucks can destroy what otherwise could be well-manicured and highly productive farmland. They are notorious for burrowing in the middle of fine hay meadows and under valuable outbuildings (wrecking their foundations), and for raiding people's hard-worked garden patches. Along with these varmints there are skunks, possums and foxes which wreak havoc in the lives of country dwellers. Chicken houses are raided, garbage cans are upset (with their contents scattered everywhere), and the dreaded rabies epidemic is always threatening. No matter how you look at it, such pests need to be controlled. Up here in the mountains of Virginia, open war has been declared on varmints, particularly woodchucks.

There is not a teenage boy in the mountains who hasn't shot a woodchuck with a trusty .22-caliber rifle. The 22 is as reliable a gun that a young boy can learn to shoot when it comes to woodchucks. The rifle is inexpensive to shoot, light in weight, and it has no repercussion (kick) whatsoever. Many a young boy has become an excellent marksman while carrying his trusty old 22. There are, however, a couple of drawbacks to the .22-caliber rifle. Number one: they don't retain their accuracy for long-distance shooting, and number two: they lack the lethal knockdown power of the larger caliber rifles. They are fine for some shots, but terribly inadequate for others.

Plain old prayer, in some cases, is like the .22-caliber rifle. It is wonderfully efficient for some things, but not quite enough for others. Before you cut me off for implying something I am not implying, read further please.

The 22 Magnum

There is another type of .22-caliber rifle which adds an extra dimension to the regular 22. It is called the 22 magnum. The gun itself does not look much different from its weaker counterpart. The bore of the barrel, as well as its length, may be modified slightly, but the casual observer probably would not notice that. The key difference is in the cartridge it fires. A cartridge is a metal, cylindrical case that contains both the charge (gunpowder) and the projectile (bullet) the rifle shoots. A regular 22 cartridge contains only a small amount of gunpowder, and when it fires (at the pulling of the gun's trigger), it propels the bullet a certain distance, with only a certain amount of impact. The cartridge for a 22-magnum rifle contains quite a bit more gunpowder than a regular .22-caliber cartridge. When the 22 magnum is fired, its bullet projects forward at a much higher velocity than a regular 22 and strikes its target with much more impact. It has more "knockdown power."

The Magnum of Fasting

Fasting adds a "magnum" dimension to prayer. In his classic, *God's Chosen Fast*, the late Arthur Wallis wrote:

> *Fasting is designed to make prayer mount up as on eagles' wings. It is intended to usher the suppliant into the audience chamber of the king and extend to him the golden scepter. It may be expected to drive back the oppressing powers of darkness and loosen their hold on the prayer objective. It is calculated to give an edge to a man's prayers of intercession*

and power to his petitions. Heaven is ready to bend its ear to listen when someone prays with fasting.

I am convinced that more prayers aren't answered, more victories aren't won, because we have not shown God that we mean business. The Scriptures assure us that God "is a rewarder of those who *diligently* seek Him" (Heb. 11:6, NKJV, author's emphasis), and that we will find Him, "when [we] shall search for [Him] with all [of our] heart[s]" (Jer. 29:13, KJV). In Joel 2:12, we see *how* we are to seek God with all of our hearts.

"Even now," declares the Lord, "return to me with all your heart, ***with fasting...***" (author's emphasis).

When a believer willingly sets aside the appetites of his body in order to concentrate on the work of praying and fasting, he shows God his sincerity. It is no game with this believer, and he determines to get down into the "effectual fervent prayer" in which fasting plays an important part (James 5:16, KJV).

Fasting and the Artillery Christian

For the artillery Christian, fasting is a must! I would go so far as to say that without a regular program of fasting, this believer will be unable to rise to his potential. This is not because his intentions are not right, but because his body, along with its desires, will not allow it. You see, consistent prayer smacks hard against our natural tendencies to stay laid back and uninvolved. When one knows in his spirit that it is time to be about the business of praying, the forces of the body (the flesh) can raise a big fuss. Paul lamented: "I know that nothing good lives in me, that is, in my sinful nature [the flesh]. For I have the desire to do what is good, but I cannot carry it out. For what I do is not the good I want to do; no, the evil I do not want to do — this I keep on doing" (Rom. 7:18-19). Like Paul, many Christians know they should be doing much more, but they never seem to be able to rise above the dictates of the sinful flesh-nature. The "big guns" are rarely fired by the likes of these precious ones, because they are held captive by their own bodies' desires.

Fasting is designed to break the power the flesh holds over

the believer. As one begins a regimented program of fasting, the restrictive forces of the flesh begin to wane.

The effect of fasting is at least two-fold. Not only are things being taken care of in the spiritual realm when I would normally be sitting down to dine, but the lusts of my body — the desires of my lazy, self-gratifying flesh — are also being crucified. The longer I go on fasting, following a disciplined regimen, the easier it becomes for my flesh to give in to the important and consistent exercise of prayer and spiritual warfare. Your spirit-man, under the Lordship of Jesus Christ, actually finds it easier to ascend to his rightful place in your triune being.

The artillery Christian, following a regimen of effective fasting and prayer, is one of the most devastating menaces God has to put forth against satan's kingdom. He "buffets his body" (1 Cor. 9:27, NAS), that he might "buffet" the strongholds and fortresses of the enemy. He is tried, true and battle-ready, and when he drops to his knees to pray, hell trembles!

Ravenhill once asked, "Who will deny himself good food, good company and rest, that hell may gaze on him, wrestling, embarrassing demons, liberating captives, depopulating the kingdom of darkness, and leaving in answer to his travail, a stream of bloodwashed souls?" The mighty artillery Christians — that's who! They are well aware that prayer is much more than simply asking a gracious heavenly Father to do something. Prayer involves warfare, wrestling and a determined use of awesome spiritual weapons! Vicious opposing forces are intricately involved in this warfare, creating hazardous spiritual cross-currents that can set our work for God miles off course. It is not enough that our God is able and willing to do great things in answer to our prayers; there is tremendous opposition that must be overcome. Through intensified prayer and fasting we are to apply spiritual pressures to certain situations until the breakthrough comes. Men and women of violence and steel must endure the heat, see through the smoke, and ignore the pain of this warfare; and only those committed to the discipline of fasting will endure the pressures of the days to come.

I met a man in Kampala, Uganda, who was the bishop (actually the apostle) over a network of churches in that part of

Africa. Through the mid-seventies when Moslem dictator Idi Amin was in power, the bishop and his brother were cast into one of Amin's merciless prison camps. The barbaric dictator despised men of God and systematically butchered hundreds, even thousands, of Christians during his cruel reign. The bishop and his brother were kept in the bottom of a cave for months on end, and almost daily the soldiers would come, shoot one of the prisoners, and require the bishop and a few others to haul the body outside for disposition. One day, they killed the bishop's beloved brother. This terrible nightmare ended when the bishop and a couple of other Christians decided they would go on a fast, humbling themselves and beseeching God for a breakthrough in the spiritual realm that would bring an end to all the madness that their country was experiencing. Only occasionally would they eat the insipid gruel their tormentors offered to them. After no less than four months of this punishing fast, the spiritual forces of wickedness supporting Amin's regime were toppled, and Idi Amin was forced to flee the country. The bishop and his friends were liberated.

> *Is not this the fast that I have chosen? to loose the bands of wickedness, to undo the heavy burdens, and to let the oppressed go free, and that ye break every yoke?* (Isa. 58:6, KJV)

Many today are asking with despair in their voices, "Can plunder be taken from satan's warriors; can his captives be freed?" But this is what the Lord is saying: "Yes, captives will be taken from warriors, and plunder retrieved from the fierce" (Isa. 49:25). Let us arise and dare to believe that such a word from our Commander-in-Chief is true!

The captive's cries have mounted up to heaven, and so have our prayers. Satan has wreaked havoc in the lives of countless millions, but the Church has wrought glorious victory in the lives of millions as well. God is more willing to hear and answer our prayers than we are to pray. Our prayers set in motion the most powerful, far-reaching forces in the universe. When we pray, heaven moves; and as we persevere in prayer, heaven's purposes are accomplished on the earth. Never underestimate your importance in prayer. God desires to do exploits at your request, and satan's thrones will topple at your righteous decrees! You are very important.

4

SIGNS MUST FOLLOW

One reason the Church of Jesus Christ has not impacted the world (particularly the civilized world) with the gospel more than it has is because it has been pathetically lacking the supernatural power of God. Many people have been led to believe that God is not a miracle worker at all, or that He no longer desires to work miracles today.

Miracles were fine for the first-century Church," such a person reasons, "when God was getting the Church started, but they are no longer necessary today." That is like saying an automobile needs gasoline to get started, but once started, it no longer needs gasoline to keep running. You and I both know how foolish that is; an automobile requires an endless supply of fuel in order to keep on running. And that's the way the Church is.

God, manifesting Himself through signs, wonders and miracles got the Church started, and by these demonstrations of His power, He will keep the Church running — running until He sends Jesus back to gather His saints to His side. Without an endless supply of miracles and continuing manifestations of God through signs and wonders, the Church will be quickly reduced in the eyes of the world to an irrelevant force having no answers to the woes of the world. People with problems are looking for answers, and if the Church does not have them, those people will look elsewhere. Satan will be there to oblige them.

I was disgusted one evening when I saw a segment on a

weekly television program documenting an attractive, middle-aged woman in the western United States who claims to be the "channel" for a 35,000-year-old warrior from the lost continent of Atlantis. His name is Ramtha. He first appeared to the woman several years ago, and from that time on has used her to conduct seminars in various cities around the country. Before the audience, the channel falls into a trance, and Ramtha begins to manifest himself through her demonic words of knowledge and wisdom. He teaches that man is divine, the master of his own destiny; that God is in everyone; and that no one goes to heaven or hell when he dies, but all are reincarnated. As I watched the program I learned that the woman has a mailing list of many thousands of people, with at least 100 new names being added weekly. What's worse is that there are literally hundreds of channels just like this one, masquerading themselves as servants of righteousness, throughout America. Each one claims to be the channel through which a specific person from the past desires to communicate. In actuality they are not channels for people of the past, but are what the Bible calls "mediums," possessed by a familiar spirit. (See Deuteronomy 18:11, Isaiah 8:19, Leviticus 19:31 and 20:27.)

A familiar spirit is a demon assigned by satan to impersonate a person who has died and departed earth's scene. Satan's kingdom has a complex and sophisticated system of information and communication, and so a familiar spirit can easily become "familiar" with the persons he is assigned to deceive and also with the person he seeks to impersonate. Familiar spirits effectively communicate with persons, through their medium, and are able to relate profound information that will awe the hearers. What can a seeker be, but awed, as the spirit channeling through the medium tells them secret information that they didn't think anyone else knew? It is supernatural power — satan's supernatural power — and it is gaining ground in leaps and bounds around the country. Everyone has a taste for the supernatural, and if it is not found in Church, people will often look elsewhere.

Is it any wonder that the baby-boom generation is "seek[ing] unto them that have familiar spirits, and unto wizards that peep, and that mutter" (Isa. 8:19, KJV)? The churches many of us were raised in were void of power. I grew up in a large church in Norfolk, Virginia, and never once saw a gift of the Holy Spirit in manifestation. I didn't know such powerful gifts were available to the people of God.

One Sunday evening several years ago a family came to one of my meetings in Monterey. The parents were very eager to hear the glorious gospel taught and were like sponges soaking in the water of the Word. With them were several children, ranging in age from three years to sixteen. It became immediately obvious to me that the sixteen-year-old did not want to be there, but his parents had made him come. He was probably sick of the powerless kind of religion I had been sick of when I was his age. He looked miserable.

At the end of the meeting as I was ministering to his mother, a couple of strong demons of witchcraft began to manifest themselves in her. They threw her to the floor, bouncing her around the room like a rubber ball. The spiritual warfare that ensued was quite dramatic, to say the least, but finally she was set free. When I was finished dealing with those demons, I looked up and saw that kid standing off in the corner of the meeting with his mouth hanging open and his eyes as big as saucers. The demonstration of the power of God made a believer out of him, and my wife, Darlene, was able to lead him to the Lord.

I have found deliverance to be an eye-opening miracle as I minister the Word of God to bound-up people. People aren't quite sure demons exist, but when they actually see and hear one manifest itself, and then see it cast out in the name of Jesus Christ, they become believers in the supernatural, and often give their lives to God.

One day in the church I attended as a young boy, a child of about seven fell into the aisle in front of me. He was having a hard seizure. His eyes rolled up into his head and he swallowed his tongue as he lay there in front of me, shaking violently. Everyone stared in terror before two men finally came and carried him out. As I look back, not one prayer was offered for him, nor was one command given, directing the demon that was tormenting him to come out. The poor boy was left to suffer such indignities just whenever and wherever the evil spirit inside him wished to seize him.

In Nakuru, Kenya, one Sunday morning, as I was wrapping up a sermon on spiritual authority that I had preached to a houseful of Kenyan believers, a demon began to manifest himself in a woman seated near the back of the congregation. Her seizure was one that caused her to stagger blindly over the rows of people near her. Without a second's hesitation, my interpreter and I rushed down the aisle of the church and boldly demanded that the evil spirit depart and torment her no more. Two or three strong men carried her outside to where they could continue ministry away from the onlooking crowd; I continued preaching. A few minutes later the pastor of the church joyfully reported to me and the congregation that she was totally healed and ready to rejoin the morning's meeting. Had I witnessed such spiritual resolve in the men who were leading the church I was raised in, I might never have departed from the Church to become involved in drugs, alcohol and rock music. I remember people who died with various "incurable" diseases with nary a prayer offered for them. My parents would inform me that they were deathly sick, and before long I wouldn't see them in church any more. Soon I would learn of their untimely passing. The prayer of faith, which James says "heals the sick," was never offered; anointing oil was never applied to their person (James 5:14-15); and not one demon was ever challenged. Ours was certainly a powerless church!

When I was seventeen, I left the Church and sought supernatural power in rock music and the occult — and I found it! I tried my hand at conducting séances and found that I had something of a knack for causing things to happen. One night three other kids and I were in the home of an old man who had died a couple of years earlier. His name was Sam Patterson, and he had lived his last years on earth without any legs. He had even installed several rings in strategic places while owning the house. These were hung from the ceiling by chains and were used for lifting himself in and out of his wheelchair. Not long after his death, his widow sold the house and moved to another city. The new owners removed all the hanging rings and all of the other aids that indicated a crippled man had once lived there.

On the night we held a séance in that house, we gathered around the table in the dining room. A lone, lighted candle was placed in the center of the table, and as the four of us made contact around it, little fingertip to little fingertip, I began to summon the spirit of old Sam Patterson. Directly to my back, and not visible to me, was a large dining room mirror. As I called up the spirit of Sam Patterson, the image of an old man appeared in the mirror, with rings hanging in his background. The other participants saw it and fled the house; and, of course, I followed. That was not Sam Patterson who appeared to us that night; it was an evil spirit who was masquerading as Sam Patterson. I am sure that had we not fled, we could have carried on some sort of conversation with him.

In the years that followed, I endeavored to call up the spirits of dead Civil War soldiers in an old Confederate hospital, and even tried to make contact with dead rock stars like Jimi Hendrix, whom I idolized. Sometimes we were successful at making contact with the spirit world, and sometimes we were not. But nevertheless, I was involved with a power that thrilled me more than anything I had ever experienced while growing up in church. Little did I know that each time I dabbled in the occult, I was allowing a curse to take deeper root in my life. Areas of my life began to fall apart and I did not know why. Severe arthritis besieged me, and all hope for a fulfilling life began to slip steadily away. I fell further into bondage to alcohol, so that by the time I was nineteen, I was an alcoholic with little or no ability to stop. But then I met someone named Jesus of Nazareth. He did not barge into my life; He simply asked to come in. As I gave my life to Him, determining to walk with Him forever, His mighty delivering power began to go into effect and set me free from the awful effects of the occult. When I met Jesus, I met the genuine article that all professional wizards, witches and mediums are seeking to replace. They may not realize this, but the demons indwelling them understand clearly. Every supernatural phenomenon that satan's forces execute through the occult is a counterfeit of something wonderful that Jesus gave to the Church. In place of true signs and wonders, he will produce "signs and lying wonders" (II Thess. 2:9, KJV). In place of the revelatory gifts of the Holy Spirit, he will produce the demonic insight of witches, wizards and mediums. In place of the utterance gifts of the Holy Spirit, he will produce the deceitful babblings of wizards and false prophets. And in place of the power gifts of the Holy Spirit, he will work such lying wonders that the world will believe it's the "great power of God" (Acts 8:9-11, KJV). Jesus warned, "... there shall arise false Christs, and false prophets, and shall shew great signs and wonders: insomuch that, if it were possible, they shall deceive the very elect" (Matt. 24:24, KJV). Be forewarned, Church! The occult is destined to increase in these last days, and multitudes will be deceived. But we can make a difference if we will open up to the supernatural ministry of the Holy Spirit and allow Him to show forth His power through us, declaring Jesus as Lord.

Another argument against the miraculous power of God in the Church today is found in the absurd statement that once the full canon of Scripture was completed, we were no longer in need of signs, wonders and miracles. It is argued that we now have the Bible in its entirety and need only to look into it for a revelation of God. This argument sounds very logical, and it is supported by the Bible itself. But the Bible never says that signs and wonders will pass when its pages are completed. Uninspired men came to such a conclusion, but they find no support in the Scriptures. While it is true that the Bible is the primary and complete revelation of God, as given by God to man, it is not true that His miraculous power is no longer for today. The purpose for signs and wonders is that man might have proven to him that the revelation the Bible brings is true. Miracles confirm the Word (Mark 16:20).

Bible scholar, Derek Prince, said, "You are deceiving yourself if you talk about New Testament Christianity without the supernatural." The supernatural realm is revealed in every chapter of the Book of Acts. The supernatural power of God set the Church on its way, and it will assist it in becoming all that it is destined to become in the future. The Holy Spirit is pregnant with the signs and wonders we've only dreamed about, and faith and obedience will be the ingredients that will unleash them on the world. May we all begin to exercise the militant kind of faith that will enable this great outpouring to happen.

The Impact of the Miraculous in the Old Testament

When the children of Israel were released from bondage in Egypt, God worked a series of miracles that are still talked about in Sunday school classrooms around the world. His crowning wonder was beheld as He parted the Red Sea, allowing the people of God to walk through the midst of it on dry ground. When the Egyptian army tried to follow, God caused the waters of the Sea to return to its place and the entire army was drowned. On the eastern side of the Sea, Moses led the children of Israel in a song of victory, and his sister, Miriam, led all the women in a celebration dance. "Israel saw that great work which the Lord did upon the Egyptians: and the people feared the Lord, *and believed* the Lord, and his servant Moses" (Exod. 14:31, KJV, author's emphasis). But it wasn't only for the sake of the children of Israel, it was "so that all the peoples of the earth might know that the hand of the Lord is powerful and so that you might always fear the Lord your God" (Josh. 4:24). Wherever the Israelites journeyed in the years that followed, there went out a fame of them. They were known far and wide as the people of the God who parted the Red Sea. When they walked in obedience to Him, God was faithful to send His fear before them (Exod. 23:27), so that they might drive their ungodly enemies out of the lands God was giving them. God's miraculous power was that effective.

The prophet Elijah was a man who moved in the miraculous power of God, and because of that he was known and feared throughout the land. One day he was instructed of God to go to the home of a widow who was living in Zarephath, a little town on the coast of the Mediterranean Sea. Upon his arrival he found the woman gathering sticks for a fire. Her intention was to prepare one last meal so that she and her son could eat it and die. A drought was ravaging the land and food was in poor supply. People were dying of starvation throughout the city and there was no relief in sight. In the midst of such a desperate situation, Elijah had the audacity to ask the poor woman to prepare him a meal first. When she did, a miracle happened. God began to miraculously involve Himself in the situation, supernaturally multiplying the supply of oil and flour she needed in order to make bread each day. It seems to me that such a miracle would have convinced her that Elijah was the man he claimed to be. But as we read this ongoing saga, we learn that it wasn't until her son died and Elijah raised him from the dead that she was able to exclaim, "Now I know that you are a man of God and that the word of the Lord from your mouth is the truth" (1 Kings 17:24). It took a mighty miracle like resurrection to fully convince that woman that Elijah was indeed a spokesman for Almighty God.

Further on in his story, Elijah journeys to Mount Carmel where before all the people of Israel, he challenges 450 prophets of Baal to call on their god to burn a sacrifice that they'd placed on an altar. No fire falls from heaven, proving that their god is vain and void of power. Elijah mercilessly mocks them as he watches them jump up and down on the altar, cutting themselves with knives and lancets, beseeching their puny god to send fire down to consume the sacrifice. After a full day of such antics, Elijah instructs them to step out of the way. They were absolute failures in invoking their god to do anything for them. Elijah steps forth before the entire nation and cries: "Lord God of Abraham, Isaac, and of Israel, let it be known this day that thou art God in Israel, and that I am thy servant, and that I have done all these things at thy word. Hear me, O Lord, hear me, that this people may know that thou art the Lord God, and that thou hast turned their heart back again" (I Kings 18:36-37, KJV). Fire falls from heaven, consuming the sacrifice on the altar. With such a mighty display of God's power, all the people fall to their faces on the ground and cry out: "The Lord — He is God! The Lord — He is God!"

Mahesh Chavda relates the story of several sorcerers who got saved in one of his crusades in Africa. Within days of their conversion to Christianity, they were scheduled to meet with all the sorcerers from the region in order to sacrifice to satan and go through other wretched rituals. A massive old tree called "The Sorcerer's Tree" was the site of this meeting. On the night of their rituals, the converted sorcerers went out to the tree to share with all the others how they had met Jesus Christ, who possesses the greatest powers, and how He had filled their hearts with love. What they encountered was anything but favorable. The evil sorcerers turned on them with murder in their demonic eyes and began closing in around the small group of converted men. Suddenly, out of a night sky full of stars and moonlight, a bolt of lightning blazed, striking the old sorcerer's tree, and burned it up! A number of the sorcerers were converted to Jesus Christ after that supernatural display of God's favor on His new-found men.

The Book of Daniel records how King Nebuchadnezzar fell prostrate on the ground, exclaiming to faithful Daniel, "Surely your God is the God of gods and the Lord of kings[!!!] "(Dan. 2:47). This happened because Daniel was the only man in the kingdom able to interpret the king's puzzling dreams. By God's supernatural power, Daniel continually stood head and shoulders above the king's magicians, astrologers and sorcerers. God's living Word, coupled with Holy-Spirit power, sets men and women apart from all others.

The Impact of the Miraculous in the New Testament

After Jesus was tempted by the devil in the wilderness, He "returned to Galilee in the *power* of the Spirit, and news about him spread through the whole countryside" (Luke 4:14, author's emphasis). His fame was predicated on the miracles He was doing wherever He went. Popularity went before Him and drew great crowds of sick and impotent folk. The sick were healed, demons were cast out of people tormented by them, and the multitudes were fed. In the course of His three and one-half years of ministry on the earth, He worked so many mighty and undeniable miracles, signs and wonders, that if they were all recorded in books, the world probably wouldn't be able to hold the books (John 21:25).

Wherever He preached or taught the Word of God, the

miraculous was commonplace — except where His listeners were filled with doubt and unbelief. Mark recorded that in His hometown of Nazareth, Jesus could do no mighty work, "save that he laid his hands upon a few sick folk, and healed them. And he marvelled because of their unbelief" (Mark 6:5-6a, KJV). It was not because He didn't have the Father's permission or that He didn't have the power to work signs and wonders among the people of Nazareth, but it was clearly because the awful doubt of its residents had a nullifying effect on the flow of His ministry. Doubt and wretched unbelief have the unique ability to stop *redemptive* power right in its tracks.

I wonder what would happen if Jesus were to examine the faith level of America's, Canada's and Europe's Christian populations. Would He again marvel at such horrendous unbelief?

Unbelief is an ugly thing. This condition of heart darkens the countenance of a people when they are confronted with God's truth. It may not have been apparent prior to the confrontation, but it sure shows up when the truth is presented.

One gifted songwriter and performer I know has often said that he has seen the faces of some congregations gather spiritual darkness as he has stood to proclaim the truth in song. It is not a physical thing, but is spiritual. Unbelief is the thief of God's great blessings.

The writer of Hebrews defines the heart of unbelief as being sin, disobedience and wickedness (Heb. 3). We are exhorted to become alarmed if we find a heart of unbelief within ourselves and to make certain we do something about it. It must be conquered as an enemy!

Once when Jesus was in Galilee, a multitude of Pharisees and doctors of the law, which were come out of every town of Galilee, Judaea and Jerusalem, came to hear (skeptically) the wisdom which proceeded from His lips. The Scriptures reveal, "The power of the Lord was present to heal *them*" (Luke 5:17, KJV, author's emphasis). However, as you read, you learn that only one man received healing that day — not because Jesus did not want to heal more, but because the others were in doubt and skepticism. God cannot be pleased by anything but a child like faith, and He will only reward those who diligently seek Him (Heb. 11:6).

One day, while Jesus was walking along with His disciples and a mob of curious seekers, a little lady with an issue of blood came through the press of people behind Him and touched the hem of His robe. She had to struggle to get that far, and when she did, healing virtue flowed into her and she was gloriously healed. Jesus declared that her faith had made her whole (Mark 5:34). I am sure that others were touching Jesus as He walked down the road that day, but the touch of faith — the touch of the diligent seeker — was what tapped into that miraculous power. The touch of curiosity will not do it, neither will the accidental touch; it takes the touch of faith to receive a miracle from God! Wherever He went, operating in the power of the Holy Spirit, miracles flowed out to needy humanity and the fame of Him was spread abroad. The Scriptures say, "Crowds of people came to hear Him and to be healed of their sicknesses" (Luke 5:15; 6:18). There were times when the faith level in the crowd was so high that as many as touched Him were made completely whole (Matt. 14:36). Jesus manifested the names of His Father to the people God gave Him (John 17:6, KJV) — Jehovah Jireh (Provider), Jehovah Rapha (Healer), Jehovah Nissi (Banner), Jehovah Shalom (Peace), Jehovah Raah (Shepherd), Jehovah Tsidkenu (Righteousness) and Jehovah Shammah (Ever-present). Jesus Christ of Nazareth was, and remains today, the greatest miracle worker of all time (Heb. 13:8). No one is like unto Him "... Lord, among the gods ... glorious in holiness, fearful in praises, doing wonders" (Exod. 15:11). Jesus was approved by God through miracles, wonders and signs (Acts 2:22).

God, the Miracle Worker

For the diehards who insist that miracles ceased after Jesus and the early Church fathers died, I firmly direct attention to the following verses. Please note the words I emphasize:

> *Ye men of Israel, hear these words; Jesus of Nazareth, a man approved of God among you by miracles and wonders and*

> *signs,* ***which God did*** *by him in the midst of you ...* (Acts 2:22, KJV)
>
> *How* ***God anointed*** *Jesus of Nazareth with the Holy Ghost and with power: who went about doing good, and healing all that were oppressed of the devil; for* ***God was with him*** (Acts 10:38, KJV).
>
> *Long time therefore abode they* [Paul and Barnabus] *speaking boldly in* ***the Lord, which gave testimony*** *unto the word of his grace, and granted signs and wonders to be done by their hands* (Acts 14:3, KJV).
>
> *And* ***God wrought special miracles*** *by the hands of Paul* (Acts 19:11, KJV).
>
> *... but the Father that dwelleth in me,* ***he doeth the works*** (John 14:10c, KJV).

Yes, it is true that Jesus is no longer physically present among us, and that Paul and the other early Christians have passed away, departing in spirit to be with the Lord in heaven. *But,* God the Holy Spirit hasn't passed away! God didn't die! The same God who wrought miracles by the hands of Paul, who gave testimony to His words by signs, wonders and miracles, is the God true Christians serve today. He declares in the eternal now: "I am the Lord, I change not!" (Mal. 3:6, KJV). The Holy Spirit is literally loaded with signs, wonders and miracles. He is eager to pour them out on the world through an aggressive Church that will not water down the message of Jesus Christ.

The world will sit up and take notice when the miraculous is demonstrated. It has always been that way. The people in the city of Samaria gave heed to the words Philip spoke when they *heard* and *saw* the miracles that accompanied his ministry (Acts 8:6). When Peter ministered healing to a man bedridden by palsy for eight years, "all that dwelt at Lydda and Saron saw him, and turned to the Lord" (Acts 9:35). A little later on and not far away in Joppa, Peter raised a woman named Dorcas from the dead, resulting in many people turning to the Lord (Acts 9:42). Brother Paul once encountered a sorcerer, a false prophet named Elymas, who was withstanding him in his ministry. Paul executed the judgment of God by the gift of the working of miracles (1 Cor. 12:10) and temporarily blinded the guy, getting him out of the way. When the proconsul of the country saw such a demonstration of God's power as it was unleashed on Elymas, he believed Paul, being astonished at the doctrine of the Lord (Acts 13:12). So often in this world, bare doctrine isn't enough to capture the attention of people, but a mighty miracle is, since it confirms the doctrine that is being presented.

In Acts 16, Paul and Silas are miraculously freed from prison! The miracle is so powerful that the keeper of the prison is prompted to cry out, "Sirs, what must I do to be saved?" And in Ephesus, Paul's ministry is so miraculous that "the name of the Lord is magnified" and "the word of the Lord grows mightily and prevails," getting the upper hand in a society where witchcraft reigned supreme (Acts 19:17, 20). Jesus said that the works He did bore witness of Him that the Father had indeed sent Him (John 5:36). I heartily maintain that as it was with Jesus, so ought it be with us as we proclaim His words to the world. Let us read what Paul said:

> *When I came to you, brothers, I did not come with eloquence or superior wisdom as I proclaimed to you the testimony about God. For I resolved to know nothing while I was with you except Jesus Christ and him crucified. I came to you in weakness and fear, and with much trembling. My message and my preaching were not with wise and persuasive words, but with a demonstration of the Spirit's power, so that your faith might not rest on men's wisdom, but on God's power* (1 Cor. 2:1-5).

> *Some of you have become arrogant, as if I were not coming to you. But I will come to you very soon, if the Lord is willing, and then I will find out not only how these arrogant people are talking, but what power they have. For the kingdom of God is not a matter of talk but of power* (1 Cor. 4:18-20).

Paul wasn't at all impressed with the powerless "windbags" of his day. Eloquent speech or superior wisdom apart from the power of the Spirit of God was worthless when it came to building strong churches or winning a lost world to Christ. Had Paul wanted to be impressed by intellect, he had only to look at himself. Educated at the feet of Gamaliel, a Pharisee of Pharisees; as touching the law — blameless; concerning zeal, he persecuted the Church (before his conversion to Christ). This capable man had to "determine" that he would preach only Christ. It was something he had resolved in his superior mind, because intellectually he could have blown most people away! He was ever careful to see that men saw the power of God in manifestation. He went to great lengths to keep himself in a place where the Spirit of God could work mightily through him. This is not to say that there were not times when he brought forth the full power of his intellect, because there were. We read that he "disputed and persuaded" in the synagogues of religious men. He presented superior and logical arguments for the Lordship of Jesus Christ, even among a people who prided themselves as being full of wisdom (in Athens, Acts 17). When Paul taught on the coming judgments, kings and rulers of nations trembled (Acts 24:25) and dismissed him from their presence.

Conviction: An Evidence of God's Choice

> *Brothers loved by God, we know that he has* ***chosen*** *you, because our gospel came to you not simply with words, but also with power, with the Holy Spirit and with deep* ***conviction*** (1 Thess. 1:5, author's emphasis).

The miraculous is often proof that God has chosen to do a great work among a people. One type of miraculous attestation is manifested when deep Holy Spirit conviction comes upon a person. It may come through an anointed song, a preached message, an utterance gift or an anointed personal prophecy. I have seen deep conviction come as a minister "reads the mail" of a scoffer. Those with evil intentions have been "found out" as a revelatory gift, such as a word of knowledge, has swung into effect at the Lord's perfect timing. This is precisely how Jesus dealt with many individuals in His public ministry. Not only were those with evil intentions confronted, but simple sinning folk caught in the webs of vice and sensual corruption also found it hard to escape His ministry of power. (See the passage about the woman at the well — John 4:17-19.)

In Samaria, a city roughly thirty-five miles north of Jerusalem, Peter and John confronted an ex-sorcerer named Simon, who was loaded with wrong motives for ministry. When they confronted him with the all-seeing Word of God, terrifying conviction pierced his heart as his selfishness was uncovered (Acts 8:18-24).

The Holy Spirit has been sent to convict the world of sin, righteousness and judgment (John 16:8). He will do this through believers who are yielded to Him fully and are accurate handlers of the Word (2 Tim. 2:15).

The Scriptures assure us all that our sin will find us out (Num. 32:23). If one knows he is regarding iniquity in his heart, but is trying to avoid dealing with it, he needs to understand that although God is merciful and patient, He is also not past confronting His children in embarrassing places. I have witnessed people break under deep conviction, repenting from their once secret sin, as an anointed prophet unmasks them before all. You say, "God wouldn't do that to me!" Oh, yes, He would! If you are failing to mortify sin in your life, you may be setting yourself up for a day of confrontation; and you'll have to live with the embarrassment that it brings. If there is sin in your life, run to God with it, confess it and secure His abundant grace for overcoming it. Deal with it now, while there is still time.

We are living in a day when all saints are being dealt with concerning sin. It doesn't matter who you are or what office you hold in the Church of Jesus Christ. God will have a pure house of refuge for last-day converts to flee into, so He is cleaning up the Church. Ministers are being revealed by fire. Men who for years commanded public adoration are being revealed for who they really are. Men who have an insatiable desire to be seen in public may also be judged in public. They had better deal honestly with sin now!

The Full Gospel

> *I will not venture to speak of anything except what Christ has accomplished through me in leading the Gentiles to obey God by what I have said and done — by the power of signs and miracles, through the power of the Spirit. So from Jerusalem all the way around to Illyricum, I have* ***fully*** *proclaimed the gospel of Christ* (Rom. 15:18-19, author's emphasis).

By the power of signs and wonders wrought through the Holy Spirit, Paul presented the "full" gospel to his listeners. It should be no different today. The gospel of Jesus Christ and the Kingdom of God are not merely something you *hear* about, but they are something you *see.* When the disciples of John asked Jesus if He was the one who should come, Jesus answered: "Go back and report to John what you hear and see: The blind receive their sight, the lame walk, those who have leprosy are cured, the deaf hear, the dead are raised, and the good news is preached to the poor" (Matt. 11:4-5). His was a message of power, not empty talk.

If one sits in the presence of preaching, week after week, month after month, year after year, and yet never witnesses signs and wonders taking place among the people, then he must realize that he has yet to see or hear the full gospel of Jesus Christ. While it is true that signs and wonders do not in themselves indicate that the full gospel is being presented, they do tell us that if they are not present, the full gospel is not being presented either. The power of the gospel should always be present to back up the Word of the gospel. When Jesus said, "I am the light of the world," He opened blind eyes. When saying He was the Resurrection and the Life, He raised the dead. When He said, "I am the only way to the Father," He gave up His life and was raised to glory. He backed up what He preached in practical ways.

They're Dying to Hear the Song We Sing

This world cries to be set free from its woes. Multitudes are dying at this very hour, dying to hear the song of salvation that the Church of Jesus Christ sings. High numbers of people are dying of AIDS in countries like Zaire, Africa. In "civilized" countries, like America and the countries of Europe, we are destined to witness whole families dying unless there is national repentance. But what is to happen when an AIDS victim turns to Jesus Christ? Shouldn't healing be within his grasp? Certainly. But too few soldiers in Christ Jesus' army are walking about with that kind of healing virtue operative in their ministries. They haven't paid the price necessary in order to secure that kind of anointing. How terribly sad.

John Osteen once had a vision in which he found himself in the midst of a massive field of sick and dying human beings. As far as the eye could see and in every direction diseased humanity lay. John was shocked, shaken by the sight, and speechless. At a certain point in the vision, a frail and sickly man raised himself up on one elbow and cried with the most forlorn sound in his voice, "Nobody cares! Nobody cares!" John was flooded with compassion and yelled out, "I care! I care! I care!" Since then John has given himself to meeting the needs of people throughout the world who are in the throes of human pain and misery. He cannot do it all, but together as a unified army of Christian ambassadors, we can all make a difference. Scripture said, "A faithful ambassador is health [or brings healing]" (Prov. 13:17, KJV). "Blessed is he that considereth the poor [sick, weak]: the Lord will deliver him in time of trouble" (Ps. 41:1, KJV).

Essentials for the Miraculous

If we are ever to realize the hopes that we may now dare for a world that is marvelously impacted by the gospel, the signs, wonders and miracles of the living God *must* accompany the preaching of the Word. The following pages set forth a list of essential things that must be found in the Church before it can consistently move in God's power. At best, the miraculous has been sporadic in twentieth-century Christianity and far less than what God originally intended. I trust that as the Church falls in with these essentials, it will begin to see the power unleashed that many of us have only till now dreamed about.

1. The Church Must Stop Blending With the World

Nowadays, almost any organization that calls itself the Church is accepted. Sound Bible doctrines and high moral standards are being ignored by many groups. Where a group may be strong in morality, often it is weak in Bible doctrine; and where one is strong in Bible doctrine, it is awfully weak in morality. This kind of inconsistency will not do in the Church that would move in the true power of God. Most good evangelical groups have developed expertise in pointing out the fallacious teachings of such groups as the Mormons, the Jehovah's Witnesses, the Moonies and the Baha'is. Many even go so far as to lay the axe to the root of Catholicism. But many of those same evangelical groups have taken a seriously lax stand against the blatant immorality that has invaded their own churches.

For example, people living together out of wedlock are accepted as members in good standing in many "Bible-believing" churches all over the land. Teenage kids are allowed to party on Saturday nights and partake of communion on Sunday morning with no repentance in their hearts. Wife-beaters, alcoholics and child molesters serve on church boards of directors in many such organizations, never being exposed or challenged if they are discovered. One can have all the Bible in the world backing up his claim to be the true Church, but if his moral life does not add up to what the Bible teaches, his religion is futile. God would have not only a doctrinally sound Church, but a morally pure one as well. A church that is not actively making this its aim is fraudulent.

When discussing the revelation of who He is, Jesus declared, "Upon this rock I will build my church" (Matt. 16:18, KJV). This is the first of only two places in the gospels where Jesus uses the word "Church." In most cases in the Bible when an important word is introduced for the first time, it shows us the great central truth about that word. The phrase, "I will build my church," in the original Greek shows the emphatic word to be "my." That indicates the possibility that other churches might well exist alongside "His" Church. We know, of course, that this is the case today. In Jesus' day the word for "church" was used in secular language for a governing body of a city. So it was not an unfamiliar word to the disciples; there were many governing bodies during Jesus' day, just as there are today.

But Jesus said, "I am going to build My Governing Body — My Church." In the midst of thousands of other governing bodies, Jesus' Church should be apparent, standing head and shoulders above all the rest. But alas, it doesn't. Why not? Because besides lacking other things, it lacks the miraculous. It will continue to lack the miraculous until it measures up in purity, for God will not set His stamp of approval — His "signature" — on a church that blends with the world. When a person comes to Jesus, he must make a clean break from the world and any other religious belief, and enjoy a brand-new start in the Kingdom of God. The Kingdom of God has no resemblance whatsoever with anything else. For too long the Church has looked and behaved worldly, allowing the world to enter and settle down with its corrupt, anti-Christian values. Worldliness with its impurity is contagious, so much so that Paul warns, "Do not be misled: 'Bad company corrupts good character' " (1 Cor. 15:33). When Christians keep company in the church with unregenerate sinners who are never challenged to become like Christ, the corrupt morals and values of those sinners will eventually contaminate the whole: "... Don't you know that a little yeast works through the whole batch of dough?" (1 Cor. 5:6). When the life-style of the Church is no longer an embarrassment to Him, but is lining up with His moral, ethical and biblical standards, God will be pleased to put His signature of signs and wonders upon it. If we are ever to see the world-shaking, hell-quaking outpouring of the Holy Spirit that we long for, the Church as a whole must rise to its feet in purity. When it does, He will place His weighty endorsement upon it, and our dream will come true to its fullest.

2. True Believing Is Essential

True belief in America's Spirit-filled community has been at a low level. What many call belief is not the genuine article. All they have is "head knowledge." The Greek word for "believe" contains much more in its meaning than the English word conveys. It means to trust in, adhere to, and rely upon from the heart. This kind of belief can only come from much time spent in the immediate presence of the Father. It is not only found in a genuine relationship with Him, but also in deep, abiding fellowship with Him. You see, relationship without fellowship is an insipid thing. What makes my relationship with someone I love so sweet is the rich fellowship we enjoy. If there is little or no fellowship with them, then the relationship is meaningless. Sadly, this is the way it has been for God with many of His children. No miracles will flow out of such a boring relationship.

A sister in Christ came to me recently with what seemed to be a monstrous problem. She couldn't muster the faith to believe that God could deliver her out of the situation. She also doubted His *willingness* to handle it for her. The poor woman was in the depths of despair.

After listening to her for a few minutes, I asked her about her current fellowship with God. As I thought, there wasn't any. Unbelief had her in its grasp and was choking the very life out of her.

Immediately I instructed her to begin taking twenty or thirty minutes a day to fellowship with God.

"Spend that time walking in solitary places near your home," I told her, "praising Him, and telling Him how much you want to love and enjoy Him."

I also instructed her not to talk to Him about her problem for the first few days, but to simply work on her fellowship with Him. Unless that was stronger, she wouldn't be able to believe God for the miraculous intervention she needed. Remember, miracles flow out of rich fellowship with God, not merely because we are related to Him.

It is amazing what the half-hour time of fellowship each day did for that sister. Within a few days her spirit was rejuvenated and her attitude toward God was transformed. There was a new spring to her step, and it was obvious that the merciless doubt and unbelief had been replaced by a vibrant faith toward her God. Slowly her "insurmountable problem" faded away as God became greater to her than it was.

Brother or sister, be sure your brand of believing is flowing from the continuous, rich fellowship you have with God, and not just from something you heard from others, or from something you remember from the distant past. Each day you are to receive an infusion of strength and faith from the continuing fellowship you are enjoying with your heavenly Father. Believing is essential for the release of His power in and through your life.

3. The Hearing of Faith

Paul asked the Christians throughout Galatia, "Does He, therefore, Who was supplying to you the Spirit, and was working miracles among you, doing it by the works of the law, or by the hearing of faith?" (Gal. 3:5, Worrell). The answer to that question is, of course, *the hearing of faith.* God doesn't work miracles among us because we earn them by keeping all the laws, rules and regulations meticulously. No man can be justified for anything by keeping the law. As a matter of fact, we frustrate the grace of God if we act like we can be. That's not to say we don't actively adhere to biblical laws and rules of conduct, but it does say we do not depend on our performance as the determining factor in whether or not God works miracles among us.

Miracles are manifestations of His grace, and it takes faith, not perfection, to receive them. Never will anyone be able to produce sufficient spiritual good works in order to earn the Lord's miraculous blessings. It is absurd to accredit a human being for the power of God working through him or upon him. To insinuate that such a person deserves displays of God's power because he is so faithful or obedient is incorrect. In ourselves, no matter what good thing we do, we deserve failure and death; but because of who Jesus is and what He has done, we can receive life and blessing. Our faith and obedience merely create within us a capacity to receive God's blessing or to be used as a channel of His power.

God requires that we simply believe Him. When one truly believes in Jesus, he will believe His every word. If he believes His words, he will act on them when the situation calls for it, and there will be an automatic unleashing of divine power. True Bible faith involves acting on the Word of God. God observes a person's faith by seeing it in action. The only way to gain a capacity to act on the Word of God is by submitting totally to it as your final authority. No matter what your situation, give the Word its proper place of final authority. It is alive and full of power. As you read, it speaks to you (see Prov. 6:22), and a living, active faith begins to rise up in your heart. When you hear an anointed speaker, one who either teaches or preaches, faith comes. "... Faith comes from hearing the message, and the message is heard through the word of Christ" (Rom. 10:17).

Twice in Luke's gospel it is recorded that people came to Jesus in order to *hear* and to be healed of their diseases (Luke 5:15; 6:17). Faith for healing came by hearing the Word on healing. People often forget that Jesus was a preacher first, and then a miracle worker. His anointed presentation of the Word on particular topics greatly enhanced the faith of His listeners, creating within their hearts the capacity to receive. Faith is not a condition of the mind, but a divinely imparted grace of the heart. We can receive faith only as God gives it, and He will not give it apart from a diligent and prayerful consideration of His Word on our part.

> *And He said to them, Be careful what you are hearing. The measure [of thought and study] you give [to the truth you hear] will be the measure [of virtue (power) and knowledge] that comes back to you — and more [besides] will be given to you who hear* (Mark 4:24, TAB).

If you come before the Word of God with a take-it-or-leave-it attitude, you are not going to receive a thing from God. You must have a respect for the Word, because it carries with it the power of God to save, heal and deliver.

Faith is much like a snowball that begins small, but grows larger as it is rolled around in the stuff it's made of. Roll your faith around in the Word of God and see what begins to happen. By feeding your faith the Word of God, your doubts will starve to death.

When does one act on the Word?

"We must realize that true Bible faith is not our own ability to 'count it done,' but is a deep consciousness divinely imparted to the heart that 'it is done.' There is a difference between human effort and 'straining to believe,' and genuine faith that comes from God. It is true: Faith acts! But the act comes from the faith, rather than faith from the act. You could say the act is born of faith; the faith is not born of the act. Faith is born of the Word of God, and when true faith is birthed there is no struggle to believe" (Charles Price).

Many folks think that to hear the Word of God and not immediately act on it is a form of compromise. But it isn't — it's wisdom. When healing (or whatever) becomes a realization in the spirit, that is when one should act — and not a moment before. We need wisdom when to act on the Word of God.

I know a person who crushed his eyeglasses after hearing a faith preacher teach a lesson on healing in the atonement. The "faith" he acted on was not a faith born deep in his heart, but was a "faith" in his head — a mental assent. Needless to say, he had to find an eye doctor and replace his glasses. He should have taken the word he heard on healing, begun to meditate on it, and allowed God to cause it to become reality in his spirit-man — reality within. Then his act could have secured the blessing in the physical realm.

In the city of Lystra, Paul preached the Word to a man who had been crippled from his mother's womb and had never walked. Scripture says the man "heard" Paul speak. In time, faith arose in his heart. Whether it took a long time or a short time is not known, but the text records that a day arrived when Paul perceived that the man had faith to be healed. He looked directly at the man and called out, "Stand up on your feet!" At that, the man jumped up and began to walk. The miracle took place as a result of "the hearing of faith." We should expect no less today.

4. Let There Be No Shame

Many Christians today are ashamed of a God of miracles. It's not popular in today's world to believe that the God who worked miracles 2,000 years ago would want to work them today. The anti-Christian news media has done a thorough job of making faith preachers and healers out to be charlatans and frauds, and most believing Christians are afraid to be identified with them. But Paul boldly stated: "I am not ashamed of the gospel of Christ: for it is the power of God unto salvation" (Rom. 1:16, KJV). If we are ashamed to be identified with those who believe that Jesus Christ heals today, then we will go through life devoid of His miraculous power. Jesus said, "Whosoever therefore shall be *ashamed* of me and of my words in this adulterous generation; of him also shall the Son of man be ashamed, when he cometh in the glory of his Father with the holy angels" (Mark 8:38, KJV). We see a basic Bible principle here: The part of the gospel you're ashamed of will be ashamed of you. There are literally hundreds of ministers who secretly believe in the validity of the Baptism with the Holy Spirit, but they will not openly pass it on to their members. Others believe God heals today, but they would never dream of hosting a healing meeting or miracle service in their churches. The thought of running an ad in the local newspaper stating that they were hosting a service where the sick could come and be healed would appall them. Many of God's ministers are "closet believers" where the miracle-working power of God is concerned, not wanting everybody to know they believe in a God of modern-day miracles. They are not ashamed of the name of Jesus, but they are ashamed of the ministry of Jesus. It's too bad, because their shame defeats them and makes their congregations susceptible to the sickness and disease that satan desires to bring upon them.

We worry about our reputations. Paul wasn't even worried about his life. Because he was so visibly joined to Jesus, he suffered much disgrace in the world. Yet he said, "I am not ashamed, because I know whom I have believed, and am convinced that he is able to guard what I have entrusted to him for that day" (2 Tim. 1:12). He exhorted the young man Timothy, "So do not be ashamed to testify about our Lord" (2 Tim. 1:8), and like other apostles, he rejoiced because he was counted worthy of suffering disgrace for the Name (Acts 5:41). Jesus is not ashamed to call you brother (Heb. 2:11). Are you ashamed to call Him Savior, Healer or Lord? The Almighty is not ashamed to be called your God (Heb. 11:16). Are you ashamed to call Him your God? Peter encourages us by saying, "However, if you suffer as a Christian, do not be ashamed, but praise God that you bear that name" (1 Pet. 4:16).

5. Become a Faithful Servant or Handmaiden of the Lord

> *And it shall come to pass in the last days, saith God, I will pour out of my Spirit upon all flesh: and your sons and your daughters shall prophesy, and your young men shall see visions, and your old men shall dream dreams: And on my servants and on my handmaidens I will pour out in those days of my Spirit; and they shall prophesy: And I will shew wonders in heaven above, and signs in the earth beneath; blood, and fire, and vapour of smoke* (Acts 2:17-19, KJV).

Signs will be seen "in the earth beneath." I don't know about you, but I am sure believing for that. But notice who is directly connected with this marvelous outpouring of the Spirit of God with signs and wonders. The servants and handmaidens of the Lord. If they do not take their places, we may miss what God wants to do in our generation.

When we speak of servants and handmaidens of the Lord, we are not speaking of the rank and file of Christendom on the earth. Mere family membership is not in view here. One is not a servant or handmaiden simply because he believes in Jesus Christ and has trusted Him as his Savior. A servant or handmaiden is one who has chosen to give his or her life to God in self-sacrificing ways. One translation refers to this type of believer as a "bondslave," that is, one who gives himself up to the will of another. A bondslave forfeits his rights to a life that serves self so that he might fully serve his master. The bondslaves of the Lord make up His royal knighthood. They wait on God in worship and praise, and when occasion for it arises, they launch forth into battle for His cause. Again, if there are not any of this class of Christians in the earth, then there will be no signs and wonders in demonstration, pointing fallen men to God. The servants and handmaidens of God walk in the spirit and do not fulfill the lusts of the flesh (Gal. 5:16). They are purged vessels, "sanctified, and meet [fit] for the master's use" (2 Tim. 2:21).

Stephen was an excellent example of a bondslave or servant of God. Acts 6, while recording the earliest days of the Church, reveals that "the word of God increased; and the number of disciples multiplied in Jerusalem .... And Stephen, full of faith and power, was doing great wonders and miracles among the people" (Acts 6:7-8, KJV). Stephen was not an apostle; he waited on old widow ladies. But I am convinced that the great miracles done by ordinary Christians like Stephen were the key ingredients in the miraculous growth of the Church. Stephen was full of faith, not only in Jesus Christ, but also in His Word to "go into all the world, and preach the gospel .... And these signs shall follow them that believe" (Mark 16:15,17, KJV). Because he was full of faith, he was also full of power — healing power — miracle-working power. And where does the text say Stephen did these miracles? "Among the people." In the various Christian gatherings of that day, I'm sure that the sick were wandering in or being carried in for healing, but the brunt of the miracle ministry of the early Church went on out in the streets where the people were.

A sister in the Lord was recently telling me how her mother has been taking advantage of the Meals On Wheels program for the elderly and shut-ins. Not only does she take food to them, but she takes the Word of God and prayer as well. When they have been receptive, she has seen God's power bring healing to their bodies. One elderly woman, for example, was crippled and bent over with a debilitating disease. As my friend's mother laid hands on the old woman, she was immediately able to stand upright without pain. Needless to say, they both commenced to worship and praise God for His great mercy.

A bondslave gets a baptism of power as he waits quietly on the Lord in prayer and Bible study. Actually, his greatest joy is found in seeking the Lord when no one else is around. The highlight of his life is his intimate communion with God. His attention is focused on the upcoming time of prayer, not the upcoming "people meeting." He lives from prayer time to prayer time. For whatever happens in between he is very grateful, but that is not his focus.

Jesus' own ministry was birthed, bathed and maintained in

intimate prayer with the Father. Scripture shows us that He was continually withdrawing into the solitary places to be alone with God, and this was the great secret of His success. Our Lord would return from His times with the Father with His eyes full of vision for the purpose of God and His heart full of passion to see it fulfilled. His schedule was as follows: from prayer to ministry, back to prayer; from prayer to ministry, back to prayer. Jesus was the ideal example of what a servant of God should be. When He said, "If any man will come after me, let him deny himself, and take up his cross daily, and follow me" (Luke 9:23, NKJV), He was speaking from His own worthy example. A handmaiden or manservant of God will bear his cross by being devoted to prayer. Too few Christians ever dare to take this cross upon themselves and so are miserably lacking the power of God. The handmaiden and manservant type of prayer is sometimes very hard — excruciating! The flesh resists its practice with all its force, because it doesn't want to experience the death that such prayer brings. But it is essential if one ever expects to walk in the awesome power of God.

6. A Life of Fervent Prayer and Fasting

This essential goes right along with being a faithful servant or handmaiden. As one serves in sacrificial ways, hard and seemingly impossible situations will arise that will only respond to the faith and authority of one who leads a fasted life. It's like when Jesus said of a particular demon, "This kind goeth not out but by prayer and fasting" (Matt. 17:21, KJV). Fasting is calculated to add a "magnum" dimension to our prayers and spiritual authority; it proves to be necessary when facing the warfare of serious Christian service. Much like the 22-magnum cartridge delivers more velocity, range and long-distance accuracy than the 22-short cartridge, so prayer and warfare with fasting heightens the Christian's effectiveness in engaging the enemy in battle. (See chapter three.)

The Christian who never employs the added dimension of fasting to his prayer life is rarely placed on satan's "hit list." Not that his hit list is the most wonderful place to have your name registered, but if it is not there, you are probably not threatening him.

The non-fasting Christian is somewhat dangerous to satan's kingdom, but the fasting Christian is *very* dangerous to him — particularly if he uses the time he would spend eating for deep intercession and prayer for God's purposes to be accomplished on the earth. This man becomes an awesome weapon in the hands of God.

Mahesh Chavda, a friend who wrote the foreword to my first book, *Kingdom Commandos*, is walking in one of the more miraculous ministries of our day. In third-world countries he has witnessed literally tens of thousands of people receive healing in their bodies and minds. Under his ministry, blind eyes are opened, deaf ears unstopped, crippled bodies are healed, the dead have been raised up to life again, and the ugly power of witchcraft has been stunned on the spot. If you ask Mahesh where he gets that kind of power, he is quick to tell you about the fasted life. Extended fasts, twice a year, have made up his life since early in his ministry. God honors the servant who seeks Him with fasting.

The Church that overpowers the gates of hell in the final days of this age is going to be a Church full of the Word of God, unified under the banner of Christ's love, convinced of the authority invested in Jesus' name, and fortified by fasting with fervent, effectual prayer.

7. We Must Know God as He Really Is

Paul's prayer was that he might "know him [God], and the power of his resurrection, and the fellowship of his sufferings, being made conformable unto his death" (Phil. 3:10). The Amplified Bible says that to know God is to recognize and understand Him. I believe that too few Christians in our western world are growing in a recognition and understanding of God. Many have had a genuine encounter with Him in the new birth experience, but have not gone on in the relationship that was begun at the time of that experience. The result has been a lack of *knowing* the power of His resurrection. Examine the following verse:

Then shall we know, if we follow on to know the Lord: his going forth is prepared as the morning; and he shall come unto us as the rain, as the latter and the former rain unto the earth (Hos. 6:3, KJV).

The awesome power of Jesus' resurrection has yet to be fully realized as it should be in the context of the former and latter rains. Because the Church has not followed on to know the Lord as He would be known, our attitude, by and large, has been far too offhanded for Him to be able to unleash His power in the way He would like to. The character and integrity of the Church has reeked with the stench of religious hypocrisy, and when God does bestow His miracle gifts, too often men have used the gifts as playthings or personal charms for their exalted egos.

The Lord tells us, "Let not the wise man glory in his wisdom, neither let the mighty man glory in his might ... but let him who glorieth glory in this, that he understands and knoweth me" (Jer. 9:23-24, KJV). These penetrating words describe the Lord's greatest desire for our lives. It is wonderful that miracle-working power is available to us. It is terribly exciting that we are saved from the wrath to come. But that is not enough. We must *follow on* to know and understand the Lord in a more intimate way; we must serve Him in spirit and truth, not merely in mind or rote tradition. The verse in Hosea said we would know His power in the former and latter rain *if* we follow on *to know* Him. The outpouring of His mighty power is contingent on that.

The most glorious thing we have going for us as Christians is the fact that we can actually come to know and understand God as He really is — as our caring Father and as the one in life to whom we can be closest. But alas, for many Christians He is nothing more than a spiritual formula or a principle to be used. How this must sadden His great heart!

I once heard Bible teacher, Charles Simpson, expound a significant story that actually took place in the lives of Jesus' disciples. It is found in Mark 6, verses 32-56. I would like to share with you the high points of that particular story so you can be as blessed as I was when I first understood its significance.

The story is told of how Jesus fed thousands of people with five loaves of bread and two fishes. As the disciples obediently distributed the food to the masses, God's power was manifested and the loaves and fishes were multiplied. Imagine what being used in the outworking of that mighty miracle made the disciples feel like. I believe that following the miracle, they were beginning to feel very confident in their understanding and knowledge of the Lord. At times I too have felt pretty accurate in my understanding of God, and it has usually been on the heels of something powerful that He did through my ministry. I am glad the Lord gives us such times, because it strengthens our faith and our resolve to go on in Him. But at the same time, it can be the beginnings of a "divine setup." Let me explain.

Following the miracle of the loaves and fishes, Jesus insisted that His disciples get into a boat and start out for the other side of the Sea of Galilee. Actually, the Bible says that He *made* them go. There was probably a reluctance on their part to follow His instruction. Some of them were fishermen, and perhaps they saw negative weather signs on the late evening horizon. Nevertheless, they set out to cross the Sea of Galilee while Jesus remained behind to dismiss the crowd, and then to ascend into the nearby mountains to pray.

Complete darkness descended upon the entire region not many hours after the disciples had embarked on their journey; but Peter, John and a few of the others were veteran seafarers who knew how to navigate their vessel after nightfall. Everything was under control.

Meanwhile, high on a mountaintop, Jesus ascended into deep degrees of prayer and fellowship with the Father, having what I would call a countenance-changing encounter. It happened on the Mount of Transfiguration (Matt. 17), so who is to say it didn't happen many times as Jesus communed with the Father in solitary places? God's glory came down, engulfing Him, changing His appearance until His face began to shine as the noonday sun and His clothes became bright-shining as the light and glory of God. It happened to Moses when he encountered the God of glory on Mount Sinai, and I'm sure it happened to Jesus when He spent prolonged periods of time with the Father in prayer. We need to remember that He was incarnate deity, that He was in unbroken fellowship with the Father.

Jesus spent much of this prayer time interceding for His

disciples. By nature, He is an intercessor and a priest, two godly functions that represent others before God. Jesus knew more than anybody that His disciples' understanding was immature and shallow. Sure they had seen Him work mighty miracles and had even been used in their outworking. But as verse 52 says, "Their hearts had grown callous [had become dull and had lost the power of understanding]" (Mark 6:52, TAB). So Jesus prayed. He sought God for them, that they would see, know and understand Him for who He really is and not merely for what He can do.

In the midst of night's darkness, a severe windstorm swept down on the Sea, catching the disciples in the angry waves it stirred up. They turned the boat's bow into the wind and kept rowing. High up on the mountaintop, while fellowshipping with the Father, Jesus saw that His beloved disciples were in trouble. The lesson was underway. It is interesting to note that Jesus did not see the disciples' situation with the natural eye (it was dark and they were far from land); He saw their dilemma with the spiritual eye. In the midst of the sea in the black of night, the disciples were straining at the oars, but going nowhere. All of their experience on the high seas, all of their wisdom and understanding couldn't get them through this one. They had been commanded to cross over to the other side of the Sea of Galilee, but they couldn't do it! How frustrating it must have been. Have you ever been sent to do something you couldn't do sent to do the impossible, and yet you couldn't quit? Had the disciples given up, they would surely have been capsized by the angry waves. Their only hope was to keep the bow into the wind and waves, and hope for the storm to pass.

"Row harder, Peter! Keep the bow into the wind!" John is crying through the howl of the wind.

"I am rowing, John, but my hands are full of blisters!" Peter screams back in frustration.

"I can't keep this up much longer!" comes a shaken voice from the back of the boat. "I'm totally exhausted!"

"Where is the Master?" someone complains. "How could He send us into a furious storm like this and forsake us?"

"Yeah!" replies another tormented disciple. "What kind of man is He?"

Can you see what might have been happening? The very disciples who had been following the great preacher, healer and miracle-worker were likely bringing His character into question, proving that they really didn't know Him as they should have. Could it be that until this time all of their understanding of Him was what "flesh and blood" had revealed? Were they yet in need of a grand revelation from the Holy Spirit? (See Matthew 16:17.)

In the early hours of the morning, sometime between three and six o'clock, Jesus came near to them, walking on the water. Scripture says, "He would have passed them by." That is frightening.

"What in the name of Jehovah is that?" asks a disciple with great fear in his heart.

"It looks like a phantom, a spirit that foretells disaster and death!" cries another as he continues struggling at the oars.

Our compassionate Lord was revealing Himself in a way they had never seen before. Fresh from His time with the Father, He was aglow with the majesty and glory of God! The disciples cried out in great fear. The Greek implies, "a deep cry out of their throats." They had not been too terribly frightened by the storm; they were more frustrated than anything else. But when Jesus came near them "glowing in the dark," they were terrified. Their problem was that they didn't really know the glory of God. They only related to Jesus as a healer, a miracle-worker or perhaps as the greatest of all prophets, but not as the Almighty God of creation. But on that eventful night, Jesus came to them as a spirit in a supernatural way; not merely *doing* something supernatural, He *was* supernatural! He came to them as God Almighty!

As Jesus revealed Himself to them by saying: "Be of good cheer: it is I; be not afraid," He climbed into the back of the boat, and the fury of the wind and the waves ceased. A new revelation of who He was produced a great calm. The disciples were totally amazed, and the literal Greek says that they "stood out from Him." In awe, they crowded to the front of the boat and stared at Him in wonder. Actually they "gawked." Never again would they only be "familiar" with Him, because they were beginning to know Him as He really was: The God of all creation!

What brought the disciples to this awesome understanding? They had pridefully assumed they knew the Lord much better than they actually did, so He commanded them into a storm, a storm through which they would be unable to go without His intervention. By their own power and cunning, and by a current revelation of Jesus, the disciples would be helpless to deliver themselves from the storm's fury. Charles Simpson said: "When one finds himself in the midst of such a storm, he is at the threshold of seeing God in a new way." This type of growth to spiritual maturity happens periodically in the lives of truly committed Christians. It is much like experiencing intense growing pains. We all need an ongoing revelation of just who Jesus really is. We know Him as Savior to begin with, but often that revelation is vague. There is so much more to Him that He wants to unveil to us. His ways are not our ways, nor are His thoughts our thoughts. We must forever be willing to have Him renew and broaden our understanding of Him, so that we might take hold of Him and know Him as He really is.

Jesus doesn't tell us everything when He gets us to do some things. Often what He tells us is only enough to get us started, only enough to get us into the midst of the sea. Once there, situations arise where we desperately need Him, and attempting to proceed with past revelations of Him simply proves to be futile. But He knows where we are; He sent us there! When we are desperate enough, He comes to us in a new way. Not in old, familiar ways, not in ways in which we expect to see Him come, but often in ways that frighten us! Is this in line with the written Word? Oh yes! But in a way you've never understood it before.

Many of you have been struggling intensely, rowing for all you are worth; but the winds and waves of adversity are much too strong for you to manage with past or present revelation. You have been deep in the midst of darkness, doing what you feel God has called you to do; but you can no longer see your way through. You're spiritually and mentally exhausted! I encourage you to open your eyes wide and broaden your mind, because perhaps Jesus is coming to you now — coming to you in a way that you've never seen Him before, meeting you in a place you've not been before. Let Him into your boat and you will see the glory of God! Stand aside and take another look at Him, a better look at Jesus. If you do, you will see more of Him, love more of Him, and experience a greater release of His power in your life.

The final verses of Mark 6 reveal an unleashing of the power of God in the ministry of Jesus and His disciples that had not been seen before that incident on the high seas. I believe that as the Church of Jesus Christ grows up in its knowledge and understanding of God, it too will witness an unleashing of divine power that it heretofore has only dreamed about. May Jesus continue to reveal Himself in greater measures to all of us.

8. Refrain From Envy Concerning the Miraculous Ministries of Others

Envy is the feeling of displeasure produced by witnessing or hearing of the advantage or prosperity of others. Envy desires to deprive another of what he has, because the envious one doesn't have the same. The chief priests delivered Jesus over to be crucified because of envy (Mark 15:10), and in the days of the early Church the high priest and Sadducees cast the apostles into prison, for they too were filled with envy (Acts 5:16-18). By godly inspiration, Paul categorized those who were "full of envy" as being of reprobate mind (Rom. 1:28-29) and declared them not to be inheritors of the Kingdom of God (Gal. 5:21).

Envy is a shameful sin in the eyes of God, and yet there are ministers of the gospel who are guilty of it every day of their lives. For example, a couple of years ago I was in attendance at a meeting in a small West Virginia church where a close friend of mine was delivering the evening's message. People were saved, challenged in their walk with God, and generally built up by the man's dynamic preaching. After the meeting, while walking to my car, the pastor of one of the other local churches began to criticize my friend for his style of ministry. He then went on to question certain well-known healing evangelists, asking whether or not the healings that reportedly took place in their ministries were for real. As I listened to him, it became obvious to me that he was filled with envy because he wasn't seeing the miraculous taking place in his church and ministry. So he attacked.

If you ever expect to witness the miraculous in your ministry or the ministry of your church, then you will have to bless and not criticize the ministries of men and women who do move in God's signs, wonders and miracles. Your future success will depend on this.

9. Seeking the Lost: The Poor, Maimed, Halt and Blind — Those Who Cannot Repay

Essential to seeing God's power poured out is the simple obedience to these instructions from Jesus.

> *Then Jesus said to his host, "When you give a luncheon or dinner, do not invite your friends, your brothers or relatives, or your rich neighbors; if you do, they may invite you back and so you will be repaid. But when you give a banquet, invite the poor, the crippled, the lame, the blind, and you will be blessed. Although they cannot repay you, you will be repaid at the resurrection of the righteous"* (Luke 14:12-14).

I firmly believe that Stephen's ministry was effective because he spent time among those who were "down-and-outers" in society. Acts 6:8 said, "Stephen ... did great wonders and miraculous signs among the people." Like Jesus, his Master, he lived to "seek and to save what was lost" (Luke 19:10). Filled with compassion toward those who were hurting around him, Stephen tapped into God's healing power and it flowed mightily. Not only did Stephen operate in the reality of fulfilled prophetic Scriptures like Joel 2:28, which declares that God will pour out His Spirit upon all flesh, but he also moved in fulfillment of those verses from Joel which state, "And I will restore to you the years that the locust hath eaten, the cankerworm, and the caterpillar, and the palmerworm ..." (Joel 2:25, KJV). In its spiritual application, we know that satan's host of demons has gobbled up many of the precious belongings of God's people. Like locusts, cankerworms, caterpillars and palmerworms, they have ravaged the inhabitants of this world in a merciless fashion. But God's promise for the last days is: "I will restore what was taken from you." Men and women like Stephen simply believed that. Health was recovered to physical bodies as they preached Jesus to the masses. Sanity was restored to demon-oppressed minds. Families were restored, financial disasters were corrected, and hosts of other woes were eliminated by the power and authority these guys walked and ministered in. But the main objects of their ministries were the needy ones of humanity, and we mustn't forget that.

It is wonderful when the rich and affluent get saved and begin to attend our services. Often these will prove to be pillars of strength for years to come. They have money to give in abundance, and because of their upbringing and background they are able to project an attractive image of Christianity to society around us. Churches are quick to cater to this type of person — the lovely ones. But what about the others? What about those who cannot benefit us? If we miss these people, we'll miss the heart of God for our generation, because God cries, "Go out quickly [more perish every minute] into the streets and alleys ... and bring in the poor, the crippled, the blind and the lame. ... that my house will be full" (Luke 14:21, 23).

In order to reach the man in the alleys of life, you'll need to be willing to get your hands a little dirty. You'll have to go where they are. You may have to lay your hands on the greasy head of a ghetto bum, or compassionately embrace the sobbing frame of a syphilis-riddled prostitute. At times the stale breath of a sin-doused reprobate will set you back several steps, but you must stay with him until deliverance comes. The rancid smell of certain kinds of cancer is enough to keep most Christians away from the cancer ward in hospitals, but the man of God will possess sufficient compassion to love cancer's victim in spite of the way he looks or smells. The same will be true with regard to ministry to someone with AIDS.

My sister, Pam Whitelaw, and I went to seven cancer victims in the terminal ward at the University Hospital in Charlottesville, Virginia. It wasn't pleasant to our senses, but five out of the seven prayed to receive Jesus as their Lord and Savior.

We must be quick to lead the blind by the hand, to carry the crippled in our arms, to provide a way for the poor to attend the Lord's banquet. It will slow us down a bit, but Jesus always slowed down for the needy and He's our excellent example. The Good Samaritan stopped to help the victim of thugs when nobody else cared (Luke 10:33). All over this world there are people who have been soundly beaten and robbed by a "thug" named satan, and they desperately need someone of your nature to come to them in their misery and bind up their wounds.

I once read a poem that gave me much spiritual incentive for the task of reaching out to society's unfortunate ones. Its author I do not know, except that I am positive the Holy Spirit gave it to this understanding saint for the purpose of stirring the Church to action. I am sure that in eternity we will meet the one who penned it.

But What Do We Care?

You have builded temples in His name
of mortar, and brick, and stone;
with windows of glass so beautifully stained,
with tower, and spire, and dome.

But what do we of the byways care
for structure, and line, and trim?
Out in the dust of the lonely road
we only ask for Him.

You've robed your choir and trained them well
in proper and intricate song.
You've bought fine organs to edify,
and lull the weary throng.

But what do we care for your black-robed choir,
and the organ's deep amen?
We want you to walk beside us here,
and show us the way to Him.

O, the paths of the world are a crooked maze,
and we are woefully lost.
For the road to Him, and the paths of men
are vague, and hidden, and crossed.

What do we care for the trophies of art
when our soul's high hope is dim?
We seek the touch of His healing hand;
isn't there somebody to show us the way to Him?

Come, my brothers and sisters, let's go to those of the byways, to love and liberate them with the awesome love and power of the glorious gospel of Jesus Christ of Nazareth.

10. Return to Biblical Apostolic and Prophetic Authority.

It is a sad fact that the Church, by and large, has relegated the offices of apostle and prophet to a bygone era. Such unfounded action has reduced the effectiveness of the Church the world over. This is a major cause in the decline of the miraculous. See what the Bible has to say:

> *And in the Church God has appointed **first of all** apostles, second prophets, third teachers, then workers of miracles, also those having gifts of healing ...* (1 Cor. 12:28, author's emphasis)

I once heard well-known Bible teacher Charles Mahaney make the humorous statement when commenting on this verse: "In the Greek, *first* means *first.*" All who were present that day chuckled, but we also saw the important point her was making. If the Church does not allow God to bless her with *first* apostles, and *second* prophets, *then* we will not see the great outpouring of signs and wonders that we long to see. To date they are sporadic, not flowing on a worldwide basis the way they were intended to.

Apostolic men lay the foundations upon which the Church is to be built in any given locality. Not only that, apostles and prophets are to make up some of the very foundation stones themselves. (see 1 Corinthians 3:10 and Ephesians 2:20.)

For God to accomplish something in as thorough a fashion as He desires, He must see that it is founded properly. Without such a firm foundation, the winds and floods of time will cause a major collapse, resulting in much loss (Luke 6:47-49). The earthshaking outpouring of the Spirit of God with signs and wonders that we so long for must have the proper foundation beneath it, or it will not produce lasting results. Apostles and prophets make up that foundation, with Jesus Christ being the Chief Cornerstone. Without such a foundation, much of our fruit is sure to be lost with the passing of time. Persecutions, afflictions, grievous wolves, false doctrines, perils among false brethren, etc., will surely come against a true working of God in order to destroy it. The master-builders of the Church, the apostles, and the gifted "seers" of the Church, the prophets, are ordained by God to provide a safeguard against the loss of blessing that He is pouring into the earth through the Church. Read the Acts of the Apostles and examine the roles apostolic and prophetic men played in the formation of strong communities of believers. Were it not for their anointed discernment and their bold defense of the truth, many young churches would have been destroyed before their own elders were strong enough to detect and repel danger. It is God's intention that apostles and prophets equip the churches they serve, enabling them to become "the pillar and support of the truth" in their localities (1 Tim. 3:15, NAS). Churches don't become guardians of the faith and blessings of God all by themselves; they require the loving, fatherly oversight of anointed apostles and prophets, and their team.

In this day of restoration, God is helping us to recover these all-too-often forgotten offices. As we allow them to funtion among us, the Lord will increase the instances of the miraculous in our midst, the evangelization of the world with signs following will be realized, and we will literally be hastening the Lord's return. He will come upon a white horse to make the kindoms of this world to become the kindom of our God!

11. True Spirit-Engenderedunity

> [Jesus prayed,] *"I in them and you in me. May they be brought to complete unity to let the world know that you sent me and have loved them even as you have loved me* (John 17:23).

The world will come to know Jesus as we reveal Him by signs and wonders. A key foundation for these signs and wonders will be unity in the Body of Christ. What kind of unity are we talking about? Jesus said, "Complete unity." How will we ever have that? I will attempt to answer that question in a moment.

The Scriptures speak of a "unity of the Spirit" (Eph. 4:3) and a "unity of the faith" (Eph. 4:13). We are exhorted, as Christians, to *maintain* the unity of the Spirit, but to *come to*, or *arrive at*, the unity of the faith.

What Unity of the Spirit is Not

True unity of the Spirit, or unity that is produced by the Holy Spirit, is not the extreme "ecumenical" brand of unity being propagated today by many "men of the cloth." These deceived leaders would have God's people embrace, in joyful fellowship, members of groups whose teachings and beliefs are contrary to fundamental Christian doctrine. With non-Christian religious groups, there can be no unity of the Spirit, because they are of a different and strange spirit. Paul warned of those who would preach "another Jesus, another gospel," and who would present "another spirit" (2 Cor. 11:4). Yet, many of today's Church leaders would have us embrace everybody, counting them as brothers and sisters in God.

Unless we can agree on the fundamental principles and standards of God's Word, we will not be able to fabricate genuine unity. Authentic Christianity is a very "narrow" walk. It is narrow in that it is the *only* way to walk in fellowship with God.

Will Ecumenical Unity Work Among Christian Groups?

Ecumenical unity will work among varied Christian groups, but only so far. We may be able to embrace one another in true Christian fellowship, having been baptized into one Body (the Church) by one Spirit (Eph. 4:4; 1 Cor. 12:13), but because we fail to see eye to eye on many other important issues, it would be rather foolish for us to try to build the Kingdom together in a very close way. I have a great deal of respect for other bona fide Christian groups and organizations, but because I know we approach certain situations very differently sometimes, I will not attempt to build too closely with them. I respect their right to pursue the vision they feel God gave them, and I hope they can respect my right to pursue the vision God gave me. Let me explain a few ways we might have difficulty in building the Kingdom together.

Suppose you believe in passive, non-aggressive evangelism and I believe in aggressive "power evangelism." How then will we move forward together? What if your conviction is to allow abortion to be practiced in our country unhindered, but mine is to prophetically decry it as murder and horrible sin? How then will we march together? If your church or denomination allows homosexuals to be ordained into the ministry and mine does not, how can we build the Kingdom of God together? If you believe God inflicts His children with sickness and diseases in order to reach and instruct them, but I do not, then how will we minister to and pray for the sick together? If I believe a Christian can have a demon, but you do not, then how will we minister to that one together? If I believe in present-day apostolic and prophetic ministry and you do not, then how can we establish churches together? If I believe the Bible to be the inspired and authoritative Word of God, and you do not, then how in the world will we be able to accomplish very much of significance together? We must look at things realistically.

Should we be willing to forfeit certain biblical truths God has graciously revealed to us for the sake of unity? The late Arthur Wallis, in his classic book, *The Radical Christian*, said, "We pay too high a price for unity if it costs us the truth." If we, therefore, abide by the truth we have received, division will result. The division should not be one of anger and bitterness, but should be of the type that allows the different factions to pursue their own particular visions. If they are wrong and need correction, allow the Lord of the Church to correct them. You should only stay true to what God has called you to do and remain open to correction in case you've been the one who has been wrong.

We must all realize an important truth when we look at the subjects of truth, unity and division. The truth of the glorious gospel has always divided families, communities and even nations, dividing those who receive it from those who reject it. When the Spirit of God is on the move, powerful things begin to happen. If our so-called peace and unity is blown apart by the moving of the Spirit of God, then I dare say that our unity was shallow and defective. Wallis said, "The little world of Judaism was relatively peaceful till Jesus stepped into it. He didn't come with an olive branch, but with a sword (Matt. 10:34). He didn't come with a call to unity, but with a message He knew would divide the nation." Do we really think it will be any different when we proclaim His message? In the divided Christianity of today's world, do we really need to hear more voices crying out for unity — trying to patch the unpatchable and join the unjoinable? Wallis said, "We need an incisive word that will confront the professing church with the government of God!" Accept that sword and afterward call for unity!

How Will True Unity Come?

Genuine unity of Spirit and unity of the faith, being the *complete* unity Jesus prayed for, will only come by the Holy Spirit working to break through the vain traditions, shabby beliefs and weak moral standards of much of the professing church. All of us have been guilty of living by a lower standard than what God calls for. True unity centers on dedicated adherence to the Word of God. Once a people come together on the Word of God they are able to see eye to eye. This speaks of singleness of vision. A prophetic verse out of Isaiah 52 says, "Thy watchmen shall lift up the voice; with the voice together shall they sing: for they shall see eye to eye, when the Lord shall bring again Zion" (Isa. 52:8, KJV). The bringing again of Zion is the latter-day restoration of God's people. In this time of restoration, watchmen, those who are looking out for what God is doing by the Holy Spirit, are going to sing together and see eye to eye. Singing together speaks of harmony. Seeing eye to eye speaks of having the same perspective, the same overall vision. When we arrive at this kind of unity, we will move together to demolish the work of satan and establish the Kingdom of God. We must *come to* this unity! The enemy has no respect for the kind of unity that is created by our compromising the Word of God and the life-style it demands. He will roll right over anything but the best of true Spirit-engendered unity.

My belief is that as the heat of the last days is turned up on the professing church, those standards that are less than what the Word calls for will fall by the wayside. All the garbage that we have picked up through the past decades, and even centuries, that keeps us from becoming the Church God intended will serve us no purpose. The Bible informs us that God has said, "Once more I will shake not only the earth but also the heavens" (Heb. 12:26). The expression "once more" indicates the removal of those things that can be shaken (things that are man-made), so that those things that cannot be shaken may remain — namely, the Word and Kingdom of God (Matt. 24:35; Heb. 12:28a). Every man-made substitute, every cleverly devised program or committee that was created by men to replace the Spirit and anointing of God will be shown for what it is worth and discarded. We will all begin to see more clearly that the only way to build the Kingdom is by strict adherence to the Word of God.

God desires that we seek, discern and walk in His perfect way before hardship or failure drive us to it. But if we fail to follow the heavenly blueprint, the Bible, then we will have to learn the hard way. One way or the other, we will line up with the Word of God, and we will be brought to unity.

How should we relate to brethren who see things differently than we do? Be nice to them, but stand by the revelation you have. If they can't bear it, don't try to discuss it with them. Leave them to God.

Our unity of faith is found easily, if we are both believing on the name of Jesus Christ and are able to love one another unconditionally (1 John 3:23). I am finding out that if we will fellowship and rejoice around these two commandments, we'll all get along much better. All Christians ought to be able to obey these commands and get along with all who do. Whether they be Church of God, Presbyterian, Methodist, Baptist, Pentecostal or Charismatic, all should be able to rejoice around Jesus' Lordship and our mutual commandment to love one another.

City-wide crusades to reach the lost can be sponsored by everyone naming the name of Jesus. The poor can be supplied by our churches working together. Together, we can support moral politicians, picket abortion clinics, feed the hungry, and break bread together. We can do these things without compromising our convictions. This is a type of unity, but don't think it is the kind of unity that God will settle for, causing Him to unleash great amounts of His marvelous power through the Church. No! Not until we are all operating according to His Word and by the leading of His Spirit will we see the greatest demonstrations of His divine power. Until then, there are some things we should not attempt to do together. They will only produce more division.

Allow other groups, denominations, etc., to pursue, unhindered by your criticisms, the vision they believe God has birthed in their hearts. If you'll do that, then maybe they'll be more apt to be gracious when they see you pursuing things that don't fit their fancy. Let us have grace, one toward another, and let God unite us on His eternal Word. He will do it in due time.

Good news for those Christians who are trying to obey God and order their lives by His Word is this: God will not wait until the whole Church comes together in unity before He starts pouring out His Spirit with signs and wonders. While it is His desire that we be in complete worldwide unity before He unleashes them through us in their totality, it is also a fact that He will honor His Word, no matter how small the number of people, as long as it is presented with Holy Ghost authority in an uncompromised way and through an uncompromising people! Walk in unity with believers of like precious faith and expect outpourings of God's Spirit and power. We wish we could walk in complete unity with all believers without jeopardizing truth, but we can't. In the meantime let's expect God to set His stamp of approval on us for our obedience and willingness to adhere to His Word.

Differences Are Inevitable

> *No doubt there have to be differences among you to show which of you have God's approval* (1 Cor. 11:19).

While differences are unedifying, they are, at the same time, inevitable. So God brings a positive thing out of them. He shows who's got it, and who does not! Remember Paul said, "I will come to you shortly, if the Lord will, and will know, not the speech of them which are puffed up, but the power. For the kingdom of God is not in word, but in power" (I Cor. 4:19-20, KJV). Universal signs of God's favor and approval are power and ongoing success.

Explosions of Almightiness: An Outcome of Unity

One of the gifts the Holy Spirit gave the Church was "the workings of miracles" (1 Cor. 12:8-10). The Greek text says: "the operations of powers." *Powers* can be transliterated to say "explosions of Almightiness."

It thrills me to read such passages as the one in Acts where, as the people of God "lift their voice in one accord," the place is shaken wherein they are assembled. But not only that, a mighty outpouring of signs and wonders among the people is a result of their being in one accord. (See Acts 4:23-31 and 5:12.) When the Church unites, praying in one accord and being brought together in Word, faith and Spirit, we will experience the fullness of the Holy Spirit. When we are filled with the Spirit like Jesus wants us to be, we will open our mouths to boldly speak the Word of God to the nations, and the gates of hell will be devastated. Until then, someone must hold the standard of His Word high! It doesn't matter if the entire religious world adulterates His Word, you must stand by it. God told His prophet, Jeremiah, concerning those who had departed from taking the Word of His covenant seriously: "Let them return unto thee; but return not thou unto them" (Jer. 15:19c, KJV). God is looking for a people who will not compromise His Word for the sake of ecumenical unity.

True unity produces explosions of God's power, explosions of Almightiness! When God's power explodes on the scene, satan's fortresses crumble and fall to the ground, allowing the people of God to put them beneath their feet (Luke 10:19).

12. Refrain From Criticizing God's Ministers

> *Another time he went into the synagogue, and a man with a shriveled hand was there. Some of them were looking for a reason to accuse Jesus, so they watched him closely to see if he would heal him on the Sabbath. Jesus said to the man with the shriveled hand, "Stand up in front of everyone." Then Jesus asked them, "Which is lawful on the Sabbath: to do good or to do evil, to save life or to kill?" But they remained silent. He looked around at them in anger and,*

> *deeply distressed at their stubborn hearts, said to the man, "Stretch out your hand." He stretched it out, and his hand was completely restored. Then the Pharisees went out and began to plot with the Herodians how they might kill Jesus. Jesus withdrew with his disciples to the lake, and a large crowd from Galilee followed* (Mark 3:1-7).

Several insights may be gained from a close look at the above passage. Notice at the end of the story how it is recorded that Jesus withdrew Himself from the midst of the congregation at the synagogue. When Jesus withdraws, the healings stop. When Jesus vacates the premises, the miracles are no more, because the anointing goes with Him. Jesus and the Holy Spirit were grieved, distressed and angered at the stubborn hearts of the religious crowd present that day. Among them were a number of Pharisees who were not desirous of seeing a poor, bound soul healed of his physical infirmity; but rather, they were concerned only with their insipid Jewish doctrine and lame traditions. On top of this, they were overly critical of Jesus' every move. Their spirit of criticism (not necessarily a demon, but definitely a condition of heart) was what drove Jesus and the anointing of God from the midst of the assembly. The Holy Ghost is always grieved and saddened by the critical, judgmental spirit of a people aimed at the ministers of God.

Upon witnessing the miracle Jesus performed on the man with the withered arm, the high-minded Pharisees marched out of the meeting with not so much as a "Hallelujah!" over the healing of their needy brother. They were just too busy criticizing and condemning Jesus' ministry. There were no more healings in that synagogue that day, and probably never again.

In many churches today, the same conclusion can be drawn. The people of God are so critical and judgmental, bound by such stubborn hearts, that the Holy Spirit has been forced to withdraw, taking with Him His anointing and blessing. Not only is the Lord grieved by such ungodly attitudes in the midst of the assembly of the saints, He is angered as well!

Many thousands of churchgoers pick apart their pastors on Saturday night, criticizing and judging them as being incompetent, and then pray for a mighty moving of God's Spirit on Sunday morning. When it doesn't come, they blame their leaders all the more. What a terrible error they have fallen into.

God never called perfect men to the ministry. If I, for one, lived to be 300 years old, I would never reach perfection. And yet so many Christians expect their spiritual leaders to be everything they want them to be. When they don't add up to those standards, they are removed from their pedestals and pelted with the stones of judgment and criticism.

For the Church in our generation to come to the place where mighty signs and wonders become everyday occurrences, we as a whole must repent of the destructive words that have poured from our criticizing mouths. We must also have a change of heart, determining to become a part of the solution and not a part of the problem. Believe me, criticizing the leaders in your church and not praying for them consistently is a big part of the problem.

We must commit ourselves to walk in love towards all men, especially the ministers who we don't think are doing a good enough job. If you cannot keep a positive attitude of heart toward them, remove yourself from their influence (and them from yours), and for the Church's sake, don't criticize them. After all, who are you to judge another man's servant? By Jesus these men will stand or fall.

It is interesting to note that when Jesus withdrew from the religious crowd in the synagogue, a great multitude of sincere folks went after Him. At the side of the lake — away from that religious, judgmental setting — He was again willing to pour out His miraculous blessing upon the needy.

Before I close this chapter, I want to ask this question. Was Jesus right in withdrawing from the inflexible, religious congregation? You know, if He were to do such a thing today many would accuse Him of division.

And Paul. Was he correct in his action of removing his ministry from the Ephesian religious community and "separating the disciples" (Acts 19:9) into the borrowed classroom of the secular school teacher Tyrannus? Examine the result of such a radical "unecumenical" move and judge for yourself.

I know a man who separated some disciples into an old store building one time, and the surrounding religious community had a fit. Yes, the store building was fixed up inside and quite comfortable, but what Christian minister in his right mind would remove worshipers of God from "respected" religious establishments and teach them in an old store building?

A certain "threatened" pastor wrote a letter to him, hoping to catch him in a divisive statement so he could show his answer all over the religious community. The pastor asked: "If Jesus Christ were to come in the flesh to our area, where would he go? Would He go to the jail? Would He go to the tavern? Would He go minister at the Methodist Church or the Presbyterian Church? Or would He come and minister only in your church?" He thought he had him. He thought he had him figured out. But this is what the man of God wrote in reply:

Dear Pastor:

> Thank you for your letter, and thank you for asking me the question, "Where would Jesus go if He were to come to our area?"
>
> First of all, I would like to think that if Jesus were to physically visit our area, He would meet such a crowd on the outskirts of town that He'd be busy healing the sick and casting out devils for days. But if the crowd was not there to meet Him, I believe He would visit the jail, the tavern, the Methodist Church, the Presbyterian Church and our church. He would visit and continue His mighty ministry anywhere the people would eagerly receive His Word and anointing. But if they persisted in shunning His radical message, disgracing His forever-settled Word, and hindering the working of the Holy Spirit, He would be sure to withdraw Himself from their midst and seek out those hungry people who would receive gladly what He had to say and offer.
>
> Now, brother, you be the judge of that. Would He find it easy to stay and minister in your church and among your people?

Sincerely,

He received no response from the foolish pastor. I hope he learned something that has helped him understand Jesus' ministry a little better.

Now let me ask you the same question the man of God asked that pastor. Would Jesus find it easy to abide and minister in the midst of your local assembly? If so, great! Keep doing what you are doing. But if not, find out why and give it a whole lot of prayer. Jesus wants to do a mighty work in your midst. Make it easy for Him.

13. Be Love-of-God Motivated

Whatever you pour your prayers, your energy or your finances into, be sure that it is God's love that motivates you. Don't be "cause" motivated.

Many thousands of Christian people are doing the things they do because they have rallied around a cause. Perhaps the cause is a worthy one; but unless the foundation for their involvement is the love of God, they will run out of steam and resources before the task is completed.

Never let anger be the force that motivates you to rally around a cause. For instance: There are those people who march energetically on abortion clinics who aren't motivated by God's love, but by extreme indignation. As heroic and righteous as their action may be, their foundation is faulty. You see, the Word of God tells us that "the anger of man does not achieve the righteousness of God" (James 1:20, NAS). When all is said or done, unless the love of God is the motive behind it all, it will not stand the day of judgment.

I believe with all of my heart that God's love must be the motivating factor behind all we do in the area of signs and wonders. If our activity in the miraculous is so that we might get a name for ourselves, then we would do better to place ourselves deep in a wilderness, far away from all people, until the love and compassion of the Lord becomes our motive for ministry.

5

OUR AWESOME AUTHORITY

Many years ago, at the entrance to what is now a world-famous harbor, there stood a formation of very dangerous rocks and cliffs known by mariners as "Hell's Gate." Many ships had been smashed against these formidable rocks by the treacherous seas that often whipped in and out of the harbor, and many lives had been lost.

A very wise old man who was considered an expert in the use of dangerous explosives was hired by the harbor officials and given the job of eliminating the seemingly impregnable rocks.

After days of laborious work, drilling holes into the cliffs at strategic points and filling them with powerful charges of dynamite, the old man was ready. People came from miles around to see if his painstaking efforts would pay off.

Thousands of feet of wire were unrolled and connected to each charge of dynamite. All these were connected to one heavy-gauge lead wire which, in turn, was connected to a detonator hundreds of yards from the cliffs.

When the moment arrived for the charges to be detonated, the old man lifted his little granddaughter onto his lap and allowed her to press the button. In one mighty burst of electrical power every charge of dynamite that had been strategically placed within those formidable rocks went off with a mighty explosion. When the smoke cleared there was not a rock to be seen, only foaming ocean water. Hell's Gate was no more!

One touch of the young girl's finger, in obedience to her grandfather's word, unleashed the forces his wisdom had provided for the demolition of those formidable rocks. How it was accomplished was beyond her comprehension; that was Grandpa's business. But together they saw Hell's Gate destroyed.

Like the small girl who destroyed Hell's Gate, the Church has been given authority in God to demolish the works of hell. Exactly how it is accomplished we do not always need to know. All that matters is that when we exercise our authority in obedience to God's command, the hideous gates of hell will crumble.

When Do We Use Our Authority?

There is no doubt concerning the authority to wage spiritual warfare that the Lord has given the Church. Jesus said, "Behold, I give unto you authority to tread on serpents and scorpions, and over all the ability of the enemy ..." (Luke 10:19, author's paraphrase). But that doesn't give to you the authority to do anything you want. To run out and attempt to do some things would spell disaster for you. Unless your authority is founded correctly, it will backfire on you, bringing much shame and defeat.

It is true; as a member of the Church of Jesus Christ I have all authority over all the work of satan, but I also know that I dare not run out and wield that authority in every situation or against every principality.

My sons have authority over my horse, Topknot, but they do not have the maturity or the ability to lead him into a stall, saddle him and ride off into the sunset. They are just not able to exercise themselves in such a great matter as that, because they are only small boys. Topknot is a rambunctious, rearing-to-go, thousand-pound colt needing someone with much more experience than what my boys possess in order to train him into the kind of horse boys can handle. One day after they have grown a great deal, they'll be able to exercise their authority over such a horse as Topknot.

Scripture says "...as long as the heir is a child, he is no different from a slave, although he owns the whole estate. He is subject to guardians and trustees until the time set by his father" (Gal. 4:1-2).

Not long after I was saved, I learned about the authority of the believer. It thrilled me through and through, and I felt as though I could take on any situation and whip any evil spirit in satan's kingdom. So I'd run out looking for the devil, and the moment I found him I would blast him with the Word of God. Though, as a child of God, I had the right to do that, I did not always possess the wisdom and ability to carry through with what I would start. So, many times I would be forced to retreat from the situation because of my inability to handle the enormous pressures it would bring upon my life.

I will never forget the time I foolishly decided to start a church in a small mountainous community where I saw great need. My enthusiasm far outweighed my ability to withstand the terrible spiritual warfare I encountered not long after I began meetings there. Up until that time, no one had been successful at establishing a strong Spirit-filled church for the people of that area, so I should have taken much more time than I did to pray, to seek God's strategy (if there was one for that particular time), and to count the enormous cost I might have to pay. Had I truly sought the Lord concerning that tremendous undertaking, I might have heard what Paul heard as he endeavored to go into Asia to preach the gospel. The Holy Ghost forbade him (Acts 16:6). After having preached the Word in Galatia, it seems Asia would have been the next obvious move, but it was not God's time yet. When Asia was denied him, Paul sought to take the next obvious step and preach the Word in Bithynia, but again he was denied (Acts 16:7). The Holy Spirit knew things Paul didn't know, and Paul had to follow His leading. Eventually Paul was allowed to go into Asia (Acts 19), and while there he was given times of great revival. His patience and obedience paid off.

The first few meetings I held in that needy, mountainous community were relatively successful. There were new faces at almost every meeting, the folks were enjoying the worship, and they all seemed to be receiving the Word of God as I energetically preached it. On the surface things seemed to be going the way we wanted, and only after I had made a tremendous investment in time, gasoline, wear-and-tear on my automobile, etc., did I begin to see that things were not as good as I thought they were.

Some of the key people began rejecting some of the topics I chose to speak about in my messages. An argumentative, critical spirit began to pervade the meeting, and before long I began to dread driving the many miles to meet with those people. Because of the resistance I so keenly felt from certain "pillars" of the group, I lost the incentive I needed to preach and teach on anything. After discussing our differences one cold winter's night, following a particularly frustrating meeting, we decided to shut the meetings down. I left that area and those people in defeat. To this day I know of no substantial work of God that has been established in that rock-hard region. I believe there is a tremendously powerful principality who rules that area (Eph. 6:12), and it will require much more than what I am presently able to offer to dethrone him and establish a solid, lasting work for God's glory there.

Did I have the authority to preach the gospel in that area? I certainly did! But I lacked the wisdom, anointing and backing to carry out my lofty plans. One day, by God's grace and in His exact timing, someone will be used to topple that evil spirit's seat of authority in that area and will be privileged to build a solid, enduring New Testament work there. I long to see that day come.

It is imperative that our authority be rightly founded before we assume we can take on the devil in any given situation. The following are several essential foundation stones of authority that any believer must come to grips with before he dares to step out to injure the work of satan. I have learned these foundations from the Word and from the school of hard knocks.

Foundation for Authority

#1 1. *Is one a Christian?* A right relationship with God through Jesus Christ is absolutely necessary before anyone can dare to confront the kingdom of darkness. Only a bona fide Christian has the right to use the weapons of God against the enemy. If any other person attempts to use the authority reserved for Christians who know who they are in Jesus Christ, he is likely to receive the same response the seven sons of Sceva did when they attempted to command a demon spirit: "Jesus I know, and Paul I know; but who are ye?" (Acts 19:15, KJV). With that the demon caused them to be beaten badly.

2. *Is one under authority?* The centurion who besought Jesus for the healing of his servant boy prefaced his request with the statement, "I am a man under authority, having soldiers under me ..." (Matt. 8:9a, KJV). He knew that because he was under authority himself, his own authority would work. He also recognized in Jesus an authority much like his own — only it was a spiritual authority. Because Jesus was under authority, His authority would work properly; therefore, the centurion requested, "Speak the word only, and my servant shall be healed" (Matt. 8:8, KJV).

Are you under proper authority? Do you show the respect to authority that the Word calls for? If you do not adhere to the authorities God has placed over you, the days are coming when your authority in Christ will not serve you, and you'll have to submit to defeat and shame. God hates insubordination among His people.

There are a couple of things we need to know about being submitted to authority. First, submission does not mean inferiority. The one in charge is no better or no worse, in the eyes of God, than the one who is in submission. It is, however, God's placement in a chain of command; a placement that should be honored and submitted to by everyone.

Secondly, one can be obedient to authority without being truly submitted. This is evil in the sight of God. For example: I may do what you tell me to do, but if my attitude is not right I'm not really submitted. Submission is an attitude of heart; obedience is an action.

There is something else to consider. It is possible to be submitted and yet not obey the orders of an authority. We are always to be submissive whether we obey or not. Rebellion is not necessarily an action of disobedience, but it always comes from a non-submissive attitude.

A woman in our church was told by her husband not to attend any more church meetings. She came to me and expressed her desire to continue in Christian fellowship even though he threatened to kick her out; but she also wanted to be submitted to him as the head of her family. She was confused as to what to do. If she continued to attend church meetings wouldn't she be disobedient and rebellious? "Disobedient to your husband's wishes perhaps, but not rebellious," I pointed out. I then showed her a verse in Hebrews where God instructs Christians not to forsake assembling together with other believers. So it came down to her husband's word or God's Word. Which would she obey?

She approached her husband in a submissive manner and a submissive attitude and told him that although she loved and respected him as her husband, she was going to obey God's Word instead of his. She continued to wash his laundry, fix his meals, raise his children, and do all the things a submissive wife can do to honor and serve her husband, but concerning the issue of church attendance, she had to disobey him and follow God's higher command. She was submissive in attitude, yet disobedient in action.

If the United States government instructed me to perform abortions, I would disobey. That does not mean I am not submitted to its authority in and over my life, because I am and God instructs me to be; but I will not transgress God's higher law, "Thou shalt not murder." If it were to cost me the friendship of this government, too bad. I am committed to a God who easily supersedes and transcends the laws of any nation.

If a wife loses her marriage over the issue of church membership and attendance, what she loses isn't worth much anyway. What one compromises to keep, he'll lose in the long run. It is best to put God's law above all others; and you can do so while still remaining submissive to the lawmaker you disobey. Remember, submission is an attitude.

As long as a human superior doesn't instruct you to do something that crosses the Word of God, do it. Do it humbly and submissively.

Are you under authority? If you are serving faithfully in God's chain of command, in the family, the church or on the job, you can expect your spiritual authority to work for you as you seek to build the Kingdom of God in this sin-sick world.

3. *Is one called to the task before them?* It is an age-old truth: The need is not necessarily the call. Moses saw the need Israel had in being set free from Egyptian bondage, but he did not have the call, at least not when he was a young man of forty. But he acted in haste, killed an Egyptian and wound up in the wilderness for another forty years. When eighty years of age, Moses was called to deliver Israel, and with that call came the authority and ability to do it. I would that young Christians could learn this lesson early in their walk with God. We assume far too much, run out ahead of God and get into much undue trouble. The Bible says, "To be over-hasty is to sin, and miss the mark" (Prov. 19:2b, TAB). A divine call is necessary to receive spiritual authority. To run when you are not sent is presumptuous and categorizes you as one with false pretenses. The false prophets of Jeremiah's day were those of whom God said, "I have not sent these prophets, yet they ran ..." (Jer. 23:21, KJV) The ultimate outcome of your ministry as a Christian is rooted in your initial call and its ensuing authority. Abraham, like Moses, was successful because God sent him. If God sends you, He will vindicate you and protect you in times of trouble; if you run out, He won't!

Second Peter 1:10 exhorts us to make our calling sure. If we know it is sure, we will not stumble and fall when times get tough.

4. *Are one's motives correct?* Many believers endeavor to battle the enemy, or endeavor to take a position of authority in the Church, so that they might be seen and admired of men. Others step forward in authority so that they might take possession of something their greedy hearts desire. Their motives are incorrect, and God will not honor their efforts. What one gains with incorrect motives, he'll often have to maintain with incorrect motives.

5. *Are one's attitudes correct?* To place yourself in an authoritative stance of spiritual warfare when attitudes in your heart are not right is to flirt with disaster.

Wrong attitudes can take many forms. A few common ones are resentment toward God or man, wrong attitudes of submission to authority, those of spiritual pride and self-importance, attitudes of self-pity and thinking people owe you, attitudes of indifference to important issues, and attitudes of self-abasement and false humility. Such attitudes are totally ungodly and will render you vulnerable to satan's attacks.

It isn't hard to correct a bad attitude. It begins with a decision of the will. Choose to change it and do whatever is necessary to see it change. Also, we need to repent of the bad attitude, crying out to God for the grace needed to see it changed. Then we must begin to order our speech with the Word of God that counters the bad attitude. I realize that all that sounds easier than it is to carry out, but I can guarantee it will work if you'll apply a little "spiritual violence" to these areas (Matt. 11:12), demanding something of yourself that, till now, you've been unwilling to give.

6. *Does one have the proper equipment?* Scripture speaks of our need of being "thoroughly equipped for every good work" (2 Tim. 3:17). Unless we are supplied with God's equipment, we will see continual failure in all we attempt to do for Him. It is not enough to be wise in your own natural mind — you need God's wisdom. It is not enough to be eloquent in your natural ability to speak — you need God's unction. It is not enough to have a pair of hands to lay hands on the sick — you need God's healing power. It is not enough to have the desire for doing great things for God — you need His call and the authority that comes with it.

Paul said, "God enabled me, putting me into the ministry." (See I Timothy 1:12, KJV.) It wasn't just any ministry that Paul was enabled for and called to; it was a particular ministry. Because he was faithful to his particular call in life, he was uniquely equipped by God Himself and placed in effective ministry. It provided him with fulfillment and joy all his life. Had he tried to be something else, he would not have been equipped. Had he ventured forth without proper equipment, the devil would have eaten him alive! And so will it be with you and me; examine yourself to see if the equipment you've been given as a Christian coincides with the call you feel is on your life. If it doesn't, you had better reexamine your purpose in the Kingdom of God.

7. *Is one acting in unison with wise and godly counselors?* #7
Scripture states that "Where no counsel is, the people fall: but in the multitude of counsellors there is safety" (Prov. 11:14, KJV). However, one must be sure his counselors are honest and godly men who have a faith and steadfastness in God worth following (Heb. 6:12). Proverbs also says, "Every purpose is established by counsel: and with good advice make war" (Prov. 20:18, KJV).

Paul was called as an apostle to the nations, but it was obvious that he pursued his calling on the foundation of good counsel and advice. (See Acts 13:1-4.)

The Church today is filled with people who have run out ahead of God, never once stopping to consider the godly advice older men and women could give. Many of these "storm troopers" have run smack into solid brick walls, and are now filled with bitterness toward the people of God because they aren't running to rescue them. They have learned the hard way that you do not initiate war on your own.

Well-known leader, Ern Baxter, returned from a trip to New Guinea several years ago, a battered and shaken man. He told a few of his colleagues that while he was there he had made the mistake of trying to take on a principality by himself. It nearly cost him his life! As great and seasoned a spiritual warrior as Ern Baxter is, he was unable by himself to pull down one of the vicious ruling spirits over that country. You or I could have done no better. It will take the united warfare of a spiritual army to rout it.

We must seek the counsel and war support of seasoned, trustworthy men and women of God. Our independent mentality will lead us to certain defeat in the coming days if we fail to get a handle on it.

Do not do things of great spiritual significance without seeking the advice of your leaders. Do not do things on your own initiative. If you do, then be prepared to take care of the consequences by yourself. Don't expect the brothers and sisters to get in it with you unless you've asked them about it before you get started. Once you say, "This is what God has led me to do," you preclude any one's speaking into it. You've single-handedly put God's stamp of approval on it, and in so doing, you've pretty much obligated people to say, "Well, if God is telling you to do it, you'd better do it!"

Take counsel, not after you've gotten into trouble, but when the possibility is just an idea growing in your mind and you haven't yet stepped out. Never ask your brothers and sisters to give their lives to something they are not committed to. When a member of a church, or a member of a ministry team, steps forth to do something of significance, it has implications that affect everybody. Counsel is essential for successful ministry. A lack of it could mean the downfall of an entire company of people.

#8 8. *Is one under pressure to act?* Often the unbearable pressure of certain situations will cause us to step out ahead of God's timing. Again, "To be over hasty is to sin and miss the mark." We can't focus on that statement enough.

A number of years ago I was offered the opportunity to broadcast my daily radio seminar, "Victory In Life," on thirteen radio stations up and down the Eastern Seaboard of the United States. At that time it seemed to be the opportunity of a lifetime, but an essential ingredient was missing as I tried to make the decision whether or not to seize the opportunity: the peace of God! Without the peace of God ruling in my heart, I would have been a fool to undertake such a responsibility.

The man with whom I was dealing wasn't helping matters any. He warned that a list of ministers were in line behind me, yearning to secure the slots available to me, and that I had to let him know within twenty-four hours whether or not I wanted them. That brought increased pressure on me, and so, without the peace of God ruling in my heart, I accepted the offer. Without going into the details, I want to say I got burned. The man with whom I dealt proved to be an irresponsible charlatan and fraud — at least where my involvement with him was concerned. If it were not for God's grace and protection, I could easily have lost thousands of dollars instead of the hundreds I did lose. God enabled us to catch a glaring inconsistency in the man's dealings with us, and so we were able to get out of our ungodly contract with him after a month of broadcasting. God's mercy and faithfulness to me, even when I blow it, never ceases to amaze me.)

I learned a valuable lesson through my involvement with that man, and it has stayed with me ever since: Never allow pressure to force you into any decision before you have the peace of God on it.

Of course there are times when you are under satanic attack and you are pressured to use your faith and authority immediately. At such times you have no choice in the matter; you either use your authority or go under. But when you are considering a possible course of action that could involve much time and effort, you had better take the time to seek God's will concerning the matter and hold out until the peace of God flourishes in your heart. Nine times out of ten, weighty decisions do not have to be made overnight. If you are told they do — that's a clue: It's probably not God.

God's peace in your heart is an essential foundation for authority.

9. *Does one have a God-given strategy for success?* It is one thing to have a goal; it's another thing to know how you're going to reach it. Too many of us are far too random in our efforts to achieve certain goals. Often our goals are praiseworthy and in keeping with the will of God, but we have no idea how we're going to reach them.

Some people are natural goal-setters and achievers. Working out the strategies that enable them to reach their goals comes easy to them. Others of us are the exact opposite. I, for one, have a heart full of visions and goals, but knowing how to reach them is often grossly missing in my makeup.

If you are like I am, it is important for you to be a part of a team of people who can help you bounce around ideas, and who can assist you in collocating a strategy that will enable you to reach your goals. In spheres of authority and spiritual warfare this is extremely important for your success. A council of peers and superiors can also insure that you don't prevaricate in seasons of stress and temptation to take another course of action. Proverbs says, "Without counsel purposes are disappointed" (Prov. 15:22, KJV); goals are rarely realized, and satan's wishes continue to succeed unencumbered. In council with godly brothers and sisters who share the burden of God, strategies can be formulated that will accomplish much for the Kingdom of God. See that you have a strategy.

10. *Is one prepared for the long haul?* Basic to a sure foundation is the understanding that not all goals are reached in a short period of time. The exercise of spiritual authority often requires painstaking commitment to the path God has laid before us; if we forget this and look for a path of least resistance, we will see eventual failure.

God never promised us a rose garden, at least not in this life. We mustn't forget that we are in a battle zone that is destined to remain until Jesus comes to subjugate His many foes.

It is "through much tribulation [that we must] enter into the kingdom of God" (Acts 14:22b, KJV), and "all that will live godly in Christ Jesus shall suffer persecution" (II Tim. 3:12, KJV). As we press into the government of God for our lives, the lives of our families, and the lives of our churches, we will meet with horrendous opposition. We must be prepared to ride it out to the end.

Let's examine the anatomy of a good goal.

> *I press toward the goal for the prize of the upward call of God in Christ Jesus* (Phil. 3:14, NAS).

First, the pursuit of a good goal nearly always introduces tension and opposition into your life. The fact that Paul said he had to "press on" reveals this reality. There was no coasting into the fulfillment of his godly goals; rather, he had to press on in faith and steadfastness.

Secondly, a goal holds a prize for the achiever. Paul did not press on through all the opposition for the fun of it. He was after definite results! Good goals always hold a prize for you.

Thirdly, our goals, and the call from God to achieve them, are always upward, bringing us into a closer walk with God. The diligence involved in reaching for these goals always produces more of the image and character of Jesus in our lives. The intense opposition that stands between us and the achievement of our goals serves to stretch us, purify us, and conform us more into Christ's holy image.

Fourthly, a laudable goal always begins with a call. We are never to decide for ourselves what our goals in God's Kingdom should be, but we are to discover the good works that God "before ordained that we should walk in" (Eph. 2:10, KJV), and give our lives to them.

The next time you are deciding what goals you want to reach for, take the time to judge them by this four-point anatomy; I believe you'll find it very beneficial.

11. *Is one in the fear of God?* Essential to well-founded spiritual authority is a genuine and healthy fear of God. This involves more than simple respect and reverence, but convolves into its framework a sound understanding that there are limitations to His grace and a wrathful side to His nature. God is Judge of the universe and He answers to no one! Thank God He is love (1 John 4:16), but He is also a consuming fire (Heb. 12:29). As much as He dislikes His office as Judge and Avenger, justice demands that He bring retribution upon the evildoer.

As the Father of redeemed people, He must carry out unpleasant disciplinary action against their persistent rebellion. Against them He stands, not as Judge, but as stern Father! A person with a healthy fear of Him understands this and seeks to live before Him on pleasant terms.

There is too little fear of the Lord in today's modernized Christianity. In losing it we have lost the authority essential to powerful, earth-changing Christian practice. Without true, God-given authority, we stand before the world, the flesh and the devil powerless — a joke, an unconsidered race of human beings.

There are three aspects to the fear of the Lord.

First, it must be chosen. Proverbs 1:29 indicates that the problem with the wicked is that they "did not *choose* the fear of the Lord," would not accept His advice, and spurned His rebuke.

Eagerly accepting godly advice and embracing the Lord's discipline is a proof that one fears God. Such action must be chosen, because the natural tendency is to recoil when the Lord's advice or correction comes our way.

Secondly, the fear of God must be taught. Psalm 34:11 records God as saying to us, "Come, my children, listen to me; I will *teach* you the fear of the Lord."

A person doesn't just wake up one day and find that suddenly he has the fear of God. This fear must be taught, *and* it must be learned. One must become a bona fide disciple (student) of the Lord Jesus Christ in order to learn the fear of the Lord. Having prayed the sinner's prayer at one time in your life doesn't qualify you as a disciple of Jesus. We are talking about laying down your life to Him daily and learning of His ways.

God thunders from Deuteronomy "... and I will make them hear my words, that they may *learn* to fear me all the days that they shall live upon the earth" (Deut. 4:10, KJV, author's emphasis).

At another place in the book of Deuteronomy, God teaches His people that the discipline of tithing diligently will teach one the fear of the Lord. (See Deuteronomy 14:22-23.) Giving God His due breeds a healthy fear into a believer.

The fear of the Lord is essential to effective spiritual authority.

Thirdly, the fear of the Lord must be understood. Proverbs 2:5 promises that if we will seek God, His Word, His wisdom, His understanding and His knowledge in the same way a money-grubber would seek silver and hidden treasure, *then* we will *understand* the fear of the Lord, and find the knowledge of God.

The fear of the Lord is foundational to spiritual authority because it "is the beginning of knowledge" (Prov. 1:7), and God's people "are destroyed for lack of knowledge" (Hos. 4:6, KJV).

The fear of the Lord is foundational to spiritual authority because it "is the beginning of wisdom" (Prov. 9:10), and "wisdom is profitable to direct" (Eccles. 10:10, KJV). Without godly wisdom our authority will have no direction.

The fear of the Lord is foundational to spiritual authority because it "is the instruction of wisdom" (Prov. 15:33, KJV). Wisdom standing alone will do very little for us. We need it to instruct us.

The fear of the Lord is foundational to spiritual authority because it is clean and pure, enduring forever (Ps. 19:9). As an antiseptic, it kills corruptive, detrimental influences that would paralyze our spiritual authority.

The fear of the Lord is foundational to spiritual authority because it "prolongeth days," or as the literal Hebrew says, it "adds" days (Prov. 10:27). We need all the days we can get in order to carry out our marching orders and fulfill our God-given destinies.

The fear of the Lord is foundational to spiritual authority, because in it "is strong confidence" (Prov. 14:26, KJV). Without strong confidence in our God's ability and willingness to act on our behalf, we would not step out to exercise our spiritual authority against the forces of darkness.

The fear of the Lord is foundational to spiritual authority because it is "a fountain of life, to depart from the snares of death" (Prov. 14:27, KJV). God's fountain of life can only be tapped by the fear of the Lord. It will bring us health, peace, prosperity and assurance, and we'll be able to avoid the snares of death, thereby remaining strong to take action against the enemy.

The fear of the Lord is foundational to spiritual authority because by it are "riches, and honour, and life" (Prov. 22:4, KJV), three ingredients that make the work of spreading the gospel easier.

The fear of the Lord is foundational to spiritual authority because it "tendeth to life: and he that hath it shall abide satisfied; he shall not be visited with evil" (Prov. 19:23, KJV). In this verse I see four wonderful promises. Number one is life. This is the God kind of life that He desires all of us to experience. Number two is the ability to abide, to remain steadfast and unmoved. It is not God's desire that the storms of life or the enemies of our soul be successful at washing us out of the way! Number three is the ability to abide satisfied. It is very difficult to exercise our spiritual authority from a place of continual frustration and dissatisfaction. The fear of the Lord gives to us the ability to abide satisfied. Number four is the promise that we will not be visited with evil, or as the New

International Version says, we will be "untouched by evil." It is not that evil will not come, but we will not be leveled by it. What more can we ask for? "There shall no evil befall thee, neither shall any plague come nigh thy dwelling" (Ps. 91:10, KJV).

The fear of the Lord is foundational to spiritual authority because "The Lord taketh pleasure in them that fear him, in those that hope in his mercy" (Ps. 147:11, KJV). What can be better than having the Lord of creation smile down upon your life?

My brother and sister, choose, learn and seek to understand the fear of the Lord God, and you will find the practice of your spiritual authority abounding with success and fulfillment.

6

STRATEGIES OF SATAN

I have always enjoyed studying the histories of the world's great military strategists. Men like Napoleon, Thomas "Stonewall" Jackson, George Patton and Douglas MacArthur have always commanded my respect. These men were masterminds when it came to managing man power for the good of their countries. In our own Virginia county of Highland, "Stonewall" Jackson successfully routed the advancements of the Union army as it sought to enter from the west the famed Shenandoah Valley of Virginia. Here at McDowell, Virginia, he successfully executed a strategy that proved to hold off the wishes of the North for more than two years. In times of war that kind of strategy means a whole lot.

As great as men like Jackson have been, figuring out and executing their strategies for victory, not one of them holds a candle to the stategems devised by satan against the people of God. Other than God Himself and His armies of heaven, satan has probably the most cunning military mind in existence. He is a strategist's strategist. He is the great deceiver, God's number-one enemy; and he is no spring chicken when it comes to deceiving the people of God. Deception and trickery are what strategy is all about, in the final analysis, and satan is a master at both.

*Put on God's whole armor [the armor of a heavy-armed soldier which God supplies] that you may be able successfully to stand up against [all] the **strategies** and the deceits of the **devil*** (Eph. 6:11, TAB, author's emphasis).

There you have it: the strategies of satan. His passion is to steal, kill and destroy everything that is dear to you and God, and he'll use every form of trickery and deceit to accomplish his mission. But the Word of God declares, "we are not ignorant of his devices" (II Cor. 2:11b, KJV). In Jesus we have the potential to walk in absolute victory over all that the devil would bring against our lives. Satan is the author of unconventional warfare, but thank God, we aren't limited to conventional things when it comes to handling him. The weapons of our warfare are "mighty through God to the pulling down of strongholds" (II Cor. 10:4, KJV). There is nothing conventional about using the mighty name of Jesus on somebody, and Philippians 2:10, The Amplified Version, says: "That at the name of Jesus every knee [must] bow!" I believe the Body of Christ on the earth must come to a greater understanding of the awesome power that is invested in that glorious name. Voodoo priests talk about God. Most of the anti-Christian cults acknowledge a christ. But it is the all-powerful name of Jesus of Nazareth that they find easy to avoid because Jesus is the Christ! Jesus is the conquering Christ, and none other can lay claim to the throne He claims for Himself. He declares, "All authority has been given unto Me in heaven and on earth" (Matt. 28:18). He declares, "I am the Alpha and the Omega, the beginning and the ending" (Rev. 1:8, 17; 22:13). He is the first and the last! All human history will be consummated in Christ Jesus (Eph. 1:10), and when He has annihilated the last enemy, "Death," He will put all things under God the Father, that God may be all in all. (See 1 Corinthians 15:25-28.) So it is to this almighty name that we owe our allegiance, and it is to this powerful name that the enemies of God must bow!

There is nothing conventional about drawing the sword of the Spirit and using it on somebody. Hebrews 4 has a few very exciting things to say about the sword of the Spirit, which is the Word of God.

> *For the word of God is living and active. Sharper than any double-edged sword, it penetrates even to dividing soul and spirit, joints and marrow; it judges the thoughts and attitudes of the heart. Nothing in all creation [including satan and his*

schemes] is hidden from God's sight. Everything is uncovered and laid bare before the eyes of him to whom we must give account (Heb. 4:12-13).

What we need to realize when preparing to engage the enemy in warfare is that everything is "laid bare" before our Commander-in-Chief, Jesus Christ! Since He and His Word are one, everything is laid bare before His anointed Word as well. The words "laid bare" in the original Greek mean: "with head thrown back and throat exposed" (W.E. Vine, *Vine's Expository Dictionary of New Testament Words*, p. 660).

When I was in my twenties I did a lot of coon hunting in the mountains of Virginia. A couple of black and tan coonhounds were always in my possession, and I hunted with men who had hounds as well.

Dog fights were something I was no stranger to. When you take a handful of dogs that don't know one another and throw them together for the first time, a fight usually results. Hunters must exercise caution when introducing hounds to a pack. If done correctly, the chances of a fight are cut considerably and the hunters can get on to the joy of hunting. However, regardless of how cautious hunters are, fighting between dogs occasionally occurs.

Something I have noticed when two dogs get in a fight is that the more timid of the two will often give up first. He will roll over on his side, throwing his head back and exposing his neck to the stronger dog. In dog communication that is the universal sign of surrender and a plea for mercy. Most dogs at that point will show mercy to the weaker opponent, allowing it to live, but will themselves emerge as the undisputed victor.

When we go at satan and his hordes of demonic spirits, it is God's intention for us to use the Word He's given us to defeat the enemy. There is a powerful anointing that is released when the believer speaks forth the Word of his God. As I read how Jesus combatted the devil in the wilderness (Luke 4), I see the Word defeating His weaker opponent. The idea that the Word of my God, spoken in faith and boldness from a pure heart, will cause my enemy to throw his head back and expose his throat generates a lot of excitement in me. When your enemy exposes his throat you have won! Complete the job, showing no mercy to him. Take the sharp, two-edged sword of the Word of God and cut his stinking throat! He has had no mercy on you; have none on him! Scripture tells us that Jesus "cast out the spirits [demons] with his word" (Matt. 8:16, KJV), and that the Word of God can "grow mightily and prevail" (Acts 19:20). The Church of Jesus Christ must recover a greater appreciation of and dependence on the prevailing Word of God. It "runs very swiftly" (Ps. 147:15, NKJV); and if it is allowed to "have free course and be glorified" (II Thess. 3:1, KJV), it will indeed prevail in our generation.

The strategies of satan are varied. Let us take the time to examine a few of his time-proven ones, those that have been most effective through the centuries.

Strategy #1 — Fear

King David of Israel prayed, "Hear my voice, O God, in my prayer: preserve my life from *fear* of the enemy" (Ps. 64:1, KJV, author's emphasis). David obviously understood the devastating effects fear could have on his life if it were allowed to run unchecked. An evil enemy was bad enough, but fear of that enemy would prove to be worse. Fear will paralyze you before your opponent, making you vulnerable to his attack.

President Franklin D. Roosevelt once made the statement: "The only thing we have to fear is fear itself," and the great English evangelist, Charles Spurgeon, said, "Fear to fear!" Your welfare depends on it.

According to the Word of God, oppression can be held in check if we will walk free of fear. Isaiah said, "thou shalt be *far from* oppression; for thou shalt not fear" (Isa. 54:14, KJV, author's emphasis). How clear do we have to get in order to drive this important truth home? Overcome fear in your life and the enemy will find it hard to oppress you. John said, "Fear hath torment" (I John 4:18, KJV), which indicates that if we are free from fear we will also be free from the torment that comes with it.

There were times in my struggle with arthritis that a demonic fear would come on me, attempting to overtake me. Gloomy forecasts of physical agony and confinement to a v would pelt my mind like a barrage of machine gun those times I would nearly sink to total despair, doubting my God's ability and His willingness to do anything for me. To make matters worse, the kingdom of darkness would see to it that I saw someone suffering from the advanced stages of arthritis and tell me that was going to be me in just a few more years. The fear that assaulted me was horrible.

Satan's strategy in this type of attack is to get us to dwell constantly on the doom of our situation and to get us to forecast it with our mouths. He knows, all too well, the verse from Proverbs that says, "As [a man] thinketh in his heart, so is he" (Prov. 23:7, KJV). A person who continually dwells on his problems literally becomes all that he fears and worries about. This is our enemy's strategy, to saturate our thoughts with his tormenting words of doom.

Along with this strategy comes his desire to hear us speak out of our mouths those thoughts of doom. Jesus said, "Out of the abundance of the heart the mouth speaketh" (Matt. 12:34, KJV). So what you spend your time dwelling on in your thought life will eventually come out of your mouth — in abundance. This unleashes the enemy to bring it all to pass in your life. Things go steadily from bad to worse, and you don't know why.

His strategy was first to cause you to dwell on your problem until it became a part of your innermost being — your heart and your mind. Secondly, he labored in causing you to speak out your problem with your mouth. His third step in this strategy is to go to work bringing it all to pass — just as you've thought it and spoken it. In essence, you help bring to pass the full potential of your problem with the words of your mouth. See what James had to say:

> *For we all stumble in many ways. If anyone does not stumble in what he says, he is a perfect man, able to bridle the whole body as well. Now if we put the bits into the horses' mouths so that they may obey us, we direct their entire body as well. Behold the ships also, though they are so great and are driven by strong winds, are still directed by a very small rudder, wherever the inclination of the pilot desires. So also the*

> *tongue is a small part of the body, and yet it boasts of great things. Behold, how great a forest is set aflame by such a small fire! And the tongue is a fire, the very world of iniquity; the tongue is set among our members as that which defiles the entire body, and sets on fire the course of our life, and is set on fire by hell* (James 3:2-6, NAS).

When a bystander watches a man on horseback turning the horse in whatever direction he chooses it is not likely that he will notice the bit that has been placed within the horse's mouth. If it were not for the fact that the bit was present within his mouth, the horse may well have gone where he wanted. But the bit, concealed within his mouth and controlled by the rider, was the means by which power was achieved over the horse's entire body.

When a person observes from a distance a massive ship that is being maneuvered into its berth at a harborside pier, it is virtually impossible to see the rudder beneath the water's surface at the stern of the ship, and the important role it is playing. The fact is that the rudder, though a small piece of hardware, is responsible for turning the entire ship.

James says that is how the tongue is — small, but very important. With our tongues we form words that either build up or tear down, minister life or minister death. He explains that a great forest can burn to the ground as a result of the tiniest flame being allowed to burn unchecked. Once the forest has been destroyed, one would rarely look for the tiny flame that started it all.

Our lives are like this. The words we have carelessly slung about have been the cause of so much grief and woe. Many people are experiencing today what they unknowingly called for yesterday. James said that the tongue is the bodily member that "sets on fire the course of your life." That can either be a positive fire fueled with the power of God, or a negative fire fueled by the will of satan. What course is your life on today?

Solomon wrote, "A fool's mouth is his destruction, and his lips are the snare of his soul;" and also that "death and life are in the power of the tongue" (Prov. 18:7,21, KJV).

The grand finale to satan's time-perfected strategy is **death!**

Careless, fear-filled words, spoken again and ag
heart and mouth of a human being, will unleash the de
forces of satan's evil kingdom. That is why it is imperative that we put the Word of God into our hearts in abundance. With our hearts chock-full of the Word, the enemy will be given very little to work with. Our mouths ought to be speaking the Word of God on a consistent basis, and we should be energetically confessing God's victory over our lives each and every day. By doing so, we will build an impenetrable shield against the works of the enemy, and when times of pressure are upon us, our mouths will act like the popvalve on a boiler — out pops the Word of God!

The Psalmist said that even the angels respond to the Word of God as it comes forth in faith from the mouth of an obedient believer. In David's actual words, they "hearken unto the voice of his word" (Ps. 103:20, KJV). The Christian is to be God's voice on the earth, working with the angels, allowing them to minister freely on his behalf.

David also said, "I will take heed to my ways, that I sin not with my tongue: I will keep my mouth with a bridle [and bit], while the enemy is before me" (Ps. 39:1, KJV). Why? Because satan's strategy is to ensnare us by the words we speak. I believe satan assigns certain demons to every one of our lives in order to catch us in careless, destructive speech. They are then to go to work in bringing what we say to pass.

Have you been giving voice to your fears? Determine to stop that, to bridle your tongue with the Word of God, turning life from its destructive course. Feed your faith with the Word, and your doubts and fears will starve to death.

Once I learned the veracity of this dynamic faith principle and put it into practice, God's hand began to work more mightily in my behalf. I saw in the Word that by Jesus' stripes I was healed (Isa. 53:4-5), and so I ordered my words to line up with that. In the face of arthritic pain I confessed loudly and boldly that I was healed. When I learned that the literal interpretation of Hebrews 10:35 says, "Cast not away your *all outspokenness*," I did exactly what it instructed me to do. I became very outspoken about my healing from arthritis. I told the devil and his demons, I told my mother, my father, the clerk at the corner market, and I would have told you had I known you. But most importantly I told God, in the form of thanksgiving and praise. I praised Him for His Word that heals me. I thanked Him for sending Jesus to die on the cross for me. I rejoiced in the reality of His wonderful fellowship. Day after day, month after month, year after year, I spoke forth His Word. I had been given the gloomy prognosis that I'd be in a wheelchair by the time I was thirty, but it didn't happen. I passed the thirty-year mark a number of years ago and I'm still growing strong. No one will ever convince me that faith in God and His Word doesn't work. The Word of God, in my heart and in my mouth in abundance, literally starved out fear and doubt! The Word of God will drive out any form of fear if it's built into one's life on a regular basis. I heard it said recently, "Fear knocked at the door; Faith answered and there was no one there." Build your Faith with the Word of God.

One night several months ago, the symptoms of a certain physical disease came upon my body. Actually, it had been lurking about for several days, pushing a little discomfort and a lot of fear on me. On that particular night, Darlene and I were relaxing in the living room, reading and watching TV. As the evening wore on, the fear became unbearable and the physical discomfort became more obvious to my mind. I tried to dismiss it from my thinking and continue doing what I was doing, but I was unable to. Finally, I got up out of the chair, told Darlene where I was going, and headed to the deserted road that runs in front of our house. Once down there, I began to cry out to God for His mercy and help. The fear that engulfed me that night was one of the worst I've ever had to deal with. A little praise and crying out to God in tears failed to remove it. I lifted up my voice in other tongues for a good while, and that too failed to remove it. It was incessant and unrelenting. Finally, I began to quote the Word of God concerning healing and to make my confessions accordingly. As time went on, the strength of my confessions began to increase, the "gusto" of my all-out-spokenness began to intensify, and sweet release began to be manifest. Like a stylish boxer, I reached the summit of spiritual warfare in a flurry of "faith's confession punches" and sent my opponent sprawling on the canvas of defeat. The fear that had stalked me for days and that had finally pounced upon me to destroy was gone! And with it went every symptom. My victory was the Word of God — returning to it, claiming its truths, confessing it boldly, and seeing it wash out my enemies!

One morning I was in my study reading. My oldest son, Bruce, who was three at the time, was out in the hallway playing. That morning I was reading and meditating on the verses in Psalm 34. The seventh verse says, "The angel of the Lord encampeth round about them that fear Him, and delivereth them." The nineteenth verse says, "Many are the afflictions of the righteous: but the Lord delivereth him out of them all." The twentieth verse reads, "He keeps all their bones: not one of them is broken." I confessed the validity of those precious promises in the form of a prayer to God, thanking Him for mighty angelic protection for my family. Within minutes of confessing those verses, and after I had moved on to another portion of the Scriptures, I heard a most horrible sound out on the stairway. Bruce had gotten too near the head of the stairs and had fallen headlong, banging and bouncing all the way down. I rushed downstairs to pick him up, and rejoiced in my God, finding nary a bruise on his body. I again thanked God that He keeps all our bones: not one of them is broken.

At another time, Darlene and I were out cutting a truckload of firewood. Half of the tree I was working on was suspended somewhat precariously in the air above me, with its butt-end jammed against its standing counterpart. All of a sudden, within a split second, the tree came down on top of me, pinning me to the ground on my back. My chainsaw went one way and my hat went the other. There I was, with better than a ton of tree trunk laying across my legs. Darlene cried out, "O Jesus!" She began to pray in the Spirit, calling on God for help; but the miracle had already taken place. A limb ten inches in diameter that had not been around prior to the accident had been mysteriously thrown to my side as the tree plummeted on top of me. It caught the full weight of the falling tree, which would have crushed my legs beyond repair. I quickly wiggled my way out of my

..icament, stood to my feet, and began to shout praises to my God for His mighty delivering power. That limb had been sawed off earlier and placed flat on the ground, far from the scene of the miracle. An angel of God, "hearkening unto the voice of God's Word," had swiftly moved it to my side just in time to catch the weight of the falling tree. Needless to say, Darlene and I had an anointed worship and praise service on the side of that hill, one we will never forget.

Such are the stories that come from the lives of those who give voice to the Word of the Lord. I encourage you to get actively involved in speaking the words of your God, daily and without hesitation. Fear can be stopped, and God's power can be unleashed on your behalf.

Strategy #2 — Weariness + Exhaustion = Knockout. Satan's Equation for Your Defeat

A Christian who has even a little experience in the conflicts of life knows that "the race is not to the swift" (Eccles. 9:11, KJV). You cannot waltz gingerly through life and receive all God has for you in a short time. The successful Christian life is one that endures the long haul, refusing to give up when conflicts arise and persist. What we receive from God in the way of blessing is too wonderful a testimony to the power of the gospel for satan to sit idly by without contesting it. When we launch out in faith for any Bible blessing, nine times out of ten there will be a fight. Paul exhorted, "Fight the good fight of faith" (I Tim. 6:12, KJV). What we receive from God by faith is much more endearing to us than what we receive when there is no effort on our part. It is God's abundant grace that gives it to us, but it is our faith that receives it from His hand.

If there is a fight of faith, then there must be an enemy to faith. Of course we know there is, and he is as wily an opponent as one can face. But if you're aware of his strategy, you can win the fight.

Let us consider a boxer entering the ring for a big fight. His opponent is a tough, highly trained and seasoned veteran; the man is definitely no pushover. Through years of experience this veteran boxer has developed quite an arsenal of punches, combinations and strategies with which to defeat any c There are jabs of pain and discomfort; combinations of fear, doubt and weariness, the punches of others' failures and misfortunes; all are designed to strip his opponent of a vision of victory. Satan has but one goal for us all, and that is death by a knockout!

A veteran boxer knows better than to stand toe-to-toe with a hungry young fighter. Often a young boxer's strength is superior to that of the older veteran. In Christ Jesus our strength is superior to satan's, and he knows that all too well. The veteran's strategy is to make his younger opponent move around and throw many wasted punches, thus slowly wearing himself out. With high levels of energy being expended early in the fight, the young boxer will become increasingly more exhausted as the fight progresses until, eventually, he'll drop his guard and allow the veteran to throw the punch he's been waiting for. With perfect timing and an ample supply of seasoned power, the veteran can deliver the knockout blow that will send his opponent sprawling across the floor.

In the army, this kind of strategy is known as attrition. The enemy is gradually worn down and weakened, thereby being made vulnerable to the offensive action of his opponent.

Many a sincere Christian has crawled into the ring of spiritual conflict only to discover that the opponent he faces is as capable a fighter as can be found. Satan, or one of his demons, is a master at employing the strategy we are considering. The enemy knows he cannot defeat the Word of God. He knows he cannot defeat us if we are standing on the Word. But he is convinced he can move us off the Word. He will attempt to wear us down by attrition until we become exhausted, lose heart, and relax our guard, thereby allowing him the knockout shot he desires. No matter what it is that you stand for in faith, this strategy will be used against you.

The Enemy's Two Choices

When a believer steps out on the Word of God in order to receive a blessing, he must do so by faith. As he does, he is automatically stepping into a ring of conflict where satan will meet him and try to defeat him. At that very moment, satan (or one of his imps) must do one of two things. He will either oppose the believer's understanding of the Word with an immediate argument, or he will bring forth no argument at all, hoping that the believer will make a hasty, non-quality decision to receive from God.

When, as a young Christian, I was besieged by a ruthless enemy called arthritis, I desperately searched for God's will concerning healing. An abundance of revelation knowledge on the subject began to come my way from the Spirit of God as He opened His Word to me. Steadily I grew in my understanding of the "good, and acceptable, and perfect, will of God" (Rom. 12:2, KJV). Satan's kingdom realized the superlative quality of the decision I would make if I were allowed to grow unhindered in my understanding of God's will. Therefore, he sent his emissaries — demon-deceived people equipped with argument upon argument against the Word of God concerning health. Whatever these dear people said cast doubt on the veracity of the Word of God. They undermined teaching on positive confession of God's Word, saying it was not in the Bible. They spiritualized healing in Christ's sacrifice. They told me of many people they had known who believed the way I did, but had died without securing God's healing. They warned me not to be presumptuous. They said they were afraid I was going off the deep end, taking my religion too seriously. Had it not been for the fact that they were too late, that the good Word of God had already taken deep root in my heart, they might have swayed me from my stand on the Word. When I sent them on their way, they were disgusted with my hard-nosed allegiance to God's Word. But my reaction was not like many others. Only eternity will tell how many dear Christian people have failed to appropriate the blessings of God because of someone's confusing, doubt-filled arguments against the Word.

The enemy's other choice is to do nothing at all, at least not until the believer has rushed through a hasty decision to receive from God. Satan and his demons have a blast with this type of person. Jesus taught that they do all right for a little while, but then when "affliction or persecution ariseth for the word's sake,

immediately they are offended" (Mark 4:17). Once o
they often quit.

Often when one steps out in faith on a promise of God, the symptoms and circumstances will grow worse. At times like this the person better be standing on a quality, no-turning-back decision to believe God's Word regardless of the adversities that surround him.

As a young, unmarried Christian, I greatly desired to be married to a woman of God who was as on-fire as I was. I didn't know very many like that, but I knew there must be one for me somewhere. Dating just any ol' girl wasn't the answer, and so I went to the Lord in prayer, basing my conviction and my standing on His Word. He had said "... when ye pray, believe that ye receive them" (Mark 11:24, KJV), so after I prayed according to that instruction I went my way rejoicing that, by faith, I had a wonderful, Christian wife — sight unseen. Mine was a quality decision and I'm glad it was, because in the months and years that followed I was offered every chance to take things into my own hands, to go and search for the perfect woman. Family and friends pressured me to date non-Christians, to play the field, etc., but I didn't fall for it. I was convinced God would bring us together in wholesome surroundings. He did — in a church I was visiting on one occasion. What first drew me to Darlene was a powerful prayer I heard her pray in the assembly. I thought, "Man that girl knows God!" In time God drew her to me, and our marriage was made in heaven. Thank God I didn't fall to adverse circumstances. Satan had hoped mine was a hasty, non-quality decision to receive a godly wife, but he learned that it was not. It was quality.

Is there, then, anything we need to do before we step out in faith to receive a promise of God? Are there any safeguards? Praise God, there is a safeguard for us.

Our Safeguard: Time to Count the Cost

> *For which one of you, when he wants to build a tower, does not first sit down and calculate the cost, to see if he has enough to complete it? Otherwise, when he has laid the foundation, and is not able to finish, all who observe it begin to ridicule him, saying, "This man began to build and was not able to finish"* (Luke 14:28-30, NAS).

But Jesus said to him, "No one, after putting his hand to the plow and looking back, is fit for the kingdom of God" (Luke 9:62, NAS).

O Lord, my heart is not proud, or my eyes haughty; Nor do I involve myself in great matters, or in things too difficult for me (Ps. 131:1, NAS).

Desire without knowledge is not good, and to be overhasty is to sin and miss the mark (Prov. 19:2, TAB).

Some folks believe that to have knowledge concerning a promise of God and not immediately act on it is compromise. It's not; it is wisdom. Do you see the principle in Romans?

The faith which you have, have as your own conviction before God. Happy is he who does not condemn himself in what he approves (Rom. 14:22, NAS).

If a believer allows himself the time to dig into the Word of God on a particular subject in order to establish it in his heart, he is wise. When he does step out in faith to appropriate the promise, he will be established on solid rock, and the floods and winds of adversity will not topple him. Truly, anything less than this is foolishness and/or presumption.

Questions to Ask Oneself (Weighing-in and Qualifying)

Prior to entering the fight of faith in order to receive something from the Lord, it is always helpful to answer the following questions:

1. Do I really need this, cr is it just a want? If it is only a personal want, is it worth the energy that may be spent in spiritual warfare before the blessing is manifested in the natural realm?
2. Is the Holy Spirit behind me in this?
3. Do I have sufficient Scripture upon which to base my conviction and upon which to stand?
4. Can I make the quality decision that is needful in order to go the long haul if I have to?
5. Are my motives correct? Will Jesus truly be exalted in this,

and am I prepared to fight the good fight of faith to the glory of God?

Into the Ring by Faith

Once the cost has been counted and you are certain that everything checks out for the step of faith, it is time to crawl into the ring. You enter the ring by a sure faith, based on the Word of God and the Holy Spirit's conviction down deep in your spirit-man.

By the prayer of faith (Mark 11:24), the prayer of agreement (Matt. 18:19), the prayer of casting your cares on the Lord (1 Pet. 5:7), or by addressing your mountain directly and making your stand (Mark 11:23; Job 22:28), you crawl into the ring as a bona fide contender, letting everyone know that you are going for the belt (the prize).

Once you are in the ring, it is important to remember that your opponent's strategy will probably be to wear you out; most likely he will not try to knock you out immediately. Around and around the ring you'll seem to go: thanking the Lord for His provision, singing praises to your God, quoting Scriptures that assure you of victory. Your opponent will dance about, throwing a punch here and there just to let you know he's in the fight — trying to keep your energy level at a high enough rate to wear you down.

When he moves in on you with adverse circumstances or symptoms, shooting a discouraging word to your mind, you are often quick to respond with the Word of your God. As you counter his offensive action by slamming a verse at him, or a combination of verses, it bloodies his spiritual nose, knocks him off his feet, and sends him sprawling in the corner. But he gets back up and comes at you again and again, willing to endure your flurry of punches because he honestly believes you will soon become weary in the fight of faith, giving him the advantage he wants. His vicious jabs of doubt, fear, pain and discomfort are relentless; they are intended to take their toll on you. If his strategy works, your faith legs will eventually become as quivering Jell-O, and he'll successfully knock you off the Word of God and out of the ring of faith. He is tenacious —

more so than any bulldog. He fully intends to weary and exhaust you, to see you become offended and disheartened. His clever strategy, Weariness + Exhaustion, will equal knockout if you fail to pace yourself. When one becomes spiritually and mentally exhausted, it is very easy to lose heart. Once one loses heart, the fight is all but over: the gloves drop to the side, and the jaw is made vulnerable to the knockout punch.

What can be done to insure that one doesn't lose heart through exhaustion?

First, look to Jesus, the author and finisher of your faith. Consider what He went through before victory was manifested. Consider what He endured because of the joy that was set before Him. Look to and consider Him, "lest ye be wearied and faint in your minds" (Heb. 12:1-3, KJV). Consider that Jesus **authors** and completes your faith. Consider that He gives you strength to stand when your strength is no more. Consider that His is the arm that never tires when human strength gives way.

There was once a mighty man named Eleazar who stood alone against an army of wicked Philistines. He wielded his human-empowered sword valiantly until his arm grew weary and dropped to his side. Scripture reveals at that point the sword of Eleazar became the sword of the Lord. A power not his own miraculously lifted his feeble arm, causing his hand to "cleave to the sword," and the Lord wrought a mighty victory that day. (See 2 Samuel 23:9-10).

As you fight various battles of faith in the arena of life, it is going to become most important that you learn to rely on God's strength. King David learned this as a young man, and as an old man he proclaimed, "I will go in the strength of the Lord God" (Ps. 71:16, KJV).

Isaiah 40:29 (KJV) says, "He giveth power to the faint; and to them that have no might he increaseth strength." Further on it says, "But they that wait upon the Lord shall renew [lit. — change] their strength" (Isa. 40:31). Like changing shirts, the Christian can change strength. But how? By waiting on the Lord. This doesn't speak of passively waiting for God to do something. No, it means that we can exchange our strength for His strength by actively pursuing fellowship with Him. To wait

on the Lord carries with it the meaning: "to tw
like the strands of a rope, twisted together in
Ecclesiastes says it is not easily broken (
Christians we are to be about the business o
together with His, knowing that in order for the enemy to
us, he will have to break Him.

I once heard it said that when we exchange our strength for His it is like exchanging a flashlight battery for the power plant in heaven. Paul said we are "strengthened with *all* might according to his [God's] glorious power" (Col. 1:11, KJV, author's emphasis). With His eternal might we can't lose for winning!

A second way we can keep from becoming spiritually and emotionally exhausted is by taking advantage of heaven's "refreshment stand." When we are hot and tired in the natural, we often head for the nearest refreshment stand and buy an ice cold drink. If we can find one, we head for an air-conditioned room or the nearest shade tree, hoping for a cool, gentle breeze. In my thinking, the greatest picture of refreshment is the "Nestea plunge" into a pool of sparkling clear water. How many times have I desired to take that plunge after a long, hot day in the hay meadow? Too many times to count.

Thank God, there is a spiritual refreshment stand that is made available to the sojourners on earth. God calls us to come take "the plunge" into the cool waters of His Word and His Spirit. There is a place, Christian, where the gentle breezes blow, bringing refreshment to your weary soul. Let's find it.

> *For with stammering lips and another tongue will he speak to this people. To whom he said, This is* ***the rest*** *wherewith ye may cause the weary to rest; and this is* ***the refreshing*** (Isa. 28:11-12, KJV, author's emphasis).

First Corinthians 14:21 shows the gift of tongues to be the fulfillment of this passage in Isaiah. And we know that one of the uses of tongues in the life of the believer is personal communion with God. As we fellowship with God, praying and singing in tongues as well as in our natural language, we are refreshed spiritually. It helps us to enter the rest that God has made available to us as His children (Heb. 4:9).

> *Bless the Lord, O my soul, and forget not* ***all*** *his benefits: Who* ***satisfieth thy mouth*** *with good things; so that thy youth is renewed like the eagle's* (Ps. 103:2,5, KJV, author's emphasis).

Anointed Bible teacher, Helen Wallace, taught me that the gift of tongues in private prayer is a good thing with which the Lord has satisfied our mouths. When given a chance, it will renew our youth like the eagle's.

My wife, Darlene, said, "Tongues is better than Oil of Olay." We thought that was really neat in light of the fact that millions of dollars are spent annually on Oil of Olay (and similar products) as women desperately attempt to postpone the inevitable aging process. Why not use Oil of Olay and tongues?

Another way in which to partake of God's refreshment stand is by sitting under the ministry of anointed music. When King Saul was being oppressed by an evil spirit, the anointed harp of young David drove the evil spirit away. Scripture says, "so Saul was refreshed" (I Sam. 16:23, KJV).

I have often gone home in the evening after a trying day at work and put on the albums of anointed men and women of God. Whether it is an instrumental album, or one where the minstrel ministers in the Word, I have received Holy Spirit refreshment time and time again.

Scripture says that God "compass[es] us about with songs of deliverance" (Ps. 32:7, KJV). We have many albums of men and women who sing nothing but faith-inspiring Word songs. They sing of God's healing, delivering power — the power of Bible faith. They sing of the glory and majesty of Jesus' name. They carry on about the reality of our redemption from the wicked hands of the devil.

There have been times when, in the middle of the night, Darlene and I could be found downstairs with a sick child, compassing him about with anointed songs of God's deliverance. On every such occasion, fevers have broken and sickness has fled; before daylight our child has felt much better.

Still another way to receive of God's refreshing is to fellowship with Christians of like, precious faith, Christians who don't need ministry from you at the moment, but who can simply surround you with love and encouragement. At one point during Paul's journey to Rome, the centurion, Julius, "courteously entreated Paul, and gave him liberty to go unto his friends *to refresh himself*" (Acts 27:3, KJV, author's emphasis). At another time, Paul stated that the spirit of his dear fellow-laborer, Titus, was refreshed by the Corinthian Christians. The noble saint Onesiphorus was often used by God to refresh the heart of Paul while he was in Nero's prison (2 Tim. 1:16); and the great saint Philemon was regularly employed to refresh the hearts of saints (Philem. 7).

Partake freely of the Lord's refreshing by fellowshipping with saints who truly love and encourage your heart.

Yet another way, and probably the most important way, to receive continual refreshment from the Lord is to continue in the Word (John 8:31). Don't fall for satan's line: "Oh, you already know that verse." Read and examine, again and again, all those precious verses that once meant so much to you. They were faith strengtheners, and they will be again if you'll cherish them. Find joy and strength in them once more, even as you search the Scriptures for new verses that will lead you on to victory.

Search and research the Word of God — search and do it again. In science, great advancements have been made as the "researchers" have approached data from different angles — exploring, experimenting, failing and succeeding. Had they moved on too soon because of familiarity and boredom, the great advancement would never have taken place.

Many of us are only familiar with verses we think we really know. "If any man think that he knoweth any thing, he knoweth nothing yet as he ought to know" (I Cor. 8:2, KJV). God desires that we be more than familiar with His Word.

Stop reading the Bible as a book of rules and regulations. If you are guilty of doing that, you are producing a lifeless form of religion through which you will sink into a pit of indifference and death. This religious approach to God's Word causes burdens to become too heavy, growth to stop, and the joy of being a Christian to slide away. Eventually, Christianity is abandoned altogether. Begin reading the Word as an open door

…n, an open door into God's heart. Relate to Him heart …, spirit to spirit, friend to friend. Tell God you want not …o be His child, but also His friend. If you are only His child a… not His friend, then you have relationship without fellowship. Relationship without fellowship is an insipid thing.

As you get to know God as Father and friend, you'll grow in your love for Him, and it will become a genuine love. To know Him is to love Him; to love Him is to please Him. The rules and regulations will take care of themselves.

Now we have examined several ways to keep from becoming overly wearied and exhausted in the fights of faith that will arise in our earthly pilgrimage. Like faith's "Hall of Famers" in Hebrews 11, we can obtain a good report by standing steadfast in faith (Heb. 11:3), enduring, "as seeing him who is invisible" (Heb. 11:27, KJV), subduing kingdoms, working righteousness, obtaining promises and waxing valiant in fight (Heb. 11:33-34d). The evil one's strategy will not prosper when it is leveled at us, and we will obtain the "better thing" that is available to us through Jesus Christ our Lord (Heb. 11:40).

Weariness + Exhaustion = Knockout: Satan's equation for your defeat. This will not happen if you'll but learn to pace yourself in faith and steadfastness for the long haul.

Strategy #3 — The Detractor

The excellent book, *Restoring Your Spiritual Passion*, by Gordon McDonald, speaks of four types of people who come to bear on the lives of a spiritual person. They are Very Important People (VIP), Very Resourceful People (VRP), Very Nice People (VNP), and finally, Very Draining People (VDP). It is to this last group of people, the Very Draining People, that I want to devote this section of this chapter on the strategies of satan.

The enemy kingdom will always seek to utilize "draining people" in its unending effort to render us ineffective in this war of the ages. I call these draining people "detractors," and I find it is essential that I learn how to protect myself from their constant harassment.

They come in various shapes and sizes, and they are all of

those unlovely people who rarely seem to
but who pull us down, sapping us of spiritua
Often they are Christian people, and that is what
How do they come?

Some detractors come to straighten out your theology.
who came to me when I was being established by God in th
truth of divine healing were potentially very deadly. Very little Scripture backed their arguments, but they had a whole lot of experience to refer to. If not their own experience, they had someone else's to refer to — how they had believed just the way I did, but didn't receive the blessing they were after. Satan's intention in this was to get my eyes off of the Word of God and on to something far less substantial. At times like this it is wise to obey the scriptural instruction of King Solomon in Proverbs:

> *Keep thy heart with all diligence; for out of it are the issues of life. Let thine eyes look right on, and let thine eyelids look straight before thee. Ponder the path of thy feet, and let all thy ways be established. Turn not to the right hand nor to the left: remove thy foot from evil* (Prov. 4:23,25-27, KJV).

Have you ever wondered why it is so important to look straight ahead into the Word of God and not get caught up into looking to the left or right hand? Because "a thousand shall fall at thy side, and ten thousand at thy right hand" (Ps. 91:7, KJV). By gazing upon the defeat and failure of so many thousands in this fallen world, we can easily become deceived into thinking we will fail and become defeated as well. God exhorts us to keep our eyes on His Word. It is to be the final authority in our lives.

The enemy is after the Word of God in our hearts. He knows that the issues of life — those powerful forces of vision, hope, faith, patience and love — are in our hearts, and that against such forces he has no law (Gal. 5:23). By focusing our attention on the defeat of others, he successfully removes our foundation of Scripture and sets us up for his attack. When his attack comes, the one who has been gazing too long at the woes of everybody around him will be unable to believe God for the better way that the Word offers.

This is not to say that we don't reach out to the defeated and needy around us; but as we do, we must be forever considering the provision of the Word of God, lest we be overcome by the woes of the world. It is easy to forget that God is able and willing to do for you what He has been unable to do for others because of their unbelief. While you minister compassionately to the defeated ones around you, don't forget that God has provided a better way for you, and that by faith and unconditional obedience you can partake of it. You are special as a Word-adhering follower of Jesus Christ, but that is the only thing that sets you apart from the people of the world. Rejoice in the fact that there is a secret place in which you can stand by faith, and His name is Wonderful Counsellor, Mighty God, Everlasting Father, Prince of Peace, and Word of God!

There is another type of detractor that comes to bear on the lives of Christians who are dangerous to the security of satan's kingdom. The enemy utilizes them in an effort to control your time. They are those draining people who come to load you down with their latest problem, or perhaps, a longstanding problem they've failed to deal with for one reason or another. Very often they do not want real help, but they do want attention — a lot of attention. If they really received the help you offer, they would see their problems diminish in number and intensity; they would demand less of your time. But they don't want that. So they remain on their spiritual treadmill, sapping you of all the energy you need in order to remain strong and to be able to help others who have genuine needs.

We do this type of detractor an injustice by allowing him or her to continue in his or her selfish habit. If they were really helped it would be one thing, but they're not; they continue for months, and sometimes years, to rape the time of the precious people they hound. I believe swift correction to be the best thing for this type of detractor. They must come to realize that they are selfish, childish and totally out of character with the nature of the God they claim to be following. Tough love is the only hope people like this have. Don't pity them; love them, but be blunt. In the long run you'll be glad you were unwilling to let them have so much of your time.

Yet another type of detractor found in most churches is the grumbler and complainer. They are arrogant, selfish people who insist that their way is the better way, that their ideas are the best ideas. They undermine authority, continually bringing church policy into question; they are ever seeking to turn "flock opinion" in their favor. The damage they inflict is often done in darkness, behind backs, because their deeds are of the darkness. They are rarely bold enough and above-board enough to present their opinions and advice to those with whom they disagree; and when they do, it is often in the most undiplomatic tones. They do not know how to accept those who don't swing in line with their opinions and "insight," and are masters at holding grudges for years. When their leaders fail to agree with and accept their wishes, they add to their list yet another reason why they should be the ones in charge of things — instead of the present leaders. They naturally generate mistrust in the Church of God: a mistrust of authority, mistrust among the flock, and a mistrust in the overall direction and mission of the church. It is no wonder that Paul desired that prayer be made for him, that he would be "delivered from wicked and evil men, for not everyone has faith" (2 Thess. 3:2). The King James Version calls them "unreasonable and wicked men." Detractors are an unreasonable lot, raised up by satan, like Sanballat and Tobiah of old, to frustrate the work of God (Neh. 4:1-3,7-8).

One evening several years ago as I was preparing for a meeting, the Lord spoke to my heart in such an extraordinary way that I thought somebody had walked into the room with me. Of course I immediately knew it was the Lord, and could only stand there in silent awe. He had broken the silence of the room with these startling words: *"I am delivering you from stubborn and rebellious men!"* At the time I had no idea what the implications of such a statement would mean, but in the years since I have come to appreciate the mercy and infinite wisdom of God in this respect.

As I pondered the word God had given me, I began to realize that a Scripture, somewhere in Paul's writing, sounded very similar. I grabbed my concordance and found the verse to which we have referred. In it Paul desires to be delivered from unreasonable and wicked men for not all men have faith (2 Thess. 3:2). But something disturbed me. The verse's ending declared that these men do not have faith. Did it mean that they were not Christians? Some of the detractors that God delivered me from were very definitely Christians, even though they were detractors.

"Lord," I said. "Some of the folks you have delivered me from were indeed men and women of faith, and not as the text says 'men of no faith' ... What about this?"

"*True*," He replied, "*but they do not have faith for the vision I have birthed in your heart for this ministry, and if I allow them to remain they will only prove to be detractors.*"

I saw we were talking about a Bible principle here. Some of those whom the Lord had moved on, and would be moving on, were not necessarily bad Christian people, but they were, for one reason or another, incapable or unwilling to embrace the vision for our ministry that God had birthed in my heart. Therefore, we would both be better off if we were separated, not trying to build together.

It is sad that we cannot all build together. But we can take comfort in the fact that ours is a God of infinite variety. What one man finds easy and exciting to be a part of, the next man may not. That does not necessarily make him inferior to the one who does, but it does possibly say that he has yet to find his niche. God has a niche for every sincere member of the Church of Jesus Christ, and we should encourage each person to find his special place. But woe unto the detractor who will complain and cause trouble even in the place to which the Lord has called him. The persistent grumbling and complaining of detractors will work to spoil the pure work God desires to do, and eventually God will have to judge them severely.

Returning to that word the Lord gave me concerning my deliverance from detractors has proven to be an anchor of my soul in the years since it was given.

Without that awesome word imprinted indelibly in my heart and on my mind, there would have been times when I'd have panicked to see certain detractors angrily leave our midst. I might have run after them, begging them to stay, and compromised my godly convictions, only to bring reproach down upon the work of God. There were even a few times when, as I was seriously contemplating an attempt to retrieve them, God had rebuked me, demanding, "*Don't become yoked again with those from whom I have delivered you*!"

Give little or no place to detractors. They will only prove to sow disharmony and great discouragement in the Church of Jesus Christ. They are a number-one cause of stress lines in pastor's faces, and additional gray hairs on their heads. With noses perpetually out-of-joint about things, they are anything but a joy to be around. Believe me, you are much better off without them.

Still other types of detractors deliberately come to frustrate the purposes of God in your life and work. Some are wolves sent by satan, and they often come in fine sheep's clothing.

When Zerubbabel, Jeshua and the rest of the heads of Israel were rebuilding the Temple in Jerusalem, their enemies came to them saying, "Let us build with you, for we, like you, seek your God" (Ezra 4:2, NAS). The heads of Israel replied, "You have nothing in common with us in building a house to our God" (Ezra 4:3). The enemies were greatly angered, so much so that they did all they could to discourage and frighten the people of Judah, hoping to keep them from building. They hired counselors against them, to frustrate their purpose (Ezra 4:5).

The heads of Israel were wise to the strategy of the enemy, and so were able to avoid deception from the beginning. But suppose the detractors had been able to infiltrate the ranks of the builders, what would have transpired then? Sabotage, no doubt!

The history of Christianity reveals the success of many thousands of detractors who have infiltrated the ranks through the centuries and have ushered in enormous damage to the cause of Christ. If it were not for the glorious fact that, in the end, Jesus will restore that which has been destroyed, I would have to say that the detractors' damage has been irreparable. They've always come in the name of Jesus Christ, very often carrying hearty doses of gifting and anointing to deceive the gullible. People have always been too easily influenced by a person's charisma, and not by the Christ-like qualities that are supposed to be apparent in him. We do well to remember that Jesus said, "Ye shall know them by their fruit" (Matt. 7:20, paraphrase mine), but alas, we choose to know them by their giftings.

A wolf in sheep's clothing may look like a sheep, walk like a sheep, talk like a sheep, smell like a sheep, praise the Lord like a sheep, and attend all the meetings like a good sheep, but his tracks will reveal him! Before getting so worked up and excited over a man or woman's ministry, accepting everything they say or do as being straight from the heart of God, we would do well to closely examine the tracks they've laid. What kind of people are left in their wake? Are they bruised, bleeding and broken? Or are they sound and joyful, fulfilling their destinies in God? Examine the business communities from which they came: Are reports of their business transactions commendable or questionable? By all means examine the spiritual health of their immediate family. Are their spouses joyful and fulfilled? If there are children in their homes, are they ruly? These are questions you have a right to find answers to. And of utmost importance: What do former spiritual yokemates have to say about them? Talk to several spiritual leaders who have a history of involvement with them. What is their unbiased opinion of them? What is their relationship to them now, and why?

Some may think that to ask such questions is to be far too picky. I disagree; I believe it to be wisdom, particularly if you stand to lose time, fortune or reputation because of involvement with an individual. You are not obligated to open your heart and life up to just anyone who desires entrance into them. At all times you are to exercise sound judgment for the glory of God. Beware of detractors; they'll come to you in many forms — manipulating, deceiving, coercing, grumbling. But be as Paul of old, who stated after having to deal with certain detractors: "To whom we gave place by subjection, no, not for an hour; that the truth of the gospel might continue with you" (Gal. 2:5).

Strategy #4 — Strife, Bitterness and Unforgiveness

Our enemy knows well that if he can involve us in

interpersonal conflict to the point where we are filled with bitterness and unforgiveness, then he will successfully bring us into bondage, making us useless to God and His purposes.

Jesus said that if we fail to forgive from our hearts we will be handed over to the tormentors (Matt. 18:34-35). The tormentors are demons that eagerly await the chance to gain a handle on our lives so they can ruin us. Unforgiveness, in any situation, gives them that chance. Be on the look-out for it.

My good friends, Paul and Mary Birt of Victorious Living Ministries, wrote and published a book, entitled, *Living in Instant Forgiveness.* It is an excellent book, showing us a sure-fire way to stay free from the spiritual tormentors. If you program your mind to instantly forgive a person the moment he wrongs you, then your freedom from torment and your effectiveness in God's Kingdom will be maintained. Forgiveness involves an act of your will. You choose to forgive those who have wronged you. You may not immediately feel as though you've forgiven them, but don't gauge it by your feelings; forgive them by faith.

Unforgiveness is often very subtle — lodged within your heart before you even realize it. Beware of its working in your life. Your spiritual welfare depends on your detecting it and dealing with it.

Strategy #5 — A Formula Mentality

Satan is working overtime in the Church in an attempt to get Christians to relate to "Bible formulas" instead of to the God of Bible formulas.

One of the fundamental doctrines of Christ, as listed in Hebrews 6 is "Faith Toward God." Many mistake this as "faith for things," and this is very wrong. It is a reversal of God's proper order. Faith does not begin with you, a problem and a formula — it begins with God! It is the product of a relationship. It is not a formula; it is not the pushing of all the right buttons and quoting all the right verses. It is trusting God as a person, and it begins with the character of God. Faith has no question, whatsoever, about the character of God. Once you know Him intimately, you know His character. Once you know His character, faith is not a struggle. Beware of the formula mentality. God is not a formula. He's not a principle. He is a person.

Perhaps Joshua 1:8 is one of the more popular Bible formulas Spirit-filled believers like to use. It reads, "This book of the law shall not depart out of thy mouth; but thou shalt meditate therein day and night, that thou mayest observe to do according to all that is written therein: for then thou shalt make thy way prosperous, and then thou shalt have good success" (KJV).

That verse contains wonderful promises. Truly it is a working, spiritual formula. However, many Christians fail to apply it as thoroughly as is required for it to work properly. The Word is not to depart out of our mouths. We are to do what the Word says to do, and we are to meditate in the Word day and night. So we begin to confess those verses that suit our fancy, that promise us healing and prosperity. We observe to do what certain Scriptures instruct us to do, but we often ignore a vast host of other, more demanding verses. We also tend only to meditate on the verses that are comfortable to our flesh, verses that give to us our wants and our desires. But what of the "whole counsel of God"? We push all the buttons, quote all our favorite verses, but often remain in strife with fellow Christians, keep our prejudices against other races of people or ethnic groups, continue to cheat (just a little) on our income taxes, and drive ten miles per hour over the legal speed limit. And then we wonder why the formula isn't working for us as the teacher promised it would. It is because we don't truly relate to God and His Word the way we should. Our fellowship with Him is far too shallow, making it easy to hold back from Him important aspects of our lives over which we desperately need to have His Lordship.

Another formula that is misapplied and pillaging the Body of Christ is the "financial vow formula." Major ministries lead gullible Christians, often Christians with whom they have no face-to-face contact, into vowing thousands of dollars into their ministries (how convenient), promising them that by doing so God will supernaturally get them out of debt and make all their problems go away. Issues of morality, ethics or doctrine are rarely addressed in the lives of those who send in their vows, and soon they learn that their problems don't go away.

Many believe that by making a vow they somehow obligate God to move in their behalf. That is foolishness. Before making a vow before God, particularly to some man's ministry, check it out with God. Ask Him if He wants you to make the vow, and find out if He's willing to bless you for making it. Don't assume anything, and allow no man to pressure you into making a hasty vow.

> *It is a trap for a man to dedicate something rashly and only later to consider his vows* (Prov. 20:25).

A young Christian brother made contact with a large Texas-based ministry a couple of years ago and began believing *their* promise that if he vowed to send them so much of his paycheck every month, God would get him out of debt. I was able to step in and help him see that sending money regularly to a ministry *does not* guarantee God's miraculous intervention in your financial affairs. If other key issues in your life are pleasing to Him, then financial benevolence will certainly help. But the giving alone won't do it.

Before hastily pledging to send money to the ministry, my friend took more time to seek God's will, and in doing so discerned it was not God's will for him to pledge to that particular ministry at all. He let them know.

For months after his decision, he continued to receive mail and occasional phone calls as that ministry persisted in attempts to add him to their list of sponsors. Personally, I think they are unethical by refusing to accept his decision not to vow.

Do not be pressured by any ministry, no matter how great its name; and never be so gullible as to believe that because you give, God is obligated to bless you in return. He is often looking at other, weightier matters in your life. Seek to satisfy His expectations in these areas and stop trying to work some kind of financial vow formula. He wants your heart, primarily.

Truly Know God

Isaiah 43:10 speaks of "knowing and believing" God. If you

first know Him, you'll have little problem believing Him. Reverse this order and you'll fail somewhere down the road.

Look at Abram's experience with God. God said some interesting things to him that can help us today.

> *And when Abram was ninety years old and nine, the Lord appeared to Abram, and said unto him, I AM the Almighty God; walk before me, and be thou perfect. And I WILL make my covenant between me and thee, and will multiply thee exceedingly* (Gen. 17:1-2, KJV, author's emphasis).

If we were to read on, we would notice a series of "I WILLS" following God's revelation of himself as "I AM." He doesn't begin by saying "I WILL," but begins by saying "I AM." The "I WILLS" are dependent upon the "I AM." Many times people are trying to talk themselves into experiencing the "I WILLS," but they don't have a revelation of the "I AM." A revelation of God's nature is foundational to the quickening of faith in one's life. If one merely has a formula mentality and not a relationship with God, sudden pressure coming on his life will cause him to jump for the Bible in desperation, anxiously trying to find a way out of it; but that's not faith toward God.

The Apostle Paul prayed, "That I may *know* Him" (Phil. 3:10, KJV, author's emphasis). The Amplified Bible put it this way: "That I might recognize and understand Him." And what is God's desire? Read Jeremiah:

> *But let him that glorieth glory in this, that he understandeth and knoweth me* ... (Jer. 9:24, KJV)

Beware of satan's strategy of pulling you off into a relationship with a bunch of formulas, and not the God of the formulas. God wants you to know and understand Him. Out of this, other things will flow correctly.

Strategy #6 — Subtle Manipulation

A literal rendering of Ephesians 6:12 reveals that the Church is wrestling "the world rulers of this present darkness." The word "ruler" comes from a Greek word meaning, "to seize, retain and control"; hence, we are wrestling spirits that desire to dominate us. If their hold is solid enough in any given situation, they will dominate. If their hold is not solid enough, they will manipulate. Either way, they will get people to do what they want done.

To manipulate means, "to operate, work, or manage skillfully; to influence artfully: to control the action of by skillful management." Satan's kingdom desires to manipulate human beings — particularly Christians who pose a threat to the stability of his kingdom.

The primary tools he uses in order to subtly manipulate us are other people. Often, the people he uses most effectively are the people we're closest to. Many a grandpa or grandma has become a manipulative force in the lives of younger members of the family. Fathers and mothers are often utilized as well. The proper use of rightful authority is not in view here; I am talking about an unhealthy use of manipulation and domination that causes the one being manipulated or dominated to lose a sense of identify and confidence. They no longer feel free to think or act for themselves without an overbearing concern for what the person who controls them will say or do. This kind of influence is akin to witchcraft, and although it begins as a soulish force, it can quickly give way to the demonic. There are demons of witchcraft literally controlling whole households in the United States, and often their primary agents are strong-willed, overbearing family members.

Two types of witches exist: those who know they are witches and those who do not. In most cases, the latter type is much more destructive than the former, because no one deals with them as though there is anything supernatural involved. If we are up against a man or woman who knows he or she operates in witchcraft, one who deals in curses and spells and who cultivates satan's power in his or her life, then we can more readily know when and where to combat his or her powers. But that is not always the way it is when we're up against one who doesn't know they are being used by witchcraft. These types work their influence under a subtle covering. They may be a grandma or a grandpa or a mama or one's big sister; and in most cases they don't realize they are being used that way.

A sure-fire result of witchcraft in a family will be the absence of strong spiritual males. The men in the family may be successful in all other areas of life, but they never seem to take their spiritual position of authority and influence in the home or the church. In essence, they're spiritual wimps!

In some cases, a strong, domineering mother or grandmother will wield the brunt of her influence on one particular child or grandchild. The effects on that child can be devastating. Often the child winds up as an emotional basket case, or a spoiled-rotten brat — for life! I know of one case where the grandma usurped the authority of the child's mother and father time and time again, causing the child to lose all respect for them. This, in turn, brought onto the child the curses mentioned in the Bible for dishonoring one's earthly parents.

Witchcraft is often the hidden antagonist in homes and marriages. The spirit of witchcraft in this country is a direct cause of the tremendous breakdown of marriages. One in two marriages are ending in divorce, and I lay much of the blame at the doorstep of witchcraft.

There are also witches running churches. Many strong, domineering men and women have seized the reins in local churches across the land, stifling the work of the Holy Spirit and the prophetic unction He desires to birth in our midst. Their evil influence is felt in every sector of church life. When the elders of a church have to worry about what a strong, overbearing member in their fellowship will think of their decisions, then in all probability, witchcraft is already present and at work.

I knew a pastor's wife who ran both her super-passive husband and the four churches that were allotted to their charge. I have a nose for witchcraft, and so I couldn't stand to be around her. She was arrogant and bossy, and when she yelled, "Leap!" everyone asked, "How high?" Needless to say, their spiritual work in that community didn't amount to a hill of beans. Eventually God removed them and replaced them with a much more gracious spiritual couple.

What are some of the forms in which manipulation and witchcraft find their expression?

1. Witchcraft and manipulation sometimes find their expression through crying, whining or pouting when one doesn't get his or

her way. The intention is that everything will be made miserable and unpleasant for everyone involved. People are allowed to employ this form of manipulation from a very early age. How many times have we seen the incessant whining, crying or pouting of a spoiled child bring his parents' decisions over to his favor? Too many times to count, I'm sure. Little, whining babies grow up to be big, whining babies who cleverly utilize this form of manipulation in order to influence the people in their lives.

2. Manipulation sometimes finds its expression in the infamous "silent treatment." Many a wife (and husband) has spoken inwardly to his or her spouse, saying, "Well, if you won't see things my way, I just won't talk to you for several days." You can see how such a rude and selfish form of manipulation could eventually dry up the love that is in a marriage.

3. Another form of manipulation prevalent in society today is the "temper tantrum." People actually get down on their bellies, pounding their fists onto the floor and kicking their feet, in order to convince those near to them that they should see things their way. And it is not only children who employ this nasty form of manipulation. I have counseled couples where one of the two was guilty of this terrible reaction to not getting their way.

4. Many resort to using fear tactics on their friends and loved ones in order to get their will accomplished. One such fear tactic comes in the form of threats.

A woman sends unspoken, but definite, vibrations to her husband or other family members that if she gets too disappointed concerning a particular matter she's liable to have a nervous breakdown, go insane, or, God forbid, kill herself. By waving such possibilities before their faces, she is able to keep them all on pins and needles, cleverly manipulating them into courting her fancy. This form is much more common than you realize.

Another form of threat concerns inheritance.

I know a young man whose father threatened to disown him and cut him out of his will if he didn't stop attending a certain Spirit-filled church. The young man stood to lose a large farm and a considerable supply of stocks and bonds. He eventually stopped attending the church and hasn't darkened its doorway since he left. How pitiful; what a nasty display of manipulative witchcraft from his godless father. God have mercy on him.

Inheritance is a very common subject that manipulative and domineering people bring up to the generation following them. It is much like putting a bit in a horse's mouth. The domineering rider can turn the animal in whichever direction he chooses, or stop him at will. Threats of disinheritance are the bits that are used.

Blackmail is another common form of manipulational threat. "If you'll do this for me, I won't reveal your secret sin." Children learn how to utilize this tactic at an early age: "If you don't clean my room for me today, Jim Bob, I'll tell Mama what you did in school yesterday."

Still other forms of threatening involve harm to loved ones, physical thrashings by schoolyard bullies, the threat of vandalism to personal property, etc. The list can become rather long.

5. Manipulation often finds expression through nagging. This persistent form of manipulation has pressured many a man to give in to the desires of a highly determined wife, mother or doughter — even against his better judgment.

6. Another form of manipulation which is commonly used in households throughout the world, is sickness or disease. I am not at all implying that all sickness is used as a form of manipulation, but many times it becomes convenient for its victim to utilize it in controlling the time and energies of others.

There are folks who really don't want to be well, because being sick brings them attention and pity. Many folks thrive on this. Jesus once asked a man, "Wilt thou be made whole?" (John 5:6, KJV), indicating the distinct possibility that maybe he didn't want to be healed.

Many a mother has found it convenient to "get" a migraine headache when she has been unable to get her way. Her whole day is then spent on the couch, and from it she undertakes to make her entire family miserable through her sickness. Whether it is feigned or genuine, it easily becomes used as a subtle from of manipulative bondage through which her family becomes enslaved. Statements like, "Don't do anything to upset Mama, she might take one of those awful migraines," become commonplace. And they're correct; she might "take" one in order to make the day miserable for everybody else.

7. Manipulation often finds expression through the soulish prayers people pray. When anybody in their own natural willpower and intentions decides to get somebody else to do something, the force that they are exercising is soulish. Very often, this soulish force is expressed through soulish prayer. If carried on, it will likely open the person up to the demonic. Let me illustrate.

The warlock that I wrote about in the first chapter of this book went several times into the restroom while I was speaking. While there, he prayed that God would straighten me out and protect the people from hearing what I had to say. Those were not Spirit-of-God inspired prayers; they were demonic. And we had a confrontation later that evening. The spirit of witchcraft, of manipulation through soulish prayers and fear tactics, tried to bring me under its control.

How many of us have been guilty of praying soulish prayers in an attempt to get God to make people do what we selfishly wanted them to do? This form of manipulation greatly displeases God. Although it does not motivate Him to respond in our behalf, it does motivate the kingdom of darkness. It does so much more than we can comprehend with our natural minds. Many a life has been fouled up by the soulish, and even demonic, prayers of selfish people. If you've been guilty of this, repent!

8. Another form of manipulation is deception. It may involve the bearing of a false witness, the telling of half-truths, or the withholding of important truth concerning a matter so that decisions can be made in one's favor.

9. Flattery has also been a subtle form of manipulation that many have used in order to get people to see things their way and get them to do what they want them to do. A flatterer seeks to please by insincere praise and attention, hoping that such undue attention will win a special place of power with the one being flattered. What saith the Word?

He that goeth about as a talebearer revealeth secrets:

therefore meddle [intermix] not with him that flattereth with his lips (Prov. 20:19, KJV).

Don't get close to a flatterer, and don't let him get close to you. He is nothing more than a subtle talebearer who will treat you as the exception. He will flatter you in order to make you receptive to the poison he wants to inject, turning you against other people and in favor of himself.

A lying tongue hateth those that are afflicted by it; and a flattering mouth worketh ruin (Prov. 26:28, KJV).

A man that flattereth his neighbor spreadeth a net for his feet (Prov. 29:5, KJV).

Flattery is soft soap, and soft soap is 90% lye (American proverb).

It is obvious that a flattering tongue brings ruin to the one being flattered by it. It is very deceptive, because the ruin doesn't come all at once. It is gradual — a diabolical set-up from the pit of hell that will surely enslave its victim in the fowler's snare. Slowly the trap closes.

Daniel 11:21 (KJV) speaks of the northern king, Antiochus IV Epiphanes, who "obtain[ed] the kingdom [of Israel] by flatteries." He got what he wanted by the use of flattery. History reveals him as a great persecutor of the Jewish people, and he is a type of the coming antichrist. Antichrist, too, will be a great flatterer who will successfully deceive the nations of the earth. Daniel goes on to prophecy that antichrist, by smooth words (flattery), "will turn to godlessness those who act wickedly toward the covenant, but the people who know their God will display strength and take action" (Dan. 11:32, NAS). This is happening today in the society of the godless. Those people who act wickedly toward the covenant by not accepting Jesus Christ as Lord are being turned to more ungodliness by the "smooth talk" of the secular humanists. But those people who know their God, Jesus Christ, are rising up as never before. This agrees with the following verse from Revelation.

He that is unjust, let him be still more unjust: and he which is filthy, let him be still more filthy: and he that is righteous, let him be still more righteous: and he that is holy, let him be still more holy (Rev. 11:11, a literal amplification from the Greek).

The dividing of the way is upon us. In the coming days, months and years, it will become increasingly obvious who belongs to God and who belongs to satan's kingdom.

Proverbs speaks of a woman who "flatters" with her words (Prov. 7:5), and "with the flattering of her lips she force[s]" men to do what they ought not do (Prov. 7:21, KJV). Can't you see the manipulation through flattery?

Be diligent before God so that He might be able to give you discernment as to when flattery is being used on you; and for goodness' sake, if you have come to realize that you have been guilty of using flattery in order to win someone's approval, repent now, turning from this evil, and let your approval come from God.

10. Another form of manipulation comes from strong, logical-thinking personalities that always come across to you as though they have thought it all out and their way is the right way. They leave no room for disagreement; and if you do withstand that cock-sure confidence, you are made to feel like a moron.

Folks like this always have a condescending aura around them. They always leave people of a weaker personality feeling unsure about themselves or bad about themselves.

Such manipulating people are usually highly gifted in "gab" and thoroughly enjoy drawing their victims out into "meaningful discussion." Discuss things with them and they'll buffet you with their logic and overpowering persuasive abilities.

If you're under the influence of this type of person, you'll subconsciously be looking to them for the approval or disapproval of anything you do or say. They are like a foreboding cloud hanging over your life, and they sap spiritual joy and vitality from your being.

When tied up with a person like this, you'll find that their precious schedule means everything to them and yours means very little. When they suggest that you do something, you feel very little room for hesitation or questioning. In essence, you become their idiot.

If you find you're under such manipulation, break off your relationship with them immediately, no matter what the cost is! If you don't, you'll come to the place where you will lose all self-worth and identity. That is a godless way to live. Break free and begin to live again! (For more teaching on this type of manipulator, I suggest you read *Breaking Controlling Powers*, by Roberts Liardon.)

Forms of Manipulation That Don't Come Through People

We have looked extensively at how satan uses people to manipulate our time, energies and resources. But he also uses many other tools of the trade. I categorize these as circumatances and symptoms that hinder. They are physical illness and pain, accidents, natural catastrophes, breakdowns that come at inconvenient times (sometimes God is involved in these situations for our good), misunderstandings or a lack of thorough communication, etc. Regardless of what form it takes, the enemy's kingdom will use it to hinder you from carrying out your mission for God. That is why it is a good practice, each morning, to bind the devil and his imps in the name of Jesus. Jesus said, "And I will give to thee the keys of the kingdom of heaven: and whatsoever thou shalt bind on earth shall be having been bound in heaven: and whatsoever thou shalt loose on earth shall be having been loosed in heaven" (Matt. 16:19, lit). In other words, by the time you bind or loose on earth, it is done in heaven as well. The power of binding is a tool we can use in order to keep the devil in check. The English word "bind" translates from the Greek word "duo," meaning to fasten or tie, as with chains. It is not unlike tying up an animal to keep it from straying. Using the authority delegated to us as believers, we ought to be fastening up the cohorts of satan every day — especially in our spiritual jurisdiction.

One ought, also, to loose the power of heaven in his behalf, each and everyday. God's Spirit and His angels stand ready to minister graciously to our many needs.

I was the guest speaker in a church in an eastern city one

Sunday morning, and I taught on the power of binding and loosing. One couple who had been having many tremendous problems took my message to heart, went home and began to apply this powerful truth. I happened to see them a few weeks later and they joyfully reported that within only a few days of applying the tool of binding and loosing, their unfavorable circumatances and hardships began to turn around. I have seen this happen time and time again.

Begin to bind the forces of satan daily, not allowing them to manipulate your time, energy and resources to suit their cause. If you fail to see a turn around immediately, don't give up; in due time you will see improvement. What have you got to lose? Scripture teaches, "And let us not be weary in well doing: for in due season we shall reap, if we faint not" (Gal. 6:9, KJV). We do well when we bind or loose spiritual forces for the good of ourselves and others.

7

The Lesson of Times and Seasons

*To every thing there is a **season**, and a time to every purpose under the heaven* (Eccles. 3:1, KJV, author's emphasis).

Perhaps the hardest lesson for a warfare-minded Christian to learn is the lesson of times and seasons. As a young minister of the glorious gospel, I deemed myself fit and more than equal to the task of taking the gospel to the world — immediately! I foolishly catapulted myself onto thirteen radio stations in major cities up and down the eastern seaboard in an effort to make God use my ministry for "His" glory. In time I learned that what man builds, man must also maintain, and that his puny shoulders are neither broad enough nor stout enough to carry the load.

Understand, I was consumed with a vision of doing great things for the Kingdom of God, and that was laudable; but my timing was all wrong. It is not enough merely to do the right thing or to have the right purpose. In order to enjoy success and blessing, we must do the right thing at the right time, and we must carry on the right purpose at the right season. When our Lord says, "*Now*," it is foolish, presumptuous and vain to say, "Later." When He says, "*Later*," it is absurd for us to answer, "Now." It is the job of the Holy Spirit to tell us what and when, and it is our responsibility as spiritual people to stay in a place where we can hear Him when He speaks. Anything less than this means continual frustration.

God was extremely merciful to me in those early years of Christian ministry; I made so many unwise decisions and foolish mistakes. Had it not been for His marvelous grace I would have stumbled, fallen and never risen again. But God was teaching me lessons concerning times and seasons, and one way or the other He was going to get me through it. Of course, His perfect way of teaching me these things would have been through His Word, but all too often I failed to give the proper "measure of thought and study ... to the truth" I read therein (Mark 4:24, TAB). And so, frustration with all its bitterness became my tragic teacher. We must understand times and seasons, and stop trying to force God's hand.

Mercifully, God redeemed all things for Himself, making at least a little something out of all my failures. He taught me a number of invaluable lessons, the least of these not being the lesson of times and seasons. If I had to take my pick of the most important lesson young Christians must learn in order to be useful to God over the "long haul," I would definitely choose the message contained in this chapter. If you are relatively young in the Lord, don't read this chapter with a nonchalant, lackadaisical attitude, but seriously ponder the message contained herein. It may well mean the difference between whether you cross the finish line or not. I am dead serious. The days are going to grow no easier, and only those Christians who understand what Bob Mumford calls "the seasonal nature of the Christian experience" will keep from becoming casualties.

God's Dealings With Creation

Following the flood that destroyed the inhabitants of the world, except for Noah and his family, God made the following statement:

> *While the earth remaineth, seedtime and harvest, and cold and heat, and summer and winter, and day and night shall not cease* (Gen. 8:22, KJV).

From this verse of Scripture it is easy to see that God deals with creation in a seasonal manner. It is imperative that we know this. Solomon wrote that there is a time for birth, and a time for death; a time to plant, and a time to harvest; a time to break down, and a time to build up; a time to cast away stones, and a time to gather stones; a time to keep silence, and a time to speak (Eccles. 3). We must realize that God is outside of time and history, and that dealing with our world on a seasonal basis does not disturb Him at all. But all too often it tears us up. We are too earthbound in our thinking. We think as other men think, spend our time as other men spend their time, and judge the way other men judge. God wants us to break from this mold and dare to be "otherworldly" in our deliberations and actions. We must "set our affections on things above, not on things on the earth. For we are dead, and our lives are hid with Christ in God" (Col. 3:2-3, free translation).

Oftentimes, we have related life as a whole to one cycle of seasons. We have viewed youth as springtime, young adult years as summertime, middle-age years as late summer and fall, and old age as wintertime. We all have acknowledged that death follows wintertime. I honestly believe that this way of looking at life has robbed too many people of their spiritual initiative.

It is far better to look at life as having many spring-through-wintertime cycles, for by doing this, you'll always function in wintertime as though spring is right around the corner. You will understand what I am saying more fully as you read on. But first, let's go back to the Word.

> *If you follow my decrees and are careful to obey my commands I will send you rain* ***in its season*** (Lev. 26:3-4a, author's emphasis).

On any good farmland, rainfall must be seasonal. If it were to rain the year round, the farmers would not be able to get their plows into the fields in order to prepare the ground for the springtime planting. There must be dry times so the ground can be worked and the seeds planted. Afterwards, let it rain! The rain will cause the seeds to germinate and spring forth from the ground, and the farmer will be well on his way to having a bountiful crop. We must realize that there is a time for dry weather, a time for wet weather; a time for hot weather and a time for cold weather. They all work together to bring forth a bountiful harvest. Too many Christians simply don't understand this vital principle; so when they experience times of dryness, extreme cold or heat in their lives, they want to quit.

Let's read about another man who obviously understood the seasonal nature of the Christian experience.

> *Blessed is the man that walketh not in the counsel of the ungodly, nor standeth in the way of sinners, nor sitteth in the seat of the scornful. But his delight is in the law of the Lord; and in his law doth he meditate day and night. And he shall be like a tree planted by the rivers of water, that bringeth forth his fruit* ***in his season****; his leaf also shall not wither; and whatsoever he doeth shall prosper* (Ps. 1:1-3, KJV, author's emphasis).

Here we have the picture of a person who is "instant, in season [and] out of season" (II Tim. 4:2, KJV), plowing when it is time to plow and reaping when it is the time of harvest. Coupling the prerequisites for a fruitful harvest listed in these verses with the prerequisites listed in the Leviticus verses, we readily see that what one does when the excitement of the harvest is not taking place is very important. These are the wintertimes, the dry times, we all encounter as Christians. According to the verses we have looked at, we are to be following God's decrees for our lives: obeying His commands, avoiding the unstable counsel of the godless, and avoiding wrong fellowship. The Word of God is at all times to be the object of our meditation and our delight. I told a woman not long ago that her only problem was that she did not spend enough time meditating on God's Word and rejoicing in His presence. If she would get flat on the floor and cry out to God, beseeching Him for a restoration of the spiritual passion she once had, He would start giving it back to her. But she doesn't want to do that. She wanted me to wave some sort of spiritual wand over her head and drive all her discouragement away. I couldn't do it. Scripture says, "*Build up yourselves* on your most holy faith, praying in the Holy Ghost" (Jude 20, KJV, author's emphasis). Until she is willing to do her part, the parts other Christians can play in building her up will be of little effect.

Returning to verse three of Psalm one, we see, "he bringeth forth his fruit *in his season*." It is helpful to know that God doesn't expect fruit out of season. He realizes more than we do that fruit is seasonal. But on the other hand, every Christian is to have fruit-bearing seasons. Unless a Christian is faithful with the prerequisites we have looked at, his life will be pathetically lacking in the fruit-bearing seasons it should have. At all times we should be drawing vitality from the Word of God and from time spent fellowshiping with the Father in prayer. His will is that we be fruitful, evergreen and prosperous.

Springtime

This is the time of flowers, beautiful smells, songbirds and excitement. In Virginia the air begins to warm and everyone begins to spend more time outside, working on projects they planned for during the cold winter months. During the spring optimism replaces pessimism, the days grow longer with each new sunrise, and life seems to take on new meaning.

Farmers begin to work their soil in preparation for the coming growing season; there's expectation in the air. Springtime is a time of hard work, but the temperature is pleasant and strenuous work doesn't seem all that taxing. It feels good to be back in the tractor seat, to hear the roar of a lawnmower, to hoe in the garden soil once again. In springtime one is easily surrounded by the sights, sounds and smells of new life. What a glorious time!

Applying all of this spiritually really isn't that hard. Thank God for the wonderful experiences of our spiritual springtimes, those times when we are excited about the work of God and our role in it. These are the refreshing times we all need in order to lead fruitful lives that ultimately glorify God. But springtime doesn't last. It hurries along to summertime.

Summertime

When summer hits us, the heat is turned up. All of a sudden the labor that didn't tax our physical bodies during springtime really does a number on us. Hoeing in the garden becomes a real chore. Pushing the lawnmower around the yard suddenly loses its joy. The novelty of the work that pleased us during springtime is lost, and what carries us through these hot, dry times is a commitment to the harvest.

Summer is a time of heat, rain, growth and maturity. The grapes are green and sour on the vine, but thank God, there are grapes.

Summer is a time of keeping the weeds out of the garden so that the produce you're growing won't be choked.

Summer is a time when sweat runs down your forehead, stinging your eyes and blurring your vision, but you keep your hand to the hoe because you know the harvest is near.

Applied spiritually, we see that summer is the time when our commitment to the work of God will pull us through. The hot sun beats down on our heads, tempting us take a sabbatical from the work and let the weeds grow. But we won't do that because we see the green tomatoes and young peppers, and we know the harvest is coming. Thunderheads full of lightning and rain billow over the horizon, threatening to halt our work, but we are committed to the harvest.

When it is not the "fun" thing to do, we pray and intercede for the harvest. As all circumstances and symptoms cry out against us, we "hold fast to our confession of faith" that there will be a bountiful harvest. After the novelty of faith's confession has long since worn off, we still speak the Word of God over what we are doing. The sweatbees sting us, the hornets have built their nests, the hot sun beats mercilessly upon us, but we are committed to the harvest. My friend, this is summertime, and we all go through it. It is often what separates the men from the boys in spiritual matters.

When I was a farmer making thousands of bales of hay during the course of a summer, I found that the most difficult part of the work was rounding up enough high school boys to assist me in the hayfields. With each passing year the boys grew lazier. They didn't mind taking the easy jobs, but it was the hard and hot work of the hay meadow that they avoided like the plague. My dad and I finally wound up doing it all ourselves.

If this problem is present in your life when you face the heat and discomfort of spiritual summertimes, you had better deal ruthlessly with it and set your will to work in spite of it. If you don't, you'll enjoy little or no harvest.

In spiritual summertime we often pray when it is not fun, read and study the Word even though it seems lifeless to us, and walk close to God when no excitement accompanies it. It is during this time that we mature more rapidly than at any other time in our Christian experience. At the time we may not realize it, but afterward we learn that the discipline has "yieldeth the peaceable fruit of righteousness" for us who were trained by it (Heb. 12:11, KJV). Scripture says, "Endure hardship as discipline" (Heb. 12:7a). It is during the heat of your spiritual summertimes that you get to put this command into practice. Endure it properly and you'll be fruitful.

Autumn: The Time of Harvest

Autumn, wonderful autumn. The days are shortening now, but the harvest is abundant — that is, if one did his work during the other seasons. Apples, potatoes and pumpkin pies are everywhere now. The root cellars are filling up rapidly as the year's produce is being gathered, canned and stored away. As one old-timer said, "It's time to get what you can, and can what you get!" It is an exciting time.

We men, living in the mountains of Virginia, love to show off our woodpiles in the fall. The ladies like to show off their root cellars. There's just something special about gathering in an abundant supply of goods in preparation for the coming winter. Autumn is a time of wonderful fulfillment of one's dreams and expectations. All the blood, sweat and tears of the other seasons seems to pay off in the fall.

Applied spiritually, autumn and the harvest are those blessed times when it seems all is paying off in your life and ministry. People are receiving from you and you feel as though you're on top of the world. Time in the Word of God abounds with revelation knowledge, and prayer proves to be one of the most exhilarating times scheduled into your glorious day. You ask; God hears and answers. Nothing seems to stand in your way, and if it dares to, it does so at its great peril. Demons flee from before you wherever you go, and everything you put your hand to prospers abundantly. What an exciting time autumn and the harvest are. But then comes winter.

Wintertime

This is the time of year when all of our great projects and fun times get buried under six feet of snow. It is the time of year when everything seems to grind to a cold, lifeless halt. The weather outside is blusterous, impersonal and merciless. All the songbirds have taken a vacation in the South and the pretty colors of the other three seasons have given way to those that are cold and drab.

At our farm high in the mountains of western Virginia, we grow weary of wintertime, because the weather is so harsh and there's very little one cares to do outside. The days are short and the nights are long. Though our house is warm and snug inside, we get tired of being confined to it for so many hours of the day. But, as with all seasons, wintertime is a necessity.

> *Awake, O north wind; and come, thou south; blow upon my garden, that the spices thereof may flow out* (Song of Sol. 4:16, KJV).

God commands the cold north wind of wintertime to blow because He knows that winter helps prepare everything for spring when spices will begin to flow out of the garden. Psalm 148:8 declares that snow and stormy winds fulfill God's Word. Therefore, "he saith to the snow, 'Be thou on the earth!' " (Job 37:6). All farmers rejoice to see the snows fall and lay heavy on the earth, even though they bring their share of inconveniences. Farmers know that snow adds valuable nitrogen to the soil, out of which they will grow valuable crops in the years to come. Heavy snows replenish water supplies as they melt slowly into the ground. Wintertime is so vitally necessary.

Winter is the time of year when the land takes a rest. Christians need to begin utilizing the wintertime seasons of their lives as good opportunities to catch up on a little rest as well. In spiritual things, wintertime is the occasional season when things begin to slow down. Sometimes you feel as though all your spiritual "goosebumps" have gone into hibernation. The colors are gone, the thrill of being a Christian is nowhere to be found, and if you are young in the Lord you might begin to think you are no longer saved. But it is not a time to fret. It's a time to dig in, a time to settle in and reestablish yourself in the basics of the Christian faith.

Wintertime is the season of the year when farmers go over their machinery with a fine-toothed comb, replacing old, worn-out parts, and getting everything ready for the coming planting season. They don't view winter as a bad time at all, but as an essential time for greater things to come. Many Christians, on the other hand, fail to see the value of the wintertime season and often fall victim to fits of despair and gloom. This is the time when they figure they have a demon and so go about looking for somebody to cast it out. But the "magic wand" of casting out something that isn't there fails to alleviate their distress.

As Christians, we must learn to enter into a spiritual rest in these matters. Understanding and accepting the seasonal nature of the Christian experience proves to be essential for the long haul. "The race is not to the swift" (Eccles. 9:11, KJV), but is to him who paces himself for the duration. Paul was able to say at the end of his long and fruitful life, "I have finished my course, I have kept the faith" (II Tim. 4:7, KJV). He understood the principle of times and seasons. He knew "both how to be abased, and ... how to abound" in his Christian experience (Phil. 4:12, KJV). The peace of God kept his heart and mind through Christ Jesus, no matter what the spiritual season was; and he proved to be an overcomer in this life.

As a Christian warrior, you will have to understand the kinds of pressure the enemy will bring upon you when he catches you in a wintertime season of your life. Let's not be ignorant of his devices.

Wintertime Accusations

Satan is called the accuser of the brethren in Revelation. He is an old warhorse when it comes to the diabolical art of accusation. When you are trodding along in a wintertime season of your Christian experience, satan will send a demon or two to accuse you of:

1. *Failure.* They'll pinpoint every time or place where you fell short of God's best and harass you with it mercilessly. They will speak to you in the first person, saying things like, "That's why I feel the way I do. That's why things are so dull in my life; I failed God, and I'm in this miserable time because of it." But don't believe it! Do not begin to accept those self-condemning thoughts as your own. If you truly failed God you'll know it, your heart will bear witness to the fact; but you won't feel condemnation and remorse over it. The Holy Spirit will quickly lead you to repent, and you'll be free! But wintertime will likely remain, because it has nothing to do with your failures.

2. *Unfruitfulness.* Did you know that demons can quote Scripture? In a spiritual wintertime demons will remind you that Jesus said, "Every branch in me that beareth not fruit he [God] taketh away" (John 15:2, KJV). What they will not tell you is that abundant fruitbearing is seasonal. Remember the verse from Psalm one? "He brings forth his fruit *in his season.*" God never expects fruit out of season.

3. *Being an unprofitable servant.* From the parable in Matthew 25, demons will accuse you of being no better than the unprofitable servant Jesus talked about, who was cast into outer darkness because of his failure to put the Lord's money to good use. They'll be quick to tell you that you, like the unprofitable servant, will receive no reward, will lose the one talent that was originally entrusted to you, and, in the final analysis, will be rejected from the Lord's presence. Unless you understand times and seasons, these accusations will defeat you.

Attack on God's Character

In the time of winter satan also attacks the Lord's character, attempting to turn the Christian against Him. Job's wife encouraged her husband to "curse God, and die" when everything around him was falling apart, but "in all this Job sinned not, nor charged God foolishly" (Job. 2:9; 1:22, KJV).

Like Job, we must never question our Lord's character when we find ourselves in times of testing. He remains absolutely just in everything that comes our way, and His love is infinitely greater than the seasons that confront us. His mighty hand is always upon those of us who trust Him, and He will not leave us comfortless in times of severe trial.

I realize that in a wintertime season of the Christian experience the heavens often seem as brass, but that does not invalidate the fact that our God said He would never leave us nor forsake us. God hears our prayers regardless of how we feel, because we are His children and He loves us as He loves Jesus (John 17:23).

Satan attacks God's character, accusing Him of a lack of love and concern for us. He makes God out to be heartless, one who takes great pleasure in abandoning us in our time of real need. If we believe his lie, we will play right into his hands, allowing him to separate us from the only one who can bring us from the cold of winter into a glorious spiritual springtime.

Winter is a time to simply trust God, knowing that our times are in His hands. During the other spiritual seasons it is much easier to exercise an active, militant faith, but in wintertime, trust is all we can do. Use the time to relax in who you are in Jesus Christ. Again, don't cry and pout when you discover your projects are buried beneath six feet of cold, wet snow. Handle winter like the North Carolina farmer in the great blizzard of 1960. Because he was snowbound high in the Carolina mountains, the American Red Cross was concerned for his well-being. Did he have food? Was he warm enough? Some people had been known to crack up under such severe weather conditions and lose their sanity. How would it be with him?

The Red Cross employed the use of a gigantic bulldozer to open the narrow mountain passes that led up to the old farmer's cabin. Some of the drifts in these passes were thirty feet deep. For several days they worked, feverishly clearing a path to the farmer's door. Finally, they arrived. They knocked on the old man's door expecting to hear a feeble, forlorn response. From inside came a strong, vibrant voice, asking, "Who is it?" The workers cried out, "It's the Red Cross!" The farmer replied, "I already gave!"

The fact that there was snow piled up outside and that the temperature was dipping down into the sub-zero range at night didn't alarm the seasoned old farmer. He was prepared for it. There was canned food in the root cellar, plenty of firewood in the woodshed, and a sufficient amount of indoor work to keep him busy during the short days and long nights of winter. He knew that spring would roll around again, so in the meantime he would enjoy and make the most of the wintertime season. There was no need to panic. Somewhat like the virtuous woman of Proverbs 31, who "was not afraid of the snow for her household, because she had clothed them well," the old farmer faced each winter season with a confidence that he too was well prepared for the cold.

Christians need to adopt this mentality if they want to enjoy their walk with God in this world. Such a mentality is essential.

Wintertime passes, my brother or sister. The Word of God encourages us:

> *See! The winter is past; the rains are over and gone. Flowers appear on the earth; the season of singing has come, the cooing of doves is heard in our land* (Song 2:11-12).

One day soon you will find yourself in springtime again and the Lord will say to you, *"See! The winter is past."* Or if you are one who is presently enjoying the springtime, summer or harvest season of the Christian experience, you need to accept the fact that wintertime is coming for you. But don't fret. Develop the laid-back mentality of that old North Carolina farmer, who, in spite of what the weather was like outside, relaxed in what he knew would see him through to the coming spring. Relax in Jesus Christ, knowing that your times are in His hands. This will make following Him so much easier and more enjoyable.

One final word concerning the seasons of our Christian experience that must be remembered. If while you are in a wintertime season you meet a brother or sister who is enjoying a springtime season — all frothy and full of outward vitality — be gracious to them. Don't ruin it for them by saying things like: "Just wait, your day's coming!" Simply rejoice, if you can, that they're having such a ball following Jesus. Don't rain on their party.

Another thing. When you are in a wintertime season and you encounter a Christian who is in the midst of a fruit-bearing season, don't try to fake them out by pulling out plastic flowers and fruits. Be genuine! Too many snowbound Christians, at times like these, try to come across as "on-top-of-the-world" men or women of faith and victory. It doesn't work. A Christian with any discernment in him can spot a sham a mile away. I have laid my hands on the heads of such Christians who were trying to come across as spiritual powerhouses and it felt as though their spiritual temperature was forty below zero. Brother, you can't get by with chicanery in the Kingdom of God; you may fool me, but you won't fool everybody. And you certainly won't fool God.

Another thing. When you are enjoying springtime or an abundant harvest of fruit in a spiritual autumn, please remember to be gracious to those brothers and sisters who are trodding through winter. Think back a little bit. It wasn't very long ago that you were in the midst of the harshness of a spiritual winter season. And guess what. You will be there again one day.

Quoting Bible verses at people who are in a spiritual blizzard is not going to bring them out into your springtime. If anything, it will drive them deeper into their cave. Telling them how they should or should not feel will only serve to strain your relationship with them. Let them alone and love them where they are.

One man made the mistake of quoting a Bible verse at his wife when she was in the midst of a harsh winter season. "The way I quoted the verse," he lamented, "was so heartless and self-righteous sounding that I didn't see her for two whole weeks! Both my eyes were swollen shut." Yuck! Yuck!

That sounds funny, doesn't it? But if you've ever strained a relationship with a good friend because you didn't relate properly to them when they were experiencing tough times, you understand how serious this subject is. At all times endeavor to be gracious, merciful and understanding.

Are you in winter, my friend? Cheer up, God has not

abandoned you. He knows your name, phone number and address. There is one thing you can always do when you find yourself in the middle of a harsh winter snowstorm; and that is believe for an early spring. God be with you.

8

MIGHTY MEN OF THE KINGDOM

There was an elite group of men in Old Testament times that surrounded and fought valiantly for King David against his enemies. Commonly referred to as David's mighty men, I have taken great pleasure in reading about them so that I might glean some new insights into how I might become a better soldier of Jesus Christ.

There was Adino (II Sam. 23:8, KJV), who lifted up his spear and in one violent encounter killed 800 men. No doubt he had grasped the truth that "nothing can hinder the Lord from saving, whether by many or by few" (1 Sam. 14:6).

Like Adino, with God's power at your disposal, you can raise up your spiritual weapons and slay multitudes of a spiritual enemy army. The power in one drop of the blood of Jesus can totally obliterate satan's entire evil kingdom. The authority vested in the name of Jesus Christ can cause every spirit in heaven or on earth to bow its knee in confession of His absolute Lordship. (See Philippians 2:9-10.)

Following Adino in the list of kingdom mighty men was Eleazar. What an awesome man this warrior was. There was the time when the Philistines gathered themselves in battle array to defeat David at Pas Dammim (1 Chron. 11:13). On location was a barley field which meant a lot to the ongoing success of David's army. Barley is a cereal grass with grain used in making soups and porridge. Spiritually speaking, it typifies the rich blessings of the Lord. The presence of the Philistine army was so terrifying that David's entire army fled in fear from before them that is, all except Eleazar! With sword in hand (2 Sam. 23:10), Eleazar stationed himself in the midst of the barley field and slew Philistines until his hand grew weary; but there were too many of them. When all of his fight seemed to be gone and the host of the Philistines were about to engulf him in defeat, a power not his own lifted his hand, enabling him to wield that sword unto victory. Scripture says, "His hand grew tired and froze to the sword." The power of God literally went into action on that fateful day, empowering all that Eleazar had (which wasn't much), and God wrought a mighty victory through him. It is interesting to note that the name *Eleazar* means "God has helped." It is like when you are in the midst of a spiritual battle for someone else, attempting to defend the rich blessing of the Lord for them, and you come to the end of your grasp of how and what to pray. And then you remember that "the Spirit also helpeth our infirmities: for we know not what we should pray for as we ought: but the Spirit itself maketh intercession for us with groanings which cannot be uttered" (Rom. 8:26, KJV). The word "helpeth" literally means that the Holy Spirit takes hold with us at our side to assist us in prayer. We know that as this happens we lean into the will of God, both praying it and receiving it for the one we are praying for (Rom. 8:27). There are some victories that will never be realized if someone doesn't stand in the midst of the barley field and defend it for others. We need modern-day Eleazars — mighty men and women who know their God and are strong to take action against the forces of lawlessness invading our inheritance today.

Take a look around you today. If you'll look hard enough you will see someone who is going down in defeat to the enemy. The kingdom of darkness is mercilessly encroaching on their field of blessing, taking from them their health, finances or sanity. For one reason or another they are not fighting. Don't judge them, help them! Go to war for them! Withstand the godless forces of satan on their behalf! And when the smoke clears away, leaving you and Jesus as the only ones standing in the midst of the battle-torn field of blessing, rejoice when you see others receive the fruit of your spiritual battling. Remember, you did it for them, not for yourself. Scripture reveals that after Eleazar and the Lord had defeated the Philistines, the rest of the army returned in order to help collect the loot (2 Sam. 23:10, TLB). How would that make you feel? Everyone cashing in your victory. If you are of pure, God-like motives it shouldn't bother you; it should cause you to rejoice.

Shammah was another mighty man who faithfully served David. At a time when the Philistines rose up causing fear to fill the hearts of David's soldiers, Shammah stood alone in the midst of a piece of ground full of lentils and defended it. Lentils also typify the blessings of God. It is a true saying that an army marches on its stomach. The enemy knew this, and so was trying to destroy David's food source. Thank God for Eleazar and Shammah who risked life and limb in order to defend food supplies that supported David's armies in the field.

Somehow, spiritually speaking, this applies to us today. Our benevolent Lord has provided us with all we need to be well equipped and successful, blessed and a blessing in this life. But satan's kingdom wants to destroy God's provisions, and is doing so in the lives of countless millions. We, therefore, are in desperate need of warriors of God who will stand as bulwarks against the invading, plundering forces of satan, routing them at every turn. The enemy's weapons are varied: sickness, poverty, fear, mental torments, and the lies of the various "isms" that are infiltrating secular and religious society with their unscriptural teachings. Sadly, these "isms" have gained ground in many sectors because the Church has not challenged them. Occultism must be challenged by superior power. The mighty Holy Spirit is eager to supply that power, but will only do so through committed disciples of Christ. Mormonism, Muhammadanism, Buddhism, Hinduism, humanism, spiritism, communism, — all the isms — must be refuted by Christians who know the Word of God and are channels of Holy Ghost power! Sluggish, sleepy, half-baked Christianity will not do it. Unless an army of Adinos, Eleazars and Shammahs come forth, many glorious benefits of the gospel in our lives can be lost. But I have a vision — a vision of a finely tuned, fully equipped army of Jesus people making one massive thrust with the gospel, apprehending sinners to the Kingdom of God. I then see Jesus coming in clouds of splendid glory, upon a white horse, with justice in His hand. May we hasten His return.

There was also Abishai, the brother of Joab. (See 2 Sam. 23:18.) He was intensely loyal to David. He was chief among thirty of David's greatest warriors. Let us examine what the Word says about him:

> *And* ***Abishai*** *the brother of Joab, he was chief of the thirty. He raised his spear against three hundred men, whom he killed.* (II Sam. 23:18)

> *Then answered David and said to Ahimelech the Hittite and to* ***Abishai*** *the son of Zeruiah, brother of Joab saying, Who will go down with me to Saul to the camp? And Abishai said, I will go down with thee* (I Sam. 26:6, KJV).

Said Abishai to David after Shimei had cursed him:

> *Why should this dead dog curse my lord the king? Let me go over, I pray thee, and take off his head* (II Sam. 16:9, KJV).

> *Moreover Abishai the son of Zeruiah slew of the Edomites in the valley of salt eigthteen thousand* (I Chron. 18:12, KJV).

A Man of Great Zeal

Whether single-handedly wiping out three hundred of the enemy's choice combatants or leading a charge of men into a valley to destroy 18,000 Edomites, Abishai was always more than eager for the task. Combat was his thrill; he enjoyed killing enemy soldiers.

On the night that he accompanied David into Saul's camp, it was all David could do to keep him from spearing Saul right on the spot. But David's respect for authority and anointing, coupled with his wisdom, kept Abishai's zeal in check. David whispered to him, "Who can lay a hand on the Lord's anointed and be guiltless?"

When that "pip-squeak" Shimei came out and began to ridicule and chide righteous King David before his own men, Abishai begged David to let him go over and whack off his head. He was always ready to defend the honor of his king. I wish more Christians were as zealous over the honor of their King as Abishai was over the honor of David.

As Christians, we don't behead mortal men (though at times we've all felt like doing so), but spiritually we are to decapitate principalities and demon spirits. We ought to head-hunt for demons while we are carrying out our ministries of reconciliation. When we see where they are operating we should be eager to wield the sharp sword of the Spirit and put an end to their heartless work. Our ministry is one of reconciling lost men and women to God, but we should be mowing down demonic enemy troops as we go.

Abishai was the kind of man you could count on. There are not too many of his kind left in this sin-sick world. Often, men are cowards where spiritual conflict is concerned, and so the devil has had a heyday in enforcing his will on people. He has had a heyday in maligning the Kingship of our Lord Jesus Christ. The world does not seriously consider the claims of Jesus because lies about Him have been allowed to circulate unhindered. The ruling spirit of witchcraft has utilized the media in its gross attempt to manipulate world opinion against the true people of God. It has worked. An absence of Abishais is one reason witchcraft has enjoyed such great success.

Humanism, that dastardly religion of the modern world, has usurped God's place of authority and respect in all but a few of our institutions. It has sacked the institutions of politics, education, medicine and sadly, the institutional church. But God is still supreme, and Jesus is the King seated on a glorious throne. The Father looks at puny, self-centered, self-exalting men on earth and "laughs at them: for He sees their day is coming" (Ps. 37:13, author's paraphrase). His laughter is not a reaction to the comical, but an expression of triumph. He says, "Do what you will on earth; I've made Jesus King in heaven!" Scripture promises a time when heaven will literally come down to earth, not to be swallowed up in earth's corruption, but to override, overrule and transform earth to the pattern that God has planned. Out will go the wicked, with his fist-in-God's-face attitude, and the righteous will reign in glory with their King.

In the meantime the corrupters will reign. They will scheme

and plot and be very much like the thousands of ants on a board, floating down a great river, each one thinking he's in the driver's seat. In the natural it looks very bleak, but there is an army on the rise. It is not communist; it is not imperialistic; it is not an army with guns and hand grenades; it isn't even an army with nuclear arms: but it is destined to win this war of the ages! It is the army of the King of kings and the Lord of lords! The communists can't silence it. The Mohammedans can't stop it. The humanists can't make it go away. It is an army of modern-day Abishais, Elijahs, Gideons and Pauls, an army full of men and women who will take risks in order to see Jesus' honor upheld. And on that day very soon, as preordained by the Father, our King Jesus will physically enter earth's scene and wage war on all of those who have spurned His Lordship. The good news is that Jesus is soon to arrive to back up the claims that Christians have been making throughout the centuries concerning Him. Oh, what a glorious time that will be for all of those who love His appearing.

Benaiah was another mighty kingdom commando, a veritable lion for God. He not only performed exploits for the sake of his king, but he performed "great exploits." (See 2 Samuel 23:20). He single-handedly struck down two lion-like men of Moab — two of Moab's best fighting men. Moabites were one of the most fierce tribes of people to be found in the world at that time, and they sent the best they had. The two that faced Benaiah that day were possessors of great courage and strength. They were no mere children when it came to combat, but were mature, confident and quick — like the big cats they resembled. Benaiah took them down all by himself.

Then there was a day when Benaiah descended into a pit on a snowy day and killed a ferocious lion (the real thing). A lion in a pit depicts the devil himself coming at you when you are at your lowest. It was a snowy day, wintertime no doubt, and the lion was probably very hungry. Benaiah slew him and arose from the pit triumphant, just like Jesus was later to do on Resurrection morning.

Think of it, a lion in a pit on a snowy day. The next time you are in a wintertime cycle of your Christian experience and a devouring lion of satan shows up licking his chops for you, reread this inspiring story of Benaiah and allow the Spirit of God to produce in you a capacity for triumph. Even if your life seems in the pits, you can emerge more than a conqueror because of Jesus' ability inside you.

Another exploit of Benaiah's was accomplished on the day when he went face to face with a giant Egyptian whose appetite for little Hebrew guys was nothing short of gargantuan. Standing toe to toe, Benaiah's eyes probably leveled off at the Egyptian's belly button. But that didn't hinder Benaiah; he waded in on the guy with nothing but a club and plucked the Egyptian warrior's spear right out of his grubby hand. He then used the guy's own spear to impale him. Benaiah had "Egyptian shish kebab" that night for supper!

As Christians, we will never go out in battle against two lion-like Moabites, a lion in a pit, or a gigantic Egyptian warrior. But every day we are liable to face the spiritual enemies of God's Kingdom — giants, lions, fierce demonic entities that are out to "steal and kill and destroy" (John 10:10). But learn a lesson from Benaiah's fine example of courage. You are a spiritual giant slayer, a veritable lion killer for God. Stand tall and proud in the God to whom you belong.

Asahel was another faithful warrior who served in David's ranks. Like Abishai, he was a brother to David's general, Joab. Scripture reveals that Asahel was as fleet-footed as a wild gazelle (2 Sam. 2:18). This speaks of one who is highly coordinated, unhindered by excess weight, very mobile and able to move with determination. These are four characteristics that I wish we could find in all Christians.

There were three other men serving in David's command who were obviously soldiers of intense loyalty and devotion. Their story is told in First Chronicles, chapter eleven:

> *And David was then in the stronghold, while the garrison of the Philistines was then in Bethlehem. And David had a craving and said, "Oh, that someone would give me water to drink from the well of Bethlehem, which is by the gate!" So the three broke through the camp of the Philistines, and drew water from the well of Bethlehem which was by the gate, and*

> *took it and brought it to David; nevertheless David would not drink it, but poured it out to the Lord; and said, "Be it far from me before my God that I should do this. Shall I drink the blood of these men who went at the risk of their lives? For at the risk of their lives they brought it." Therefore he would not drink it. These things the three mighty men did* (1 Chron. 11:16-19, NAS).

There are a few things about this story that are helpful to understand. When David was longing for the water of Bethlehem's well it did not mean that he was without water. His life was not in jeopardy — he only longed for the better-tasting water of Bethlehem. David desired a blessing that was rightfully his, by God's decree, so these three mighty men set out to secure the blessing for him.

The king's wish was most likely uttered quietly — he was probably wishing out loud to himself. Therefore, you would have had to be in his immediate presence to hear it. His wish became their command!

Once they heard David's longing they had a choice to make. "Do we ignore it and remain in the safety of our fortified camp, or do we risk life and limb so that he might have what he longs for?" They knew that the choice to act would be taken at great risk — a thing few Christians know anything about.

Facing great peril, they made a breach in the enemy's front line of defense. The nature of the breach is unknown to us. Whether it happened under cover of night or in broad daylight doesn't seem to have mattered. The fact is that they broke through and secured the water. These three commandos, with a sense of great joy, presented the treasured water to their king only to witness him pour it on the ground as an offering to his God. I am not sure how they reacted, but I do not believe it bothered them. They had not secured the water to exalt their own reputations, but had secured it because of their intense loyalty and devotion to the king. I believe they were thrilled to realize that a higher authority than David was present to receive that water as an acceptable offering unto Himself.

What can we learn from the example of these three mighty

men? That we must also spend sufficient time in our King's immediate presence so that we might hear His deepest longings. The intimacy of our Commander-in-Chief's immediate presence is still something sought by relatively few people.

I wonder how many of us are willing to risk our lives so that Jesus might receive something that is dear to Him. May we all learn something about intimacy with God and loyalty to our King by the fine example of these three men.

Concerning all the mighty men we've looked at thus far, the Scriptures reveal that they "gave [David's] kingship strong support to extend it over the whole land" (1 Chron. 11:10). They were committed to that end, and it seems they were willing to do whatever it took to accomplish their mission. How much more should we be willing to serve the King of David in such a way?

Characteristics of the Army of God

> *Day after day men came to help David, until he had a great army, like the army of God* (1 Chron. 12:22, author's paraphrase).

How awesome a sight this army must have been to its foes — an army resembling the great angelic army of God! Not only was David's army impressive to behold, but it behaved itself as no other army on earth — before or since. I want to examine the men that gathered themselves to David at Ziklag so that we might gain further insight into how God's present army on earth — the Church of Jesus Christ — might better reflect His glory, dominion and might.

A look at the first verse of First Chronicles 12 will be a wonderful springboard into an insightful study of David's elite forces of fighting men.

> *1. These were the men who came to David at Ziklag, while he was banished from the presence of Saul son of Kish (they were among the warriors who helped him in battle....)* (1 Chron. 12:1).

The King James Version describes them as "helpers of the war." I like that better, because it tells us that the majority of

David's men came to him, not to be prestigious, recognizable leaders, but to be the ones willing to wage the warfare, to fight in the trenches and make David look good. Their motives for ministry were correct; none was grasping for fame, or stepping on his brothers in order to get into the limelight of glory. They were simply willing to be faithful "helpers of the war."

I remember a young man who joined himself to our church a few years ago, hoping I would immediately recognize his "tremendous" potential and place him in an authoritative place of ministry. Indeed, I saw potential all over him, and he even had an anointing on his life. But I know that tremendous gifting and anointing do not necessarily mean that a person is faithful and trustworthy. So I assigned a few mudane, non-glamorous jobs to him so that I might see what quality of character he was made of. What I saw was anything but impressive. Like a spoiled child, he pouted when he was asked to do things that didn't sport his fancy. He had no desire to help me or the church carry out some of the lackluster responsibilities, but he rather had a nagging desire to make a name for himself. His eyes were set on the pulpit, on leadership where he would be seen and admired of men, and he could not understand how setting up chairs, washing windows or sweeping the floor could ever help him arrive at a place of authority in the church. After a while he left because I would not give him what he wanted.

We desperately need helpers of the war in this hour of the Church of Jesus Christ. Somebody has to be willing to "get down in the dirt" and do the work of the ministry. Most of the work will not be glamorous, and the Christian world at large will probably never hear about what you did for the Kingdom of God. But does that really matter to you? The most important thing is that Jesus sees your good deed and He'll remember it always.

> 2. *They were armed with bows and were able to shoot arrows or to sling stones right-handed or left-handed* (1 Chron. 12:2).

The soldiers who joined David at Ziklag were well-balanced men, able to adjust to any situation. Imagine being able to use any weapon available to you, and being able to use it with either right hand or left. How could an enemy blindside such a man? And how could the enemy approach his weak side when he had no weak side?

As Christians, we should seek to be efficient in the use of the weapons our God has made available to use. The all-powerful name of Jesus Christ, the blood of Jesus Christ, and the Word of God are the primary weapons God has given to us for spiritual war. But we must know how to war with them effectively. (I suggest that you read chapter three of my book, *KINGDOM COMMANDOS*, Destiny Image Publishers, 1986.)

3. Warriors from the tribe of Gad who joined David at Ziklag were another impressive group.

> *And of the Gadites there separated themselves unto David into the hold of the wilderness men of might, and men of war fit for the battle, that could handle shield and buckler, whose faces were like the faces of lions, and were as swift as the roes upon the mountains* (I Chron. 12:8, KJV).

The first thing that impresses me about these Gadite warriors is that they "separated themselves unto David into the hold of the wilderness." I view the wilderness as a place of prayer. Men who come to a leader in his place and time of prayer are warriors who can be trusted, trained and used for God's glory. The wilderness is where the bush burns with God's presence. It is where a union to God's will takes place, and where a baptism of His power is received. In the wilderness, battle plans are formulated and explained by the Spirit of God, and all warriors are gathered unto the same vision. Watches are synchronized in the Spirit and strategies are finalized. It proves to be the only valid starting block for all Christian endeavor. If a soldier will not join his leaders and comrades in the wilderness, he is unfit for warfare.

As an elder leading a group of men and women who desire to impact the world with the gospel, I look for such participants as the Gadites. I have seen those who desire a place of ministry in the public eye, but who are not willing to come to our place of prayer. I've called corporate prayer meetings and they don't show up. As I see it in the Scriptures, the warriors are responsible for getting into the presence of their leaders whenever it is the order of the day. Unfortunately, there are multitudes of Christians who expect their pastors to run them down in order to keep them abreast of things happening in church — to keep them abreast of what the Lord is saying to him as he is seeking God's face. Often it is these very people who will put forth the most resistance to what God is working to accomplish through the faithful warriors. Why are they so out-of-tune? Because they weren't in the prayer meetings when God was clearly speaking. Believers like this are very displeasing to the Lord.

When Jesus called His disciples, He didn't say, "Give Me your schedule, and I'll order My time by it. I'll schedule My meetings during times when it is convenient for you to be there." No! Jesus simply said, "Follow Me!" He then took off with or without them, depending on their response to His command.

I have known men and women who have laid down all, when necessary, in order to be available to God. One young man, upon becoming a born-again, Spirit-filled Christian was willing to give up a profession that paid him forty-six thousand dollars annually just so he might move to a new location and be equipped for kingdom service. The high-paying job was one that insisted that he compromise his Christian ethics on occasion and he would not allow himself that liberty. He is now where God wants him, holding down a high school teaching job, making significantly less then he was making before. Will God honor that type of commitment? You know He will.

A second thing I liked about the Gadites was that they were "men of might." These were no sissies who gathered themselves unto David. Few things repulse me as much as an effeminate man who is that way by choice. A man of might is God's handiwork; this description may not necessarily involve physical might and power, but it certainly refers to internal might by the Holy Spirit. Paul prayed for the Christians in Ephesus, that God would "grant [to them], according to the riches of his glory, to be strengthened *with might* by his Spirit in the inner man" (Eph. 3:16, KJV, author's emphasis). If this is happening in one's life, he will not only become more manlike in his physical image (the way he carries himself, dresses and talks), but also in his spiritual likeness of God. To be a man of might in the Kingdom of God doesn't necessarily mean one is built like a body-builder on the outside, but he is very strong on the inside. I've known well-built men on the outside who were spiritual wimps on the inside. Doesn't the Bible say, "Bodily exercise profiteth for a little time, but godliness is profitable unto all things" (1 Tim. 4:8, author's paraphrase)? A man of true spiritual might is one who knows the Word of His God, enjoys deep abiding fellowship in the presence of His God, and is producing the fruit of such a dynamic life-style.

A third thing about the Gadites that I like is that they were "men of war, fit for the battle." The word translated "fit" could have been translated "prepared." By both instruction and ample practice, these awesome warriors were readied for battle. They were professional men of war; David didn't have to train them. At a moment's notice they were ready for the most intense types of warfare. In times of peace they readied themselves for times of war. They were not so naive as to think they would never have to face an enemy, and so they kept themselves prepared.

In the Church of Jesus Christ on earth today we can find several types of believers. First, there are those on active duty, faithfully fulfilling their God-given assignments. Secondly, there are P.O.W.s, men and women who have been taken captive by the enemy. They need to be set free, or they need to escape. Thirdly, there are Christians who are AWOL — Absent Without Leave. God hasn't given permission for the deserters to vacate their responsibilities, but they have run off. They are having problems with the rebel in their flesh and an unrenewed mind. In times of natural warfare they would be hunted down and shot for desertion. The Body of Christ today, sadly, is full of this type of renegade. Fourthly, there are those Christians who are Missing in Action. They were once among us, but nobody has seen them in a while. Somehow, the enemy has been able to take them out of the war. They pose no threat to him, and they provide no assistance for their own comrades in arms. As I stated, the Church is made of all four types. What type have you been for the past several months? Are you fulfilling your God-given assignments? Are your spiritual leaders pleased with your performance lately? Why not report to them for an evaluation of your service in the cause of the King?

A fourth thing I liked about the Gadites was that they could handle both shield and buckler. One translation says "shield and spear." This speaks of the ability to handle defensive *and* offensive military hardware. God wants us to be able to defend ourselves against the attacks of the enemy as well as to launch offensives against him. We must gain a working knowledge of the armor that is ours in Christ (Eph. 6), and we must learn how to wield our weapons of attack.

A fifth point of interest concerning the Gadite warriors who defected to David was that they had "faces like lions." As I meditated on this statement, the Lord brought to my remembrance a documentary I saw a few years ago on the lions of Etosha National Park in southwest Africa. As He brought this documentary film to my mind, I saw the faces of those lions: bold, intense, no nonsense, determined, confident and full of authority. Lions don't attack their prey unless they are convinced they can score. When a pride of lions is on the hunt, stalking a herd of zebras or other desirable game, they are as intense as anything you could ever see. Very little can get their minds off of what they are doing.

After the hunt, when their bellies are full, they relax and play with the cubs, or spend the hours stretched out beneath a shade tree sleeping off the morning's meal. But when it is time to hunt again, when important things need to be done, they are as intent upon success as ever and are determined not to have to do things twice.

I wish that more Christians had the hearts and faces of lions. Certainly the face of a lion indicates that there is the heart of a lion within the man or woman of God, or at least there should be a lion's heart within them.

One night in Nairobi, Kenya, I was involved in a very special meeting in the home of friends. Just prior to the start of the meeting two young African evangelists came in and sat down.

One of them was pure-blooded Masai, one of Africa's fiercest fighting tribes. Prior to this century the Masai tribe boasted some of the mightiest warriors of any tribe that had ever existed. At one time they literally dominated the countries of eastern Africa, and even today they demand the respect of people the world over.

After introductions were made, I began to study the face of the Masai. While he talked with other members of our group, being unaware I was looking intently at him, the Spirit of God began to give me insight on this young man's unique qualities. After several minutes of study and listening to the Lord, I began to share with the Masai the things God was saying. I said, "You have the face of a lion, but it goes much deeper than that. You have the heart of a lion as well. In times past, your Masai customs required that the rite of manhood be accompanied by the slaying of a male lion. But the needful laws of Kenya have made that an illegal act in your day and time. But the Spirit of God would say to you, young warrior, '*You need not slay a lion as entrance into manhood, because I've made you a lion. I call you more than a man, you are a lionhearted man of God! With your eyes, which are the light of your body and the mirror of your spirit, you strike fear in the hearts of your enemies. With godly confidence, determination and an attitude of no nonsense, you will subjugate your foes, pluck the prey from their teeth, and be responsible for a multitude of lost men and women coming to Me for salvation and entrance into the Kingdom of My Son!*

No sooner had I given that word to my Masai brother than the man in whose home we were visiting shouted in excitement, "That's exactly right! No better description could be given of my brother there. With boldness and determination, he witnesses to the sinners in the marketplace. With great confidence he stands on the street corners to proclaim the mystery of the Gospel. He is truly a lion at heart, and I too have seen it in his face. The face of a lion of God!"

The face of a lion of God has little to do with the physical appearance of a man's face. It matters not how deeply set his eyes are, or what the line of his jaw is like. It is not a physical thing; it is spiritual. It has to do with his countenance. Also, it has to do with his attitude toward the things of God and with the godly violence in his heart toward the works of satan. It speaks of the amount of God's wisdom he possesses in his heart, because the Word says, "a man's wisdom maketh his face to shine, and the boldness of his face shall be changed" (Eccles. 8:1b, KJV). I have seen the timid, uncertain looks on the faces of countless young Christians transformed as they have learned who they are in Christ, and who He is in them. Their sheepish faces have slowly transformed into the faces of lions of God!

The sixth unique Gadite characteristic I like is that they were as swift as roes or gazelles in the mountains. Gazelles are known as one of the fastest animals in the world. They are sure-footed animals, often able to run in terrain other animals must walk through. Grace of movement characterizes them, and they are highly coordinated, unhindered by excess weight.

Christian warriors should be like gazelles, moving with spiritual and mental grace. We should be spiritually sure-footed, dashing into and through places where others fear to even walk. We should not be hindered by the weight of sins that so easily beset others, and we should be, at all times, quick to hear and obey God.

There was a man who used to live in the county where my sister, Pam, and I live. We both had talked to him about his need for Jesus, but he never was interested. Eventually we gave up.

One day I heard that he was in the hospital, and that he was dying. It seems as though the combination of alcohol and diuretic pills had destroyed his liver, and the man's life was slipping rapidly away. When I heard this, the Lord spoke to me, instructing me to go to see him immediately. I informed Pam, so that she would be praying, and drove to the hospital. When I entered the man's room, friends and close relatives were standing around pining away.

"Lord," I sighed, "could you please get me some time alone with this poor man?"

To my delight, the Lord went to work immediately to clear the room. He simply put it in everyone's minds to go somewhere else for a while. Soon the hospital room was empty, except for me and the dying man.

I jumped right into it with the man and found that he was very receptive to the gospel he had at other times rejected. Within the hour he was gloriously born again and was expressing a strong desire to see all of his friends and family members saved. From all appearances, that man's experience with Jesus was genuine.

Needless to say, I left the man's hospital room that day walking on cloud nine. I fully intended to go back to the hospital the following day to begin building his faith for physical healing. *But that night he died!*

Brother or sister, we must be "gazelle-like Christians," quick to hear and obey God. The lives of multitudes may depend on it.

Gazelles Escape Disaster

At the slightest hint of danger, a gazelle darts for safety with lightning-fast speed. How often have Christians waited until an enemy has slipped right up to them and put a chain around their necks before they try to flee to safety? There have been times when at the first symptoms of a cold or flu I have run into the "Secret Place" of God's Word to find safety and deliverance. At that moment the attack began to wane. At other times I have failed to run into the safety of God's Word, and the result has been a "whopper" of a cold or the flu.

One night several years ago the symptoms of a cold began to fasten onto my body with vehement force. It was in the middle of deer season and I did not want to be down with a bad cold during that time; besides that, I hadn't killed my two deer yet. I grabbed my Bible and headed for the door of the hunting camp. One of the men asked me where I was going in such a hurry. I was faced with a choice. "Do I tell him I'm going out to pray and get deliverance from an oncoming cold, or do I tell him 'nowhere' and return to my perch in the cabin?" You see, the devil will not only attack you, but he'll also try to convince you not to go to the Word. I faced the very real possibility that my hunting partner (whom I didn't know very well) would think I was a religious fanatic and not want to be around me any more. But I was also facing the thought of two or three days of cold and flu misery. I chose to jeopardize my reputation. With Bible and flashlight in hand I told him where I was going and headed out into the dark night surrounding the hunting camp. When I returned about fifteen minutes later, the Word was working mightily in me, and by daylight the following morning every symptom of cold or flu was gone. Now I ask you, which is better? Hit it early and whip it, or delay (for some asinine reason) and allow it to sink its claws into me?

Gazelle Christians are also going to be quick to recognize and escape the temptations to sin that regularly confront them. Because they have spent time with God and had their minds renewed by His Word, they will be more apt to think His thoughts and walk in His ways. When "sin lies at their door, it's desire for them, they will master it" (Gen. 4:7, author's paraphrase).

Gazelle Christians are also going to be quick thinkers, because they have the mind of Christ (1 Cor. 2:16c). The Apostle Paul, on a number of occasions, was able to dodge disaster by being this type of Christian warrior. One incident that stands out in my mind is recorded in Acts 23. In it, Paul is found standing before a council of Pharisees led by the high priest, Ananias. The priestly courtroom is erupting with shouts of accusation from both Pharisees and Sadducees, Paul being the object of their scorn. Equipped with the mind of Christ, Paul perceives that this is a good time to be as wise as a serpent and as harmless as a dove. Verse 6 (KJV) records: "But when Paul perceived that the one part were Sadducees, and the other Pharisees, he cried out in the council, Men and brethren, I am a Pharisee, the son of a Pharisee: of the hope and resurrection of the dead I am called in question." This seemingly simple yet profound statement uttered from the lips of quick-thinking Paul causes a tremendous uproar in the courtroom. Suddenly the Pharisees are verbally combatting the Sadducees whom they think are persecuting Paul because he believes and teaches the doctrine of resurrection. In one swift move, Paul turns his accusers against one another, removing the heat from himself. What a superlative maneuver by this man of God.

I prophetically declare that such ingenious action must be recovered by the army of Jesus Christ for the bitter days that lie ahead. There will be times (there already have been) when men and women of God will face terrible accusations from the religious world and will have to be able to react swiftly to God's mind and counsel, as did Paul, in order to thwart sure destruction. Circumstances may be a little different and the accusations may concern other issues, but the mind of Christ made available to Christians through the blood of His cross will be there to provide "the answer of the tongue" (Prov. 16:1, KJV).

The seventh noteworthy thing about the Gadite warriors who defected to David in the wilderness was the strength and anointing for war of each soldier. First Chronicles tells us that the least of them was a match for 100 enemy soldiers, and the greatest of them was a match for 1,000 of the enemy soldiers (1 Chron. 12:14). Scripture reveals that they crossed the Jordan River when it was flooded and routed the enemy (1 Chron. 12:15). When the going got tough, these tough ones got going. Circumstances didn't have to be perfect before they would attack. Too many Christians are waiting for circumstances to get better before they attack and overpower satanic strongholds in their families, churches and cities. If you will think about it, you'll remember that there has always been a flood of some kind that you had to wade through in order to secure a victory. Don't expect the floods of evil in society today to go away on their own; wade through them and rout the enemy — beat him at his own game! His flood is designed to stalemate you in the warfare. Cross the river and catch him off guard, showing him that you are better than that!

4. Another impressive group of warriors who defected to David in the wilderness were representatives of the tribe of Benjamin (1 Chron. 12:16-18). Immediately David checked their motives for joining him. He declared, "If you have come to me in peace, to help me, I am ready to have you unite with me" (1 Chron. 12:17). David, like any good leader, was not eagerly aggressive about bringing people under his oversight. He wanted to be sure God was directing those who came to him — they could be trusted under pressure. True commitment is tested in warfare.

The Holy Spirit came upon one of their leaders, Amasai, and

he said, "We are yours, O David!" (1 Chron. 12:18) What a tremendous thing to say. They willingly placed themselves into the hands of the one God was directing them to serve.

David had a great deal of confidence in these men whose motives were right. He felt secure in making them leaders of his raiding bands. They were highly qualified kingdom commandos — hit-and-run raiders — experts in infiltration, reconnaissance, demolition and sabotage.

The Kingdom of God needs this kind of warrior today. Such ministries as Ramtha's must be stymied — blocked by the power of God. (See chapter 4, "Signs Must Follow.")

Spirit-empowered Christians ought to infiltrate a few of Ramtha's meetings, and when his "channel" begins to go into her trance they ought to run spiritual interference, binding up his deceptive lies and bringing confusion by praying silently in the Holy Ghost. Sabotage that damned imposter and all of them like him, in Jesus' name! I mean it. He is damned and doomed, and we ought to enforce it.

The next time you hear of the communists conducting a rally on a nearby campus, be brazen enough to attend and bind that anti-Christian devil in Jesus' name. Get on the offensive, Christian. Be strong and take action (Dan. 11:32b, NAS).

5. Yet another group of fighting men who joined themselves to David were Manassites. These warriors were utilized in helping David against the raiding bands of the enemy (1 Chron. 12:21).

In the spiritual war taking place today between the forces of darkness and the forces of light, there are many raiding bands sent by the enemy to infiltrate and destroy the armies of God. We desperately need Christian men and women who can find it their pleasure to withstand the work of these demonic rovers. The next time malicious backbiting and gossip start up against your spiritual leaders, be one who rises quickly to their defense, proving your true spiritual valor in the Kingdom of God.

6. There were the sons of Issachar, "who understood the times and knew what Israel should do" (1 Chron. 12:32). These men proved valuable to David's success as king.

Jesus once rebuked hypocritical Pharisees and Sadducees, asking, "Can ye not discern the signs of the times?" (Matt. 16:3, KJV) As it was in Jesus' day, so it is in our day; thousands of "religious" leaders have no idea how crucial the days are. Or, perhaps if they do know, they haven't the slightest idea what should be done about it. But that's not how it was with the sons of Issachar. They knew what Israel should do! They were obviously prophetic in their gifting, God's cabinet members, privy to His foreknowledge and equipped with His answers for the situations that confronted them.

Every church needs ministry like this in order to remain on top of the varied and changing circumstances that surround it. Without it, the church will be driven along by every passing fad or fear that drives any other group of people. Sons of Issachar are believers of "another spirit" (Num. 14:24, KJV), with their affections set "on things above, not on things on the earth" (Col. 3:2, KJV). They are "seers" who come to lead the blind.

7. Of the tribe of Zebulun, there were men who were "expert in war, with all instruments of war, fifty thousand, which could keep rank: they were not of double heart" (I Chron. 12:33, KJV). They were experienced in combat and possessed the ability to use any weapon of modern warfare with extreme accuracy. In the intense heat of battle they were faithful to keep rank, knowing that their comrades depended on them being steadfast in their positions. There is very little that is worse than an unrestrained army running wildly in the midst of battle. You turn for assistance from a man who is to be at your right hand and he's not there. How lethal that can be.

The warriors of Zebulun were not double-hearted, but were of one mind and one purpose — to make David king over all Israel! This speaks of undivided loyalty. With men like that how could David lose? They were obedient to authority, moved about in unity, and there was little or no strife among them. Before such an army no foe could stand.

These warriors who came to David in the wilderness numbered better than 340,822 fighting men. Scripture declares that they came with a perfect heart to Hebron, *fully determined* to make David king (1 Chron. 12:38, author's emphasis). Like

David's mighty army, the Church ought, with undivided loyalty and purpose, seek to make Jesus Lord over all the earth. Through aggressive evangelism and church planting we can work toward that end.

9

MAGNIFICENT ANGELS AND THEIR END-TIME MINISTRY

If we could see into the realm of spirits with the natural eye for only ten minutes, we would be awestruck by the dynamic activity that is actually taking place there. But because spirits are in another realm — the invisible realm —we easily become guilty of the error of focusing our attention only on natural things and thinking only earthly thoughts. Becoming unmindful of those eternal realities that weigh much more heavily on our lives than we know, we fall prey, as all natural men do, to the unseen forces of satan's kingdom, which are ever seeking to bring destruction to our lives.

Paul, the insightful apostle of Jesus Christ, exhorted us: "So we fix our eyes not on what is seen, but what is unseen. For what is seen is temporary, but what is unseen is eternal" (2 Cor. 4:18). If we fail to order our lives by this directive, either through consent or ignorance, we will only live as other men live, think as other men think, talk as other men talk, and become victims to the same woes that befall them.

Scripture clearly presents the truth that there are two realms of existence: the natural one which is temporary and the spiritual one which is eternal.

For by him [Jesus] all things were created: things in heaven and on earth, VISIBLE AND INVISIBLE, whether thrones

> *or powers or rulers or authorities* (Col. 1:16, author's emphasis).

Kingdoms in Two Realms

In the natural, visible realm there are many kingdoms, or governments, consisting of their leadership and their constituency.

The Word of God reveals that in the spiritual, invisible realm there are only two kingdoms, and that they are at war with one another. Within each of these two warring kingdoms — the Kingdom of God and the kingdom of satan — there are thrones, power, rulers and authorities.

In the spiritual realm there are myriads of fallen spirits. These demons are vile, grubby and deceitful spiritual creatures who are totally committed to the destruction of the human race. They literally detest God Almighty; and if a man or woman belongs to Him, the demons regard them with extra hatred, seeking to bring upon their lives every kind of destruction imaginable.

Also in the spiritual realm there are myriads of angels — angels of God — faithful, loyal possessors of indescribable strength and agility. They are unequivocally pitted against the works of the demon spirits and all enemies of God's people; they are destined to one day obliterate from the heavens and the earth every godless spirit that is in rebellion against God.

Both kingdoms possess massive armies with which they seek to vanquish their foes. When the Word likens King David's army to the army of God (1 Chron. 12:22), it is speaking of the mighty angelic army that serves under Jesus Christ, "sent to serve those who will inherit salvation"(Heb. 1:14).

The prophets of old were always amazed at their great number:

> *Thousands upon thousands attended him; ten thousand times ten thousand stood before him* (Dan. 7:10b).

> *And I beheld, and I heard the voice of many angels round about the throne ... and the number of them was ten thousand times ten thousand, and thousands of thousands* (Rev. 5:11, KJV).

While Jesus was being betrayed into the hands of His enemies He stated that it would be nothing at all for Him to receive from His Father "twelve legions of angels" (Matt. 26:53). That is 72,000 heavenly warriors who would be willing and able to set Him free! The Bible records how only "one" of these awesome heavenly soldiers went through an Assyrian camp one night and slew 185,000 elite fighting men (II Kings 19:35). Imagine what 72,000 judgment-carrying angels of God could do!

Within the great company of angels who faithfully serve in the Kingdom of God there is a very definite rank and file. Scripture indicates that Michael is one of the supreme heads of this massive spiritual army, answering to no one but God Himself. (See Daniel 10:13, 12:1 and Revelation 12:7.)

Angels are a company rather than a race. They do not marry, neither do they die (Luke 20:36). The great ranks of these awesome spiritual creatures have neither been decreased by death nor increased by marriage. I suppose they have had their numbers increased from time to time as God saw fit, but marriage and procreation through intercourse is not His way of increasing them. He merely speaks forth His creative Word, and "presto!" — an angel. A miracle? An explosion of almightiness? Call it what you will, but I believe that's the way God creates angels.

Angels possess spiritual bodies, not physical ones. A physical body like the ones we have on planet earth is subject to physical laws that bind it up and hold it back. Gravity holds us down, keeping us from being able to soar in the sky. Our lungs keep us from being able to live underwater. Let's face it, we are grossly limited in what we can do. So why would God encumber one of His mighty ones with a physical body? To do all He commissions them to do, they must be strong, swift, splendid, subtle as the winds of heaven, and elastic as the light of God's glory, unhindered by earth's natural laws.

Angels! Awesome creatures. No distance wearies them. No physical barriers hinder them. No earthly power matches them in strength. Have you ever seen an Air Force jet fly overhead? It's peanuts to an angel. The jet may be capable of flying many hundreds of miles per hour, but angels can dart about at 186,000 miles per second — at least! How? Because they're creatures of light, and light travels that fast! Don't underestimate their potential or you'll cheat yourself.

A few years ago, in southern Lebanon's Valley of the Springs, two American missionaries serving George Otis' High Adventure Ministries experienced dynamic angelic intervention right in the nick of time. They were trouble-shooting transmission problems in one of the towers belonging to Voice of Hope Radio Station, owned by High Adventure Ministries. All of a sudden they heard a walking barrage of mortar shells exploding and coming their way. They knew it was too late for them to evacuate the area, and so one of them cried, "JESUS!" The next PLO mortar shell was destined to explode right on top of them. Then the miracle happened. One of the men, having his eyes opened into the realm of spirits, looked and beheld a magnificent angel spring into action to rescue them and the tower from certain destruction. With liquid-like movement he leaped at least fifty feet from the floor of the valley, threw his right arm up over his head, caught the shell in mid air, and with one unending movement threw it back toward PLO lines. There were no more shells fired that day. The men said, "It's no wonder the PLO terrorists say there are angels around our camp." Angels are extremely capable beings.

When angels appear on earth they are youthful and commanding, and, quite often, majestic and full of awe. When Balaam's eyes were opened to see the angel sent to withstand his progress, because it was reckless, he fell face down on the ground before the angel. (See Numbers 22:31.)

When an angel appeared to the shepherds in the field to announce the birth of Christ, they were terrified. (See Luke 2:9.)

The angel who appeared to Cornelius in Acts 10:3, had an appearance that caused Cornelius to look at him in fear.

When Zechariah, the father of John the Baptist, looked up to see an angel sent from God with tidings foretelling John's birth, he "was startled and was gripped with fear" (Luke 1:12). Fear seized him, not because of the news of John's birth, but because of the dazzling appearance of the awesome messenger.

Even when angels are so obscured in their personality as to be thought only men, there is a splendor in their being which calls forth a profound reverence.

When two angels approached Lot at the gates of the city of Sodom, Lot bowed before them, calling them, "My lords." I do not believe he was aware that they were angels of God at that time, but still, there was a certain grandeur about them that set them apart from mere men. Lot had been close enough to them to sense it, but the homosexual men of Sodom had not. All they knew was they they had seen two great-looking guys enter Lot's house, and they wanted them for the fulfillment of their own sexual lust. The idea that anyone would approach an angel of Almighty God in such a perverted way tells me that they didn't know they were angelic beings. They soon found out, however (Gen. 19:10).

In their veiled appearances, that is, when they are present but unseen, strange overpowering sensations are sometimes felt by people present.

When an angel appeared to Daniel (Dan. 10) after twenty-one days of intense prayer, the men with him were unable to see the angelic visitor, but they all sensed the presence of someone powerful. Scripture says "... such terror overwhelmed them that they fled and hid themselves" (Dan. 10:7).

My wife, Darlene, was up late one cold winter's night, stoking the fire in the kitchen wood stove. As she sat on the floor in front of the stove she began to pray in the Spirit and worship God. She says that she continued in this vein for about an hour, enraptured with God's fellowship. "When I finished praying," she relates, "I sensed someone standing directly behind me, watching me intently." At this point, Darlene relates, "Goose bumps jumped up all over me, and I knew it was an angel of God."

Darlene saw nothing, but there was an overwhelming sense of his presence there in the kitchen with her. She rose to her feet and made her way through the dark house to our bedroom. Stationed in the hallway, just outside our son's bedroom, was another angelic being of enormous stature. Did she actually see him? No! But she sensed him all the same. As she entered our bedroom where I was busy "sawing logs," she sensed another mammoth warrior, with drawn sword, standing at the foot of our bed. This wonderful guy was watching over "Yours Truly." Darlene sensed all of this in the spirit, after a wonderful time of prayer and fellowship with God. Some might venture to say it was all a product of Darlene's overheated imagination. You'll never convince us of that!

Though Darlene could not actually see these majestic guardians from God, the ability was given to her to sense their awesome presence. I, too, have encountered such feelings in some of my deepest and most intimate times of prayer to God. I thank God for it and will seek never to hinder its taking place by allowing evil doubt and skepticism to find a place in my heart.

Greatest Hindrance to Angelic Assistance

Certainly doubt and unbelief concerning their existence stands paramount as an obstacle to their ministry. Aren't we earthlings such a sophisticated bunch? And how about most of the professing church world? The perils of Egypt and a burning dry wilderness don't pertain to us. No godless monarch threatens us with a fiery furnace or with savage lions. No Syrian army surround us, threatening to take our lives. We are at ease in Zion. We have hospitals and insurance policies and mutual funds and a sophisticated military and Star Wars and democratic government. But God thunders, "[I have] rejected thy confidences, and thou shalt not prosper in them!" (Jer. 2:37, KJV) You may find them sustaining you now, but what will they do for you when hell's fury breaks out against you in the last awesome days before God brings destruction upon the earth?

But that doesn't pertain to us now, for our Jerusalem is a quiet habitation. For centuries most of the Church world has vaunted itself, while angels have gone unrecognized and undesired. This has resulted in a Church that is devoid of the miraculous. They appear to have refrained their offices and withheld their visitations. Only a few pockets of Christians, scattered here and there, seem to be benefiting from the angels' unique and needful ministry.

But wake up, Church! We shall not long be able to continue in this apathy of security; for the Word of God clearly foretells that "in the last days perilous times shall come" (II Tim. 3:1, KJV). And Jesus said, "... and except those days should be shortened, there should no flesh be saved" (Matt. 24:22, KJV)! Such fierce trials, tribulations, persecutions and hardships are coming upon the earth one day, that unassisted flesh and blood will be unable to endure them. As Noah made haste to "prepare an ark" for the time to come (Heb. 11:7, KJV), so we should seek to prepare an ark of angelic safety and assistance for the terrible, hard-to-bear days that will come upon our world —if not for our generation, then surely for our children's or grandchildren's, because certainly they will see the end.

May we reject doubt concerning angels' existence and their ability to be involved in our lives; and may we teach the generations following us to have attitudes that are conducive to their regular and mighty intervention.

My sons have always believed in angels. Both have seen angels at least once in their lives as a result. My sons have always believed in the angels' ability to protect them. Both have been "[borne] up in their hands" (Ps. 91:12, KJV) in times of impending disaster.

Teach both yourself and your children about the ministry of angels. Find the many Scriptures having to do with angels and chock your hearts full of their present-day truth.

Speak God's Word in faith over your life and circumstances, and also over those of your children, knowing that the angels of God "excel in strength, hearkening unto the voice of his Word!" (Ps. 103:20, KJV). Determine to be a voice of God's Word in the earth today. The angels stand ready to help.

What Can We Expect?

Jesus, our Lord, was fed by angels, defended by angels, and strengthened by angels. The stone was rolled from the entrance of His tomb by angels. Peter was freed from prison by a mighty angel. An angel stopped the mouths of fierce lions because of Daniel's faith and obedience. Psalm 91:11, The Amplified Bible, says, "For He will give His angels [especial] charge over you, to accompany and defend and preserve you in all your ways [of obedience and service]." To be an obedient servant of God is imperative!

In Daniel, the three Hebrew boys were unharmed by a blazing hot fire inside an awful furnace because of the presence of one mighty angel of God.

Two angels took Lot, his wife and his two daughters by the hand and led them out of Sodom before it was destroyed by fire and brimstone from heaven.

Their Involvement in Judgment

The two angels blinded the perverts of Sodom when they attempted to burst through Lot's front door. An angel smote ungodly King Herod, filling his bowels with maggots, when he foolishly received praise for himself that was due to God (Acts 12:23). Angels blinded an entire Syrian army bent on destroying one lone prophet of God named Elisha (2 Kings 6:17-18). Angels will be very much involved in the great vials of judgment that are to be poured upon the earth in the evil end times. (See also Matthew 13:41-42 and Psalm 35:4-7.)

Other Things They Can Do

An angel cooked breakfast for the prophet, Elijah, underneath a Juniper tree. Elijah went forty days and forty nights in the strength of that one angelic meal. It is interesting to note that a Juniper tree depicts a defeated spirit or a depressed soul. As Elijah lay there, wanting to die, the angel was sent by God to provide just the encouragement and nourishment Elijah was in need of.

Angels ate dinner with father Abraham and then shared God's plan to destroy Sodom and Gomorrah.

An angel, with one stroke of his staff, consumed the offering Gideon had laid out. Up it went in a flame of fire!

Angels encamp around servants of God who fear Him and deliver them from the designs of satan (Ps. 34:7).

Angels guide and give directions to Christians as they seek to carry out the Master's Great Commission. An angel of the Lord spoke directly to Philip, telling him to go to Gaza where a divine appointment with an Ethiopian official was supernaturally arranged (Acts 8:26).

Angels give relief and comfort in time of need or distress. Jesus received it after that awful time of temptation in the wilderness (Matt. 4:11). Paul received it on board ship in the Mediterranean Sea as it was about to go down. The angel exhorted him to be of good cheer; his life and the lives of those with whom he sailed would be spared because of his prayers and faithfulness (Acts 27:21-35). Again, Jesus received strength from an angel after His bitter time of prayer in the Garden of Gethsemane (Luke 22:43).

Angels have charge of escorting the righteous dead into the presence of the Lord. Luke's gospel reveals that they carried the beggar, Lazarus, into paradise when he died.

If you are truly a Christian, then you can expect to receive an exciting angelic escort into the very presence of your Lord, the very moment your spirit — the real you — leaves that physical body in death. That's one reason why God's Word proclaims: "Precious in the eyes of the Lord is the death of His saints" (Ps. 116:15, author's paraphrase). Brother, it'll be homegoing time, and you'll go in high fashion.

I have read many accounts of the death-bed experiences of great men and women of God who, just prior to their glorious departure, have coherently related to their loved ones that angels were standing by, waiting to take them home.

A number of years ago in the famed Shenandoah Valley of Virginia, three Full Gospel Business Men were headed home one night after flying in from a national convention. As they headed the car west, toward Staunton, Virginia, a drunk man coming from the opposite direction crossed the road and hit them head-on. All three Full Gospel Business Men were killed instantly.

A local news reporter hurried to the scene of the accident in time to snap a couple of pictures of the car before a wrecker hauled it away. There in the pitch-black night, hovering only a few feet above the wrecked car, was a mysterious glow. None of the official law enforcement officers or rescue squad workers could explain its origin or its meaning. When the picture was developed and even run in the newspaper the following day, that mysterious glow was still present for all to see.

After several angels had departed the scene of the accident, escorting the spirits of those three men into the presence of God, one had remained behind, allowing a measure of the radiance of God's glory that was on him to show for the sake of the loved ones and friends who were left behind. Other people could not explain the mysterious glow, but to the Bible-believing saints who beheld it, there was no question. All was well with the three men of God who had departed.

I could relate scores of testimonies from my own personal life, and the lives of others, of just how intimately angels are involved in our day-to-day lives, but I believe the Lord has already gripped your heart. Now I want to talk briefly about the important place that prayer and spiritual warfare will hold in the roles angels will have in the front line warfare to come.

The Place of Prayer and Spiritual Warfare

Our commitment in these two areas of Christian service will determine the part the angels of God will play as we endeavor to take this gospel of the Kingdom to the world and establish strong New Testament churches for God's glory. Consistent prayer and spiritual warfare in the final days of this age will bring a tremendous increase in the number of angels commissioned by God to assist us.

Ruth Prince, wife of renowned Bible teacher, Derek Prince, was blessed with a powerful vision a few years ago as she and Derek sat with several other Christian leaders in a prayer meeting in Belfast, Ireland. For several days they had been teaching about and entering into spiritual warfare. A major prince of satan over that country had been identified and cast down by that army of warring believers, and a sense of great victory was in the air. On the closing day of their time together, as Derek was talking and praying with the local leaders, God granted Ruth insight into the spiritual realm. As she sat quietly in the room listening to her husband, she directed her gaze through the window and out into the atmosphere surrounding the building. Suddenly she beheld an angel descending and heading off in a certain direction. Still more followed, until after a number of minutes Ruth had witnessed a vast host of mighty angelic warriors descending from heaven, going forth to carry out the purposes of Jesus Christ on the earth.

The committed prayers and spiritual warrings of Derek and Ruth Prince, along with those of the Irish brethren who were taking part for those several days, had given the angels sufficient ability and right to knock the satanic resistance in heavenly places out of their way, enabling them to descend unhindered into the spiritual battlefield over the Republic of Ireland.

Daniel's Example

Had Daniel not prayed steadfastly for twenty-one days (Dan. 10:2,13), the evil satanic prince of Persia would have successfully withheld God's messenger angel, keeping him from getting through to Daniel with the vital information he longed for. But Daniel persevered in prayer! Suddenly, that evil Persian prince who was successfully holding back God's angel with the message felt a rush of agonizing fear come over him, for the mighty prince of God's host, Michael, appeared on the scene resplendent with God's glory to take matters into his own hands. Who was the puny prince of Persia to stand against perhaps the most awesome and dazzling of God's vast company of angels? The angel carrying the message was able to deliver it safely to Daniel, because "ain't no devil a match for Michael." Glory!

In both of these stirring accounts, we see that persevering prayer will set into motion the most powerful forces in this universe. As the people of God order themselves in holy array, praying and fasting consistently for God's purposes to be accomplished, heaven is able to move in ways that are often beyond our understanding.

I believe with all of my heart that our prayers give power and authority to the angels. They hearken to the voice of God's Word (Ps. 103:20). As we offer up prayers to God in the mighty name of Jesus Christ, the angels' work is made easier. As we pray "Word" prayers and combat the host of evil with "Word" decrees (Job 22:28, KJV), strong footholds are taken from satan! As we pray in the tongues of men and of angels (1 Cor. 13:1), angels hear and respond because they recognize "tongues" as their language. As we worship God out of full hearts, the "high praises of God in our mouth" execute vengeance and punishments upon those enemies God desires to eradicate. As we do all of these things from hearts that are not "regarding iniquity," the angels are given tremendous liberty to "chase and persecute" the spiritual enemies of God, and to furnish divine protection and assistance to the children of the Kingdom. (See Psalms 149:6-9; 66:18 and 35:5-6.)

Revelation 7:1 (KJV) speaks of "four angels standing on the four corners of the earth, holding the four winds of the earth ...." The ministry of these angels, and perhaps the legions that serve under their command, displays the exercise of relegated power over the material forces. Holding in check mighty winds blowing from every quarter, these mighty ministers preserve the earth from disaster. I believe that every small thunderstorm has the potential of growing into such a ungodly force that it could devastate entire cities and states. If it were not for the ministry of these angels, the entire population of this planet could be obliterated overnight.

During the approach of fierce thunderstorms in the summertime, I bind the principalities and powers in the heavens over our region, forbidding them to bring destruction to my property by wind, water or lightning. I ask Jesus to dispatch a regiment or a host of angels to hold the elements in check, not allowing anything of a destructive nature to happen. God is faithful.

In times of drought I often pray that the angels at the four corners will allow the winds to blow up a storm that will water our lands, bringing refreshment and relief. It is always wise, however, particularly the nearer we get to the end of this age, to ask for God's wisdom as to whether we should pray this way. I'll tell you why I say this. The Bible indicates that droughts will likely play a part in the massive shake-up that God will bring upon this planet. Beware not to pray against what God has commissioned. Woe be unto the man who attempts to steady, with the arm of flesh, what God is busy shaking. Prayers offered against the forces of nature at the wrong time could get one in trouble with his Maker. So be in the habit of seeking God's directives when you're considering prayers and warfares of this type. Not to do so could result in your praying fleshly prayers and resisting what God is doing in judgment.

Close Encounters of an Angelic Kind

It should thrill us to know that there is an "innumerable" host (Heb. 12:22, KJV) standing by to assist us in the terrible days that will come upon this planet.

The following are a few encounters some friends of mine have had with beings of the angelic kind. I pray it will encourage your heart as we close out this chapter on angelic ministry in the last days.

One friend of mine was headed home late one winter afternoon after a long day working at Wintergreen, a ski resort located in the Blue Ridge Mountains of Virginia. As he began his descent down the western side of Afton Mountain, the late afternoon sun shone brightly into the cab of his pickup, creating a cozy warm atmosphere conducive for a short snooze. The heat from the sun, coupled with that from the truck's heater, sent him into a state of slumber. While traveling at a speed of 55 to 60 miles per hour, my friend went to sleep and was headed for a low guardrail, beyond which was a deep mountain ravine.

Suddenly, the hand of an angel shoved his slumping form backwards into the seat. His eyes popped open to see a mammoth hand pressed against his chest. The hand then moved quickly to his chin, raising his face upward so that he would see the impending disaster. My friend, only a split second away from crashing through the guardrail and plummeting into the ravine, was able to regain control of his truck and guide it back onto the roadway.

He said that after regaining his composure he fully expected to be able to look to his right and thank the ministering spirit that had saved him. When he looked, there was no one there.

Another friend was ministering on skid row in Chicago at one time during his early Christian life, trying to reach the bums and the winos. Down on skid row was a giant of a man, totally bound by cheap wine and liquor, who was also prone to horribly demonic fits of temper and violence. Everyone on the row was terrified of this man. Such was the man with whom my friend one day found himself face to face, and no one was around to help. In a demonic, liquor-induced rage, the giant wino threw himself toward him, wielding some sort of wooden club with which to bludgeon him. "JESUS! HELP ME!" my friend cried out, only moments away from being struck. As the big bum's club-wielding arm was beginning its downward thrust toward my friend's head, an invisible force seized his wrist, forbidding him the ability to complete his stroke. Once more he raised his hand to try to hit him, but again he was unable to follow through with the lethal stroke. And then my friend saw it. A huge, masculine hand had wrapped itself around the wrist of the enraged wino, prohibiting his ability to deliver the crushing blow. My Bible-toting friend simply turned and walked away, leaving the bewildered wino in the grasp of an awesome angelic warrior.

Just the other night, a Christian woman living in the county south of us was sitting in her living room when suddenly five or six massive angels walked through the room. No explanation was given — they were just passing through.

A minister friend of mine went to the World Conference on the Holy Spirit in Israel in 1974. While there, he took a bus tour of some of the sights of the Holy Land. It happened that his bus driver had served the Israeli army as a tank commander during the time of the Six Day War of 1967 — the war in which Israel regained possession of the Old City, Jerusalem.

Getting to know the driver after a couple of days of travel, my friend asked him for a few specific details concerning his involvement in the war. During this conversation, the ex-tank commander related the story of how on one battle front, when the Syrian army was bearing down on the Israeli defensive line, they suddenly reversed their direction and retreated swiftly. It was inexplicable. The Syrians had outnumbered the Israelis by at least 100 to 1 on that front alone!

Several crack Israeli commandos launched out in hot pursuit, catching several of the retreating Syrians. Later that day during a time of interrogation, the captives were asked the meaning of their swift retreat, particularly in light of the fact that they had outnumbered the Israeli soldiers on that front by such a large margin. The captives' reply is worth rejoicing over. They retorted, "Outnumbered? We were the ones who were outnumbered! We saw all those men, clothed in brilliant white, ranked behind you for hundreds of meters!"

A brother in our Monterey church was working beneath his house one evening when a cement wall, weighing several tons, fell over on him, pressing him into the ground. This would have meant certain death were it not for the fact that God sent an angel to keep the full weight of the wall from coming down on him. It took rescue workers more than an hour to free him, but all the while my brother was gathering comfort from the visible presence of the angel who had been sent to save him.

If space would permit, I could tell you story after story concerning the marvelous ministry of angels in these last days. You should expect their involvement with us to increase as we get nearer the end. The front line warfare of the days immediately ahead will be impossible to endure without their constant intervention. Expect to see them many times before the end of the age, because I believe God will allow you to if you're faithful.

Beware not to be one who has to see an angel before you can trust God. Our faith is never to be placed in angel-sightings, but in the Word of God which lives and abides forever. If you are one who has been blessed to see an angel, consider it a fringe benefit, but not the paycheck. The paycheck for a life of faith is knowing Jesus and knowing His Word. Live and work for the paycheck, not the fringe benefit.

Beware, also, not to be guilty of worshiping angels (Col. 2:18). There are people who, after seeing and/or communicating with an angel, have relegated Jesus from His rightful position of Lordship in their lives and have substituted Him through the vain worship of the angel. I am confident that, in such cases, the angel involved is heartsick over such a miscarriage of worship. When John attempted to worship an angel, even though he was only caught up in the excitement of the moment, the angel was quick to instruct him, "See thou do it not: I am thy fellow servant" (Rev. 19:10; 22:9, KJV).

Now right on the other side there are evil angels that are thrilled to receive the worship of mortal men. Satan is one of them. The rulers and princes in his kingdom are others. They are even able to appear as "angels of light" (2 Cor. 11:14) to deceive the simple-minded and undiscerning. Such was that vile spirit, "the angel Moroni," that deceived young Joseph Smith, the founder of the Mormon religion. The Word of God instructs us to "try the spirits whether they are of God" (1 John 4:1, KJV). Should a glorious-looking spirit appear to you, ask it if it loves to worship Jesus Christ of Nazareth. Ask it if God came in the flesh to shed His blood and redeem mankind. Ask it if Jesus was raised for the dead, flesh and bone on the third day, and if He is now seated as a resurrected *man* at the right hand of God Almighty in heaven. Ask it to get down on its knees with you and worship Jesus, and Him alone. If it can do all of that, you've probably got a bonafide angel of God before you; hear what he has to say. But then judge his message by the Word of God. A true angel will not mind being put through such a test, particularly if he comes with a message.

In a time of disaster when there's no time for discussion, you'll just have to trust God's providence and watch the angel work. To put him through a five-point test could mean the difference between life and death.

Will we really need assistance from angels in the time to come? I guarantee we will. Revelation reveals that a time is coming when the great enemies of God under satan, the dragon, will be so infuriated over their inability to eradicate Israel, that they will turn to make war "against the rest of her offspring — those who obey God's commandments and hold to the testimony of Jesus" (Rev. 12:17). Worldwide persecution against the Church will unequivocally require the ministry of angels or it simply won't endure it. The evil spirit of Jezebel will again raise her manipulative, domineering head to "kill off the Lord's prophets" (1 Kings 18:4). Whether it comes in the form of Communism, Muhammadanism, the New Age Movement, or false brethren really doesn't matter; it will come upon the earth in the latter day, wreaking great havoc among the nations before Jesus returns upon a white horse to destroy it by "the brightness of His coming" (II Thess. 2:8, KJV).

If the Church is not raptured prior to this time, like so many believe it will be, a remnant of God's people, with mighty angelic assistance, will carry on the glorious work of the gospel. Many will give their lives in Jesus' service, "in nothing terrified by their adversaries," which will be to the enemy a sure sign of his impending judgment from God. (See Philippians 1:28.)

Many will escape the sword, the flame, the wrath of a dying devil by the direct intervention upon natural law of the mighty unseen ones who surround them. Perplexity of nations will be upon us all, but out of it will stand up a holy nation unto God, a royal priesthood whose banner reads loud and clear — "Jesus Christ is Lord!"

10

THE REMNANT

In his best selling novels, *The Present Darkness* and *Piercing the Darkness*, author Frank Perreti refers to the faithful prayer warriors of Ashton as "The Remnant." I like that, because God will always have a "remnant" carrying out His directives in the midst of "a crooked and depraved generation" (Phil. 2:15).

Merrill C. Tenney's definition of a remnant is two-fold. A remnant is:

1. A people who survive political or military crises.
2. A spiritual kernel of Israel who would survive God's judgment and become the germ of the new people of God. (Tenney, *Handy Dictionary of the Bible*, Zondervan Publishing, 1965)

God's remnant in the turbulent days to come will be comprised of those believers who keep true faith and righteousness when the majority of professing Christians are falling away. Because of their fervent love for God, and their lives of obedience to His Word, they will be hated, maligned, esteemed of little or no value, and discarded by an antichristian world and lukewarm Church.

Anyone who has worked with fabric knows what the remnants are. Remnants are those small, insignificant cuts of fabric that are taken off the beginning and the end of a bolt of material. In one of my outbuildings, I have the remnants of a nice carpet we laid over two years ago. They lay there gathering dust, forgotten, unappreciated. That reminds me of the Scripture in Hebrews where the writer is talking about the faithful down through the centuries: "Of whom the world was not worthy"

(Heb. 11:38, KJV). Like Joshua and Caleb, the remnant are of "a different spirit" than the majority of God's people. Like the three Hebrew boys, the remnant refuses to bow to idols even when it is the *safe* thing to do. Like the fighting men who left their tribes in order to rally 'round David at Ziklag, so the remnant of any generation leaves tribal, "denominational" traditions, loyalties and useless customs to gather unto Jesus Christ in totality.

Compared to the general population of a nation or the Church, a remnant is a very small number. Often referred to as "survivors" in modern translations of the Bible, I believe the remnant, in any generation, are those whole-hearted believers who "have been crucified with Christ" (Gal. 2:20), who no longer are living unto themselves, and whose lives are "hid with Christ in God" (Col. 3:3, KJV). Sin, iniquity and idolatry is regularly being judged and expelled from their lives as they seek, by the grace of God and the blood of Jesus, to "purify [themselves], even as he [Christ] is pure" (1 John 3:3). Because of godly purity, and because they "hold forth the word of life" to a dying generation, they are often misunderstood, misrepresented, maligned and murdered. Satan sees to that! That is why the Word exhorts us to "pray for the remnant that still survives" (Isa. 37:4). Two vicious enemies of God — the world and the devil — are out to eradicate the faithful remnant from the face of the earth. Indeed, satan's plan has always been to wipe out every living, breathing segment of genuine Christianity so Jesus will have nothing to return for on the last day of this age. But praise God forever, we can gratefully say as did Isaiah of old: "Unless the Lord Almighty had left us some survivors, we would have become like Sodom, we would have become like Gomorrah" (Isa. 1:9).

Much of the Church today is guilty of the sins that called for the destruction on the twin cities of Sodom and Gomorrah. Pride, fullness of bread, idolatry, abundance of idleness and a failure to strengthen the hands of the poor and needy. (See Ezekiel 16:49-50.) Sexual perversions of the vilest sorts are always found among such a host of people. But out of the rabble that often calls itself the Church, God faithfully gathers a remnant. The Word prophesies: "And I will gather the remnant of my flock out of all countries whither I have driven them [because of their stubborn pride and rebellion], and will bring them back to their fold; and they shall be fruitful and increase" (Jer. 23:3, KJV). In every nation on earth God is gathering a spiritual priesthood from among the scattered of spiritual Israel. Abundant fruit and increase is His goal for this remnant. In another place He declares, "Once more a remnant of the house of Judah will take root downward and bear fruit upward" (Isa. 37:31-32, author's paraphrase). He caps it off by saying: "The zeal of the Lord Almighty will accomplish this!"

Remnant Characteristics

In times of great temptation to do otherwise, the remnant of God will "hate evil, love good, [and] maintain justice in the courts" (Amos 5:15), thus prompting God's mercy to be poured out on them. Hebrews 1:9 reveals that *Jesus* hated iniquity, loved righteousness, and was anointed above all His companions. These cardinal characteristics found among God's remnant people will bring on a great anointing for the building of God's kingdom on the earth.

Zephaniah 3:13 declares that the remnant "will do no wrong; they will speak no lies, nor will deceit be found in their mouths." Does this sound like the Church today? This verse continues: "They will eat and lie down and no one will make them afraid." The truth will pour from their mouths, and their actions will line up with the Word they herald. Deception and manipulation will not be found among them; God will have exposed it and barred it from their number. Their every need will be supplied, because they are active in the Lord's work. No one will scare them. Death itself will not frighten them, because they know that in Jesus Christ they have already died. Though the power of hell be arrayed against them, they will stand triumphantly, because the death of their bodies will only send them to their heavenly reward.

The last days remnant should have no fear of the mark of the beast, either. Christians today ought to have a greater fear of not having the mark of God in their foreheads. (Examine Ezekiel 9:4-6.) Heaven marks the men and women who feel with God for the sins that break His heart and turn His face away from His people. These are the intercessors. In the final days of this age, these will be the ones who are spared the wrath and judgments of God!

How about you, my friend? Would you say that there is an invisible, spiritual mark in your forehead? Are you giving your life for the kingdom of God? Is intercession a part of your busy schedule? Do you stand in the gap for the defeated and dying around this world? Judge yourself.

Restoration

The Word reveals in Haggai that in times of restoration the Lord will stir up the spirit of His remnant to rise and build together.

> *The Lord stirred up the spirit of ... the whole remnant of the people .... They came and began to work on the house of the Lord Almighty, their God* (Hag. 1:14).

Take a look around you, Christian. Who are those brothers and sisters who are eagerly and actively involved in the building of God's latter-day house, the Church? Who is busy building people, living stones, into a holy habitation for the Lord? Who are the ones praying fervently for revival? Who are those actively sharing the faith with the lost? Who are the ones joyfully supporting God's appointed leadership over them, working in faith and not complaining? If you see a few folks like this, they're the remnant. Those who are not working are not the remnant. Haggai said, "the *whole* remnant ... came to work." It is always that way!

We are in perhaps the final days of the restoration of the Church. The five ministry gifts are coming forth; God's proper government is being established among His people. He's beginning to unleash more of His authority and power in the earth. Spirit-engendered unity is coming forth — God's way! Who are those taking hold of these aspects of restoration? Who are humbling themselves before it? Who are not ashamed of the gospel of Jesus Christ — the most radical, revolutionary, earth-shaking message ever proclaimed to the ears and hearts of men? Whose castigations of sin, worldliness and compromise in the Church are causing them to be rejected by the sinners and hypocrites in Zion (Isa. 33:14)? "But it is not mercy to castigate them" some argue. Sometimes the most merciful thing we can do is reprove and rebuke; if received correctly it will be kindness and oil poured on their heads.

> *Let a righteous man strike me — it is a kindness; let him rebuke me — it is oil on my head. My head will not refuse it* (Ps. 141:5).

A Dividing of the Way

Because of the stance a believing people will have to take upon the Word of God, many will find it convenient to leave their ranks. Not everyone is willing to commit themselves that far. By and large, the Christianity we have seen in modern America has been self-styled and lazy, costing the so-called disciple very little. But that is changing rapidly. The revealing winds of God are beginning to blow more briskly now and will likely reach hurricane force as God roots out and rids His Church of pride, rebellion and hypocrisy.

A dividing of the way is even now coming upon us in Christendom, and it will be very hard to remain in the Church for long without having our true hearts revealed. The prophetic ministry of Jesus Christ that is being rapidly restored to the ranks of Christianity will expose and sift the false from among the true. We dare not resist this vital ministry among us; we had best get real and honest before God, giving up our sacred cows and doing away with our secret agendas. We must do away with preconceived ideas that aren't in line with the Scriptures and be open to accept the truth as God reveals it to us.

To be numbered among God's remnant, we must be totally open; we must be eager for God's dealings in our lives. Only then will we be prepared for what is coming. Allow Him to expose, sift, analyze and judge the very thoughts and purposes of your heart, and you'll find yourself being prepared for glory!

Persecution Doesn't Sound Like Glory!

> *And the dragon was wroth with the woman, and went to make war with the* ***remnant*** *of her seed, which keep the commandments of God, and have the testimony of Jesus Christ* (Rev. 12:17, KJV, author's emphasis).

It is obvious that at some point in future events, God's people are going to have to deal with the dragon of Revelation. Times of great persecution and bloodshed will accompany it. What glory can possibly come out of one's being mauled by satan and his persecuting agents? Let's look at Scripture.

> *Dear friends, do not be surprised at the painful trial you are suffering, as though something strange were happening to you. But rejoice that you participate in the sufferings of Christ, so that you may be overjoyed when his glory is revealed. If you are insulted because of the name of Christ, you are blessed, for the Spirit of glory and of God rests on you* (1 Pet. 4:12-14).

There is a special glory awaiting those who suffer patiently for the gospel. When Jesus' majestic glory is finally revealed in its fullness, those who suffered because of their union with Him will have that glory revealed on them as well. The sufferings of this present time cannot be compared with the glory which shall be revealed in God's overcomers!

The Cooling of Christian Love: A Sign of the End

Matthew 24:12 reveals that the *agape* love of many end times Christians will grow ice-cube cold. Because of the increase of wickedness many people who at one time professed Christ's Lordship will be subtly drawn away from the fellowship of believers and, ultimately, from fellowship with God.

The New International Version says "the love of *most* will grow cold." That means the majority of professing Christians are going to allow the prevalence of iniquity to somehow lead them off the narrow path, and they may one day deny their allegiance to Jesus. What a terrible thing for a person to do. Hear Peter:

> *If they have escaped the corruption of the world by knowing our Lord and Savior Jesus Christ and are again entangled in it and overcome, they are worse off at the end than they were at the beginning. It would have been better for them not to have known the way of righteousness, than to have known it and then to turn their backs on the sacred commandment that was passed on to them* (2 Pet. 2:20-21).

Paul warned of a time at the end of the age when a falling away, or departure would occur.

> *Let no man deceive you by any means: for that day shall not come, except there come a falling away first...* (II Thess. 2:3, KJV)

The Greek word *apostasia* signifies an abandonment from true faith in Jesus Christ. One translation refers to it as a rebellion that will occur. This can only mean a rebellion as it relates to the people of God, because the world is already in rebellion.

If such a rebellion of God's people occurs, with the majority of them rejecting the pure Word of God, where will that leave those few faithful ones who actively follow Jesus to the end? I believe it leaves them in the remnant.

What About World Harvest?

In Matthew 24:14, Jesus says, "This gospel of the Kingdom shall be preached in the whole world as a testimony to all nations, and then the end will come." Will the gospel be preached in all the world to win the world? I certainly hope that will be the result! But Jesus said it would be preached "for a witness." In other words, no man shall have an excuse on Judgment Day.

It is true that a mighty harvest of converts will be swept in during the final hours of this age, but how many of them do you honestly believe will stick with the Lord till the end? Jesus spoke of "the hour of trial that is going to come upon the whole world to test those who live on the earth" (Rev. 3:10).

What About the Rapture of the Church?

Two major opinions exist concerning the belief in a secret rapture or "catching up" of the Church just prior to the greatest horrors of the tribulation period. Many believe wholeheartedly that true saints of God will be snatched out of the world by Jesus just in time to miss the wrath of God as it is poured out on the earth. Other Christians believe just as wholeheartedly that Christians will have to go through such tumultuous times, but, through faith in God, will be able to endure it.

A third group stands at the middle of the issue, desiring to be taken out of the world via secret rapture, but also willing to face the very real possibility that we may be left here to face the horrors of the tribulation.

Different interpretations of prophetic books such as Revelation and Daniel abound. What is a Bible believer to do with them all?

First of all, obey Jesus' command and "see that ye be not troubled" (Matt. 24:6b, KJV). Being disturbed over all the prospects concerning your future will only cripple your faith in God's ability to care for you in whatever may come. We must remember that regardless of our location during perilous times, we have a "secret place" under the shadow of His wings (Ps. 91:1, KJV).

Secondly, don't become dogmatic about your interpretation of the prophetic Scriptures. No one likes a know-it-all! Paul said, "If any man claims to know anything, he knows nothing yet as he ought to know it" (1 Cor. 8:2, free translation). When discussing your particular viewpoint concerning the subject of the end times, keep your words soft and tender; you may one day have to eat them.

Thirdly, determine that between now and the end of your life, or the end of this age, you are going to give your life for Jesus as never before. Determine that if there will be a remnant of only a few million believers left in the world after a possible "falling away," you are going to be a part of them.

The Church: Spiritual Israel

When God speaks of natural Israel in the Scriptures, His words often apply equally to the Church, which is spiritual Israel. With that in mind, let us examine the following verse:

> *Though the number of Israelites be like the sand by the sea, only a remnant will be saved. The Lord will carry out his sentence on the earth with speed and finality* (Rom. 9:27-28).

Many people in the world today are calling themselves true sons of Israel. But a time is coming when God will sort out the false from the genuine. Only the true seed of Abraham, Isaac and Jacob (Israel) will be saved.

The world is full of people calling themselves something they're not. Therefore, a time of exposure is at hand. Tares, goats and thistles are being revealed for what they are. The false in Zion are beginning to show up among those who are pure of heart, like an ink spot on a wedding gown.

May I ask you a question? If God were to sort through your church at this hour, how would the members fare? Judge honestly, friend. Times so perilous are coming upon the earth that weak, uncommitted Christianity will become a thing of the past.

The Winnowing Fork: How God Arrives at His Remnant

If a remnant is all that will remain of God's faithful people when the clock finally ticks down to the end of this age, then how will He arrive at this remnant?

I believe that a prophetic word, spoken by John the prophet concerning the unique ministry of Jesus, is finding fulfillment today as never before. It speaks of Jesus' winnowing fork:

> *His winnowing fork is in his hand to clear his threshing floor and to gather the wheat into his barn, but he will burn up the chaff with unquenchable fire* (Luke 3:17).

The definition of the word "winnow" is revealing. It means to expose grain or other substances to the wind or to a current of air so that the lighter particles (chaff and other refuse matter) are separated or blown away.

The winnowing fork was used to pitch wheat to the wind so that the true wheat would be revealed as it fell back to the threshing floor.

Within each of us there exists both chaff and refuse matter. Chaff often comes in the form of pride, unteachableness, rebellion, unforgiveness, resentment, dishonesty, doubt, fear, impatience, greed and tendencies toward sexual immorality. These are often hidden deep within the most sincere of Christians. God will not allow such refuse to abide in His children forever, because He desires a pure people for Himself. He therefore chooses a winnowing fork and pitches us into the air so that we might be exposed to the wind of God.

The Scriptures speak of a "stormy wind fulfilling his word"

(Ps. 148:8, KJV). The winds of God are not always gentle breezes; sometimes they are unyielding gales blowing upon our flesh and carnal minds. No one who names the Name of Jesus in sincerity will escape exposure to the winds of God. All who attempt to hide will fall, because there are unrelenting currents demanding purity, integrity, morality and conformity to the life and nature of Jesus Christ our Lord.

Everything we bring with us into the Kingdom of God from the old, unregenerate life is baggage either to hold onto or discard. Most is baggage to discard, and too often we do so with screams of sheer agony. But it must go if we are to be mature men and women in Christ.

The chaff I carried with me into the family of God was hideous. Fear of man was lodged deep within me. Procrastination and laziness oozed out of my pores. So the Lord began arranging circumstances and situations to challenge me in each of these areas. Each time He did so, my old man, the flesh, cried out. Yet His winds were unyielding. Through the years I've been changing for the better.

Winds of adversity will blow upon the Church in this hour. Even as I write, I am undergoing severe testing. Storms of hurricane force will put each Christian to the test as God works tirelessly toward a remnant. There will be sifting, sorting, analyzing and exposing. We must all fall upon the Rock and be broken (Matt. 21:44), or else have the Rock fall on us one day and break us!

How one responds to the winds of God will determine his future in the Kingdom. The tempting thing to do will be to run and hide, or to become angry, but such reactions will not work the righteousness of God.

It will help us to know a little about the winds of God, and also about the winnowing fork ministry of the Lord, if we are to pass the tests of the times to come.

What will God use to pitch believers into the air so that the true wheat in their character will be revealed and the chaff will blow away? Through study of God's Word and the experience of witnessing the work of the Holy Spirit in my life and in the lives of others, I have arrived at the following "winnowing forks." I have seen them used of God in the selection of a remnant. We must remember that "many are called, but few are chosen." What eliminates those unfit for the following list of situations and circumstances answer that.

Winnowing Fork #1: Pride

Circumstances, situations and people will challenge and reveal our pride.

What will we do with pride as it shows up in the face of God's revealing wind? That's what God is looking to see. Will we react in pride, or will we refuse it and mortify it?

One fork the Lord uses to toss our pride into the wind is to have a ministry we hold dear withheld from us or taken from us. I have seen grown people behave like children when such a thing happens. If they don't cry and pout, sulking off into a spiritual corner, they become very bitter and angry. Either way, they fail a very important character test in God's maturation process.

Abraham was willing to offer his only, long-waited-for son to the Lord without grumbling. God was then able to bless and honor him in ways he never knew possible. Not only did he get his son back, but he also made it possible for God to give His only Son as the sacrificial Lamb for the sins of the world. Had Abraham failed the test, God may not have sent Jesus to die for us.

Your unwillingness to offer up "your" ministry when God creates circumstances and situations, or brings people into your life who call for it, will stand paramount as a hindrance to God doing anything greater for you.

When faced with the possibility that a ministry may be taken from you, it is good to reflect on this truth: "If you let it go and it returns to you, you'll have it forever; but if you let it go and it does not return to you, you never had it in the first place." Be willing to put things like this to the test. Why be so determined to possess something that was never really yours to begin with?

There was a musically gifted and talented man who derived great joy and satisfaction from standing before God's people and leading them in worship. One day his pastor asked him to step back from his responsibilities for an indefinite period of time. At that moment the man was faced with a choice: "Do I ubbornly reject his wishes and raise a fuss?" he asked himself. "And if he fails to yield to my objections will I pout and make things miserable for him and everybody else? Or will I give the whole decision to God, trusting Him to do what's best for me and my place in His Kingdom?" The man showed the latter response, and within a few weeks was given back his responsible position in worship leadership. With it came a greater degree of anointing than he had ever before known. He had passed a very important test, and God rewarded him.

Another way God tosses your pride to the wind is to let you see or hear of someone receiving credit for something you did. Many a person has abruptly jumped forward at such a time, tooting his own horn and making a fool of himself. The godly reaction, at such a time, is to abide quietly in the background, allowing the Lord to see that you get the credit when and if He's ready for you to. You'll be sorely tempted to take matters into your own hands, but don't do it! React properly and God will be pleased to exalt you *in due time*. React wrongly and you'll fail the test.

Still another way Jesus tosses pride to the wind is by allowing you to see an opponent or an enemy rewarded publicly. Deep down inside, most of us would really rather see our enemies abased. But God's Word exhorts us:

> *Rejoice not when thine enemy falleth, and let not thine heart be glad when he stumbleth* (Prov. 24:17, KJV).

How often have you secretly (or openly) rejoiced to hear of calamity or misfortune sacking your adversary? How often have you grimaced at the news of him prospering? Judge yourself properly when such times arise; react properly or fail the test.

Yet another way we have our pride revealed is when someone less deserving or qualified is given something we've coveted for ourselves. Perhaps it is a position, perhaps a reward. God will have this happen in order to see your response.

One more way pride is revealed is when we are placed with a person or persons who are not overly impressed with our abilities or our intellect.

"Why don't they see what I have to offer?" you wonder. "I've got a college degree, and I'm so qualified!"

If you remain faithful (and silent, not pushing yourself forward), the Lord Himself will bring you release, by causing them to recognize and utilize you, or by releasing you to become part of something else. But give it time, and keep a right attitude.

I knew a man a few years ago who considered himself to be a highly qualified and gifted person, capable of doing anything he set his mind to. Actually, he was quite right in his assessment of his abilities. But he was also full of pride. He was so lofty in his opinion of himself that no one could stand being around him.

There is a proverb that says, "Most men will proclaim every one his own goodness [worth], but a faithful man who can find?" (Prov. 26:6, author's paraphrase). What this verse is saying is that it isn't hard to pick the "best" people — they'll tell you who they are. If you do not recognize them as quickly as they think you ought to, they'll cause all sorts of problems in the Church. They are expert sowers of discord among the brethren. The winnowing fork of delayed recognition or no recognition reveals them. Good! We need to know.

Winnowing Fork #2: Challenges to Commitment

Another winnowing fork utilized by the Lord are the many challenges to commitment that we face. We live in a world that is full of such challenges, and God allows them to confront us to see if we meant business when we accepted Him.

In such a world of adversity it is of utmost importance to rely on the power and grace of the Holy Spirit, because the natural man, even the carnal Christian, is incapable of handling all the challenges to commitment that will arise.

Are you truly committed to the Lord? Are you really committed to the Church He has sent you to be a part of? Let's find out.

One challenge confronting multitudes of Christians in this hour is seen when God asks them to submit to leaders they don't particularly like, trust or agree with. But if God has called you to a certain church or job you will have to submit to its leadership.

None of us will see eye-to-eye on every issue. However, we must stay in faith toward God for His ongoing working in all of us. In the Church our relationships must be built on nothing less than covenant and a firm understanding that God has called us to live and build together. True covenant relationships survive theological, geographical and ecclesiastical change. Covenant is binding.

Charles Simpson said: "Covenant binds God to men; and men to other men." Such binding together, performed by the working of God, is next-to-impossible to break, and yet, all over the Body of Christ we see fractures. It is because our relationships are founded incorrectly.

My wife and I are covenanted together. Our agreement or lack of agreement is no basis for our relationship. We both know God called us to live and serve Him together, and so our mutual commitment to that calling transcends anything that would attempt to separate us. Ours is not a fragile relationship because it is based on covenant. That is the way it is to be in the Church and in our relationships in the body.

I heard of a brother who fell out of fellowship with a church because the conservative political views of one of his elders did not agree with his liberal viewpoint. Rather than allowing God to assist him in an expectation for a growing relationship with this elder, despite their political differences, he allowed a fear of the elder to enter into him and motivate him to leave the church.

Another challenge to our commitment to Jesus is placement among a people with whom we have very little in common, except for our loyalty to Him. Often they are the type of people we would have avoided when we were sinners. The way they dress, what they drive, the houses they live in, the music they listen to, etc. has a tendency to repel us. They usually are not the "lovely types" we would have chosen to serve with, and yet the Lord instructs us to build lasting covenantal relationships with them.

We must allow God to bring into our lives the people of His choice. If we surround ourselves only with people who meet our liking, we are headed for disappointment. God's choices turn out to be the best ones for us.

Still another "winnowing fork challenge" to our commitment to Him is the continual temptation to deny that we know Him. How often have you found yourself among "sophisticated worldlings" whom you know would think we were nuts for believing in Jesus? Have you ever denied Him before them? You have listened to their jokes and laughed for fear of being considered "square." You have heard them deriding a Christian brother or sister behind his or her back and haven't defended him or her. You have listened as they cursed God's name and used it in vain, never once letting them know how it makes you feel. Your reaction to things such as these often reveal the strength of your commitment to Him.

Other challenges that test our commitment to Him come in the form of temptations to return to the evils of our past life. Jesus said, "No one who puts his hand to the plow and looks back is fit for service in the kingdom of God" (Luke 9:62). We must beware of the subtle temptations to look back to the lives we left behind. Look too long and you may leap.

Winnowing Fork #3: Financial Pressure

This winnowing fork seems to be applied to many people these days. It comes in the form of a challenge. What will you do if your financial stability is threatened? Rather than drawing near to God, many draw near to a second or third job. When financial hardship looms large on your horizon, will you discontinue tithing? Many people only tithe when they can "afford" to. We must remember that steadfast tithing keeps us in a place where God can move on our behalf, but if we quit tithing, the devourer is given liberty to bring cursing into our lives. Never stop giving the first fruits of all your increase (Prov. 3:9), even if your increase is at times pitifully small.

Another financial challenge: When in a crunch, will you stoop to dishonesty to save yourself, or will you remain a man or woman of integrity before God? The Lord will examine your reactions in times of financial stress. Where have you really placed your trust?

At this very moment you may be under financial stress, tempted to do something that will jeopardize your fellowship with God. Don't do it!

Perhaps you are one who is trying to support too extravagant a life-style, and so are being subtly drawn away from doing what is right in God's sight. Reverse this process and develop the godly art of contentment. "But godliness with contentment is great gain" (1 Tim. 6:6). Learn to rule your desires and confine your wants to the measure of what God has provided.

In our town there is a man who constantly groans about how much he has to work in order to make ends meet. Hearing him either calls forth great pity or extreme disgust. In my case it brings forth disgust.

He works two and three jobs, seven days a week, in order to pay for his expensive home, his three new automobiles, his brand-new satellite system and his gun-collecting hobby. Does he give the Lord His ten percent? I doubt it. Does he give generously or even sparingly to the poor? He's never been known to. He can, however, complain about how hard he "has" to work. The sad thing about this man is that he's headed for certain disaster somewhere down the road.

Winnowing Fork #4: The Challenge to Watchfulness

> *Be careful, or your hearts will be weighed down with dissipation, drunkenness and the anxieties of life, and that day will close on you unexpectedly like a trap. For it will come upon all those who live on the face of the whole earth.* ***Be always on the watch****, and pray that you may be able to escape all that is about to happen, and that you may be able to stand before the Son of Man* (Luke 21:34-36, author's emphasis).

"Be always on the watch." This directive from the heart and mouth of the Son of Man is not a suggestion, it is an imperative! We are surrounded by an anti-Christian world whose pull to godlessness is incredibly powerful. I am seeing Christians whom I never thought would fall away turning their backs on Jesus over the craziest things.

The other night Darlene and I were discussing the reality of the perilous times at hand. Up till now it always seemed that such days of testing would certainly come, but they were always off in the future somewhere. However, because of so many negative events taking place in Christianity we have come to realize that perilous times are no longer off in the future, but are upon us now!

I had always figured that the heavy heel of communism, great earthquakes in strange places, or terrible plagues and wars were the signs of perilous times — and they certainly are. But now I've come to see that one of the greatest perils to the Church is the multitude of Christian people who are falling out of fellowship with God and each other. If I didn't understand the prophetic Scriptures it would be downright depressing. There is a large and aggressive demonic working taking place in the ranks of Christianity today, and I don't see it getting better as time goes on.

> *At that time many will turn away from the faith and will betray and hate each other* (Matt. 24:10).

The demonic working of betrayal within the Body of Christ at this present time is monstrous, but we must look for the good the Lord can bring out of it. Be watchful as the Lord reveals those who can be trusted, differentiating them from those who cannot. We will need to know the loyal ones in the evil day to come.

The Bible indicates that loyalty will be in short supply during the last days, and that it will be a precious spiritual commodity. Seek to be one of the few who will remain loyal to the end — both to God and your fellow believers.

"Be always on the watch." Our spiritual affections and mental faculties are so easily distracted from concentration on serious matters. We so often waste moral and physical powers by vicious indulgence in pleasure. Paul prophesied that the last generations of human beings before the return of Jesus Christ would be "lovers of pleasures more than lovers of God" (II Tim. 3:4, KJV). The reality of this prophetic statement intensifies in our world with each passing day. The day of God's judgment will indeed close like a trap upon all who fail to keep their mind and energies set on God, and sadly, many who once expressed allegiance to Jesus will find themselves in the lurch with those who never accepted Christ.

That God would allow such trying times to confront us should neither shock us nor offend us, for He has given the Church through the centuries ample warning. Also, He spoke of the time "when I make up my treasured possession" (Mal. 3:17). Those faithful few who truly love the Lord, adoring Him to one another on an ongoing basis, will make up His jewels.

God will spare them as a man spares his own son who serves him, and they will comprise those discerning righteous ones, shining forth in the midst of gross darkness because of God's glory upon their lives.

Among this group there is no room for the brand of lukewarm Christianity we see so much of in America. God is cutting their number down to size. Are you permitting, through your own laziness or rebellion, the challenges proffered by the world and allowed by God to eliminate you?

"Be always on the watch!"

Winnowing Fork #5: Fear

Another winnowing fork — one that reveals the quality of trust we have in God — is the pressure of fear. Fear is a bold opponent to our growth in Christ, brazen in its defiance of us as Goliath was brazen in his defiance of the armies of Israel. Fear will run right up into your face and back you down in a moment's time. It is bold and showy, and yet it has a mysterious, secretive power over us as well. Most of the time it is obvious; at other times it is well-hidden beneath the surface of other reactions and feelings.

Fear of falling back into a sinful life-style will often cause men to hold, legalistically, to a pet doctrine or way of life. Let me give a couple of examples.

I knew a brother in Christ who became so legalistic in the way he lived his Christianity that he lost the joy of living and eventually walked out on the Christian life altogether. This guy was so bound up by a fear of falling back into the ways and pleasures of the world that he wouldn't allow himself some of life's smallest pleasures. For instance, he wouldn't even allow himself to hang a picture on the wall. He considered all pictures to be the graven images forbidden in Scripture. He wore black clothes, fearful that even clothing of a "slightly" stylish fashion would pull him back to the world. On top of all this, he almost insisted that all other Christians adopt his legalistic manner, saying that if they did not, they were displeasing to the Lord and falling into apostasy.

Eventually he fell away from the Lord, black clothes and all, and was reduced by fear into an even more miserable human being than he had been before. My wife and I had attempted to show him that he was being motivated by fear, and that by dealing ruthlessly with that fear, he would swing into balance and enjoy the Christian life. He wouldn't hear us.

Another man I knew had come to the Lord with two big problems weighing him down. One was bondage to a materialistic life-style, which had placed him far in debt. His means could not adequately support his thirst for more of this world's playthings. Rather than learning how to get a grip on his materialistic tendency, he rejected altogether the notion that God desires to prosper His people and adopted a poverty, "barely get by" mentality. Fear of the power of money motivated him to take an extreme position against it. Rather than deal with that fear, he became out-of-balance and isolated himself from Christians who believe differently.

The second major problem this man had was an explosive temper. Prior to his commitment to Christ he was involved in a number of fights, indicating his violent nature. As a young Christian, this tendency frightened him. Rather than deal with his violent temper in a mature way, he reacted in an immature way: He became a total pacifist. In order to protect himself from his violent temper, he adopted what I feel is an extreme position on the subject of defense. He didn't really deal with his temper, however, and if push came to shove, he would still explode.

Suppose a violent intruder entered his home one night to rape and kill his wife. Standing only upon the teachings of Jesus as delivered in the Sermon on the Mount, it would seem that he should stand idly by and allow the intruder to have his way with her. But by interpreting what Jesus said in light of the whole counsel of God, he would see that he had the right and responsibility to intervene with justifiable force, if the need called for it. True, Jesus said that if someone slaps you on the cheek, turn the other cheek. But what if they are assaulting one for whom you are responsible? What about the Scripture that says, "If thou forbear to deliver them that are drawn unto death, and those that are ready to be slain; If thou sayest, Behold, we knew it not; doth not he that pondereth the heart consider it? and he that keepeth thy soul, doth not he know it? and shall not he render to every man according to his works?" (Prov. 24:11-12, KJV)

Hopefully you can see that fear, undealt with, can lead fine people to adopt faulty positions on very important subjects.

Fear of Man

The Bible teaches that "the fear of man bringeth a snare" (Prov. 29:25, KJV). This type of fear is often more paralyzing than any other. It is easy to stand boldly and talk ferociously to unseen demon spirits, but to stand eyeball-to-eyeball with a flesh and blood opponent that naturally intimidates is altogether different for many people.

Throughout our lives, the devil will seek to bring us into bondage to people. We must beware at all times, because the fear of man is one of his most effective ways to get our eyes and ears off of what God is saying to us and onto what men are saying. If anyone is becoming louder and more influential in your life than God, check to see if you are being snared. If you are, then back off from the person and cultivate the one-to-one fellowship with your Lord that you once enjoyed. If the person you back off from presses in on you at this time, then know he's being sent by satan to gain control of your life. Break free!

Fearfulness Disqualifies

As Moses prepared a people for warfare, the fearful were cut out (Deut. 20:8). As Gideon prepared a remnant for battle, the fearful were cut out (Judg. 7:3). Eliminated along with the fearful of Gideon's army were those who weren't watchful. A lack of watchfulness will allow fear to creep in and stop us. The latter-day remnant will be comprised of men and women who remain watchful and fearless till the end.

Fear of God's sovereignty over our lies, a lack of trust in His faithfulness, fear of what tomorrow may bring, fear of satan and demons: the fears that confront us are many. But as born-again Christians we are to have no fear! Our life is hid with Christ in God. Because He lives, we can face tomorrow confidently!

Winnowing Fork #6: The Challenge to Change

God has been telling the Church that constant change is here to stay, and yet, when it actually happens, we often react negatively. A little change, from time to time, is all right, but what do we do when big changes are called for?

We have learned through our years of working with them that most people regard change as loss. Because change often alters the way we're used to doing things, we blindly accept the lie that we are coming out on the losing side. This, in turn, is usually followed by some form of anger. We think that changes mean we are being stolen from, and nobody likes to be stolen from. A reaction of anger to changing situations will *never* work the righteousness of God. The wrong reactions in times of change will cause us to lose out, but that is not God's will for us.

Change has often released people into the greatest exploits of their lives. Change can be an invigorating thing if we'll respond correctly to it, trusting God in it. Psalm 55:19 (KJV) says, "Because they have no changes, therefore they fear not God." Responding correctly when our plans are unhinged and our hopes are dashed will keep us from drifting into deadly forms of spiritual apathy. Unsettling change draws one to God.

When in a time of change it is good to consider the following:

1. Change almost always involves pain and discomfort. Examine the many changes that took place in the lives of God's men and and women of faith in the Bible and see the pain they experienced. But don't settle down on the pain; look for the results.

2. God pressures us into change because He has something better for us. It may be very difficult to believe while in the midst of great changes, but the experiences of the Bible prove it to be so. Exercise faith for it to be so in your life.

3. Moving into new things means we must be willing to let go of some old ones. A major problem with people in the midst of God-ordained change is that they often refuse to abandon old attitudes and old ways of doing things. Holding on to the existing form that God wants them to abandon has often been the downfall of a people being called to change. God makes it so that we cannot have both the old and the new. Too often we want to hold onto the old and peek up into the new, to see if we really want it. There's no faith in that kind of reaction to the call for change.

4. Change can often revitalize our faith and give us new enthusiasm for the future.

Learn to see change as a positive thing designed by God to take you from glory to glory, faith to faith, and from strength to strength.

Winnowing Fork #7: Challenge to Integrity

From time to time in the Christian life, the Lord will allow us to be confronted with opportunities where it would be easy to get by with stealing, cheating, lying, etc. Dishonesty is what He hopes He will not find.

I once rented a farm that had a dozen or so outbuildings. In one of them was a little bottle-neck hydraulic jack. Two or three weeks earlier, there had been an auction sale, where the farm, the house, the outbuildings and all of their contents had been sold. Somehow, the little jack had been overlooked and had not been auctioned off. I knew that, legally, the jack belonged with the farm, and was therefore the property of the farm's new owner. But I also figured that he knew nothing of the little jack. He lived four states away and hadn't even been on the farm since the day he had bought it. What was the jack to him? I needed it, and if I took it he would never know the difference. It was the perfect set up. So I took it. But please don't stop reading here.

> *Beloved, if our heart condemn us not, then we have confidence toward God* (I John 3:21, KJV).

On my way home from that farm, as I carried that stolen jack, all confidence toward God left me. My heart began to condemn me bitterly. "The heart knows its own bitterness" (Prov. 14:10, TAB), and brother, my heart was feeling terrible.

Constrained in spirit, I returned to the old outbuilding on that farm (some five miles away), and replaced the jack. The very moment I removed my hand from the jack, leaving it on the shelf in that rickety old outbuilding, the overwhelming guilt and conviction I had been feeling was gone! My confidence in God was restored, and I had a little praise service right there.

That incident took place years ago, not long after I had become a Christine. I am convinced that I passed an invisible rite of passage into a new level of Christian maturity that day. From then on, greater things began to happen for me in my

Christian walk; God was pleased to bless me in new ways. I'll never forget that little jack. Insignificant though it was in the natural, it served a very important part in the process of maturation in this believer.

Winnowing Fork #8: Deliverance From Demons

A final situation I would like to examine as one of the Lord's winnowing forks is the one where a demon might be involved. Perhaps your pride, your unteachableness, your fear or your rebellious attitude is demonic in nature, and God is telling you that you need deliverance. Are you too sophisticated and lofty in your opinion of yourself to even consider that your problem might be demonic? If so, you'll not make the grade.

> *But upon Mount Zion shall be deliverance, and there shall be holiness; and the house of Jacob shall possess their possessions* (Obad. 17, KJV).

It will be essential for the remnant to be both a holy people and a delivered people. Often, the unseen, vile demons, taking up residence within the body of a child of God, are the major reasons he cannot walk in continual holiness before God and man. Demons of lust, anger, bitterness, fear and rebellion hide within many, not allowing their hosts to come to maturity in Christ. These intruders *must be* identified and driven out! Not to do so can keep one out of the remnant of God. It is not a sin to have a demon; it is a sin, however, not to get rid of it once you realize you have one.

Much ground is to be gained in the lives of God's redeemed people. Many wonderful possessions are to be had and realized. But until deliverance is found in Zion, and holiness, the house of Jacob will not possess what is legally and rightfully theirs. Examine yourself.

The Remnant

The preceding list of winnowing forks is by no means exhaustive. There are many more situations and circumstances God uses proficiently to examine our hearts. Are we proven defensive, argumentative, unteachable and prideful when challenged, or are we able to give things to God and not be anxious? The winds will reveal many in these last days.

What if a man or woman fails the tests to which the winnowing fork exposes them? Are they lost? Absolutely not! If they've trusted Jesus Christ as their personal Lord and Savior, trusting in what His shed blood did for them when He went to the cross, they are saved. We are saved and placed in God's family by faith in Christ alone. However, the remnant, in any given age, is an "election within the election." This remnant is comprised of those believers who are open and eager for the purifying fires and pruning winds of God to sift through their lives and rid them of all impurity, be it demonic or fleshly. Many Christians don't want this, and yet, they still believe in Jesus. I believe they will make it to heaven when they die. They will not, however, comprise the special remnant that God will use in displaying His glory and power to a lost, dying world. And they will not be privileged to rule and reign with Him in the highest positions throughout eternity. They will have to sit on the bench, like a third string quarterback, and watch the first string man help the team on to victory. But they will be saved. That's better than eternal damnation.

It seems that the Church in America is saturated with compromise and worldliness. So where is this remnant I speak of? They are out there. Just as surely as the Lord gathered a remnant *out of his flock* in Jeremiah's day (Jer. 23:3), so is He gathering a remnant *out of His flock* today! However stubborn a people may be at any given time, there is always room for His remnant. They are the survivors among us, those who continue to grow and broaden in Jesus Christ. They can be found in both denominational and nondenominational settings. They are the humble "sticklers" to God's Word and His call on their lives. They are a spiritual remnant "chosen by grace" (Rom. 11:5). They are not an "elite," exalted group, but a humble, seriously devoted group of Christ-followers. God is offering us all a place in their number. Our choices decide.

May the winds reveal the Church in this hour. I pray we can all respond properly as God brings judgment to His house before that great and notable day of the Lord.

FINAL WORDS

The time has come for me to end this book. I long to continue, because when you are writing about spiritual things there is no end to them. The Lord Jesus is infinite; He is Jehovah. He is the self-existent One who is continually revealing Himself. Throughout eternity we will go further into our knowledge of Him. We've only just begun to move into a bright and glorious future with Him. Let that thrill you, but also realize that He wants you to be very serious about Him and wholly committed to Him in *this* life. Stop playing the religious games and draw nigh unto Him as never before. Our God is Love. But also realize that to draw nigh unto God is to draw nigh unto a Consuming Fire. The fire of His glory will reveal sin to be purged!

Feel free to teach any of the lessons or outlines contained in this book to your church or group. After *Kingdom Commandos* was published, I received requests from various Christian groups desiring to use the book in the training of disciples. I believe *Front Line Warfare* will be beneficial in this way as well.

I am also available, as God leads and as time permits, to come to your area to speak in seminars, crusades, revivals or conventions that will help to equip men and women of God to wage war against the forces of darkness and establish the Kingdom of God. It is my delight to assist you in this way, helping you to grow stronger as the Day of the Lord approaches. God bless you.

The night is far spent, the day is at hand: let us therefore cast off the works of darkness, and let us put on the armour of light (Rom. 13:12, KJV).